# Democracy, Religion, and Commerce

This collection considers the relationship between religion, state, and market. In so doing, it also illustrates that the market is a powerful site for the cultural work of secularizing religious conflict. Though expressed as a simile, with religious freedom functioning like market freedom, "free market religion" has achieved the status of general knowledge about the nature of religion as either good or bad. It legislates good religion as that which operates according to free market principles: it is private, with no formal relationship to government; and personal: a matter of belief and conscience. As naturalized elements of historically contingent and discursively maintained beliefs about religion, these criteria have ethical and regulatory force. Thus, in culture and law, the effect of the metaphor has become instrumental, not merely descriptive. This volume seeks to productively complicate and invite further analysis of this easy conflation of democracy, religion, and the market. It invites scholars from a variety of disciplines to consider more intentionally the extent to which markets are implicated and illuminate the place of religion in public life. The book will be a valuable resource for researchers and academics working in the areas of law and religion, ethics, and economics.

**Kathleen Flake** is Richard Lyman Bushman Professor of Mormon Studies and Co-Director, Virginia Center for the Study of Religion, University of Virginia, USA.

**Nathan B. Oman** is Rollins Professor of Law and Co-Director, Center for the Study of Law and Markets, William and Mary Law School, USA.

**Series Editor**
Professor Norman Doe
*Director of the Centre for Law and Religion, Cardiff University, UK*

**Law and Religion**

The practice of religion by individuals and groups, the rise of religious diversity, and the fear of religious extremism, raise profound questions for the interaction between law and religion in society. The regulatory systems involved, the religion laws of secular government (national and international) and the religious laws of faith communities, are valuable tools for our understanding of the dynamics of mutual accommodation and the analysis and resolution of issues in such areas as: religious freedom; discrimination; the autonomy of religious organisations; doctrine, worship and religious symbols; the property and finances of religion; religion, education and public institutions; and religion, marriage and children. In this series, scholars at the forefront of law and religion contribute to the debates in this area. The books in the series are analytical with a key target audience of scholars and practitioners, including lawyers, religious leaders, and others with an interest in this rapidly developing discipline.

**Series Board**
Carmen Asiaín
*Professor, University of Montevideo, Uruguay*
Paul Babie
*Professor and Associate Dean (International), Adelaide Law School, Australia*
Pieter Coertzen
*Chairperson, Unit for the Study of Law and Religion, University of Stellenbosch, South Africa*
Alison Mawhinney
*Reader, Bangor University, UK*
Michael John Perry
*Senior Fellow, Center for the Study of Law and Religion, Emory University, USA*

Titles in this series include:

Democracy, Religion, and Commerce
Private Markets and the Public Regulation of Religion
Edited by Kathleen Flake and Nathan B. Oman

For more information about this series, please visit: www.routledge.com/Law-and-Religion/book-series/LAWRELIG

# Democracy, Religion, and Commerce

Private Markets and the Public Regulation of Religion

Edited by Kathleen Flake
and Nathan B. Oman

LONDON AND NEW YORK

First published 2023
by Routledge
4 Park Square, Milton Park, Abingdon, Oxon OX14 4RN

and by Routledge
605 Third Avenue, New York, NY 10158

*Routledge is an imprint of the Taylor & Francis Group, an informa business*

© 2023 selection and editorial matter, Kathleen Flake and Nathan B. Oman; individual chapters, the contributors

The right of Kathleen Flake and Nathan B. Oman to be identified as the authors of the editorial material, and of the authors for their individual chapters, has been asserted in accordance with sections 77 and 78 of the Copyright, Designs and Patents Act 1988.

All rights reserved. No part of this book may be reprinted or reproduced or utilised in any form or by any electronic, mechanical, or other means, now known or hereafter invented, including photocopying and recording, or in any information storage or retrieval system, without permission in writing from the publishers.

*Trademark notice*: Product or corporate names may be trademarks or registered trademarks, and are used only for identification and explanation without intent to infringe.

*British Library Cataloguing-in-Publication Data*
A catalogue record for this book is available from the British Library

ISBN: 978-1-032-31343-6 (hbk)
ISBN: 978-1-032-31346-7 (pbk)
ISBN: 978-1-003-30929-1 (ebk)

DOI: 10.4324/9781003309291

Typeset in Galliard
by Apex CoVantage, LLC

# Contents

*List of Contributors* vii

Introduction: Democracy and Religion in the Market 1
KATHLEEN FLAKE AND NATHAN B. OMAN

1 Denominational Uncoupling in a Divestment Age: Religion in the History of the American University 8
KATHRYN LOFTON

2 Markets, Religion, and Moral Deliberation: The Affordable Care Act's Contraceptive Mandate 25
JULIA D. MAHONEY

3 Regulating Religion in the Public Arena: Lessons Learned from Global Data Collections 39
ROGER FINKE AND KERBY GOFF

4 Shots Not Fired in the Culture War: Commercial Litigation in Contemporary Rabbinical Courts 64
CHAIM SAIMAN

5 Go Tell It [to the IRS]: American Suspicions Around Religious Profit-Making 90
SAMUEL D. BRUNSON

6 The Liberty of the Will in Theology Permits the Liberated Markets of Liberalism 110
DEIRDRE NANSEN McCLOSKEY

7 Neutral Principles and Legal Pluralism 136
VÍCTOR M. MUÑIZ-FRATICELLI

8 Markets as Moral Contexts: An Account Based in Catholic
  Theological Anthropology 162
  CHRISTINA McRORIE

9 Regulating Religious Performance on the Commercial Stage 177
  NATHAN B. OMAN

  *Index* 194

# Contributors

**Samuel D. Brunson,** Loyola University Chicago School of Law

**Roger Finke,** The Pennsylvania State University

**Kathleen Flake,** University of Virginia

**Kerby Goff,** The Pennsylvania State University

**Kathryn Lofton,** Yale University

**Julia D. Mahoney,** University of Virginia School of Law

**Deirdre Nansen McCloskey,** University of Illinois at Chicago

**Christina McRorie,** Creighton University

**Víctor M. Muñiz-Fraticelli,** McGill University and School of Law

**Nathan B. Oman,** Marshall-Wythe School of Law, The College of William & Mary

**Chaim Saiman,** Villanova University Charles Widger School of Law

# Introduction

Democracy and Religion in the Market

*Kathleen Flake and Nathan B. Oman*

For democracies, the place of religion in the public square is a perennial question, even a struggle. We often imagine this debate in spatial terms as a public square. We believe this contemporary "square," like the ancient agora, joins two independent spheres of human action: religion and the state. Moreover, it is considered open to all and for the benefit of all, notwithstanding that in church–state debates, it is typically occupied by professionals speaking primarily in the language of First Amendment law and philosophy. Just as often, however, debates about the status of religion in a democratic society occur in relation to economic exchanges and as part of the truck and barter of market actors. This fact has not been sufficiently appreciated in political reflection on the place of religion and religions in a democratic republic. This collection of essays considers what happens when we explicitly acknowledge the commercial nature of the public square and consider questions not simply of religion and state, but of religion, state, and market. Our wager is that focusing our view on the market will better reveal the work that it does in negotiating the boundaries between religion and the state.

This book invites scholars from a variety of disciplines to consider more intentionally the extent to which markets are implicated in and illuminate the place of religion in public life. More material, in every sense of the word, than what we think of as the political public square, the market has always hosted debates over the legitimacy of public manifestations of religion in a democracy, and this seems to be increasingly true today. Consider, for example, religious entrepreneurs that pit themselves against anti-discrimination laws; for-profit corporations that claim to practice religion; and economic boycotts against states over legislation related to religious freedom or transgender rights. Such activity engages at least as many citizens as the more overtly political sphere and often engages them more directly. Though not everyone votes, all buy and sell. Moreover, they often do so with moral, even explicitly religious goals in mind, not merely material ends, making their intentions a matter of public and not merely private interest. Unsurprisingly, American law has been early and often engaged in regulating the manifestations of religion in the market, even if this fact hasn't always garnered the explicit reflection it deserves.

Both the pervasiveness of free market economics in American life and the new nation's religious diversity brought conflicting religious and economic interests

DOI: 10.4324/9781003309291-1

before the law. Indeed, the primacy of commerce in early America encouraged tolerance for religious diversity and laxity: laborers of any kind or no kind of religion, famously even Jews and enslaved Muslims, were pressed into service to maximize the extraction of wealth from Britain's colonies. Thus, the fact of America's religious diversity joined other, more principled demands for freedom of conscience to unravel religious establishments in the new republic. At the same time as the rise of "free religion," or religion untethered from the state, market economics began to shape, if not define, social relationships and, ultimately, became as significant as free religion in the organization of American life, its values, and its liberties.[1]

Though their stories are often told separately or lose their particularity in general secularization narratives, free religion and free markets are intimately related discourses that together continue to discipline democratic efforts to maintain a government that protects "life, liberty and the pursuit of happiness." John Locke, who provided Jefferson two-thirds of his trinitarian definition of natural or "inalienable" rights, had placed his third emphasis on "property," not personal fulfillment. Jefferson's emendations notwithstanding, American polity and practice evidence the conviction that free markets, no less than freedom of conscience, constitute a free people. It is not accidental that in the United States metaphors of market and religion often became intertwined.

Indeed, disestablishment has been commonly seen positively as a deregulation of religion: the creation of a market in which spiritual entrepreneurs compete for converts and religious consumers are given a wider variety of sectarian choices. This optimistic view of market religion arose amid handwringing that the hurly burley of such a religious market could threaten both a true sense of the sacred and the institutions of American democracy. The fear was that, in the name of disestablishment, religion has been impermissibly subordinated to the state: no longer the arbiter of public morality but rather subject to it, especially when expressed in the nation's laws. The ambiguous place of the market in our thinking about and experience of religion in public life can be seen in the US Supreme Court's handling of church–state cases, particularly from the dawn of the so-called rights revolution after World War II to the present. In those cases, the market and market metaphors perform important intellectual work without ever coming clearly into focus as means for determining the acceptable roles of faith within our democracy.

---

1 See, e.g., Joyce O. Appleby, *The Relentless Revolution: A History of Capitalism* (New York: Norton, 2010); Dierdre Nansen McCloskey, *The Bourgeois Virtues: Ethics for an Age of Commerce* (Chicago, IL: University of Chicago Press, 2006); Robert H. Nelson, *Economics as Religion: From Samuelson to Chicago and Beyond* (University Park, PA: Pennsylvania State University Press, 2014). For Religious Studies more specifically, see e.g., François Gauthierr, *Religion, Modernity, Globalisation: Nation-state to Market* (New York: Routledge, 2020); Francis Ching-Wah Yip, *Capitalism as Religion? A Study of Paul Tillich's Interpretation of Modernity* (Cambridge, MA: Harvard University Press, 2010); Mark Valeri, *Heavenly Merchandize: How Religion Shaped Commerce in Puritan America* (Princeton, NJ: Princeton University Press, 2010).

In the beginning, before the revolution, religion and state cases were chiefly fights about property. Slavery and the Civil War produced a bumper crop of church litigation, as numerous congregations and denominations split over the country's "peculiar institution." When the theological debates over whether slaveholders should be excommunicated got down to the legalities of who got to keep the church building, denominational battles over slavery migrated into the courts. In the 1871 case of *Watson v. Jones*,[2] the Supreme Court ultimately resolved the issue by establishing that "neutral principles" of secular property law, not religious standards for membership, were the only way to decide the rightful owner in such cases. In short, once theological contests intersected with property, the ordinary law of the marketplace—property, contract, and trusts—were to be used to resolve the case, presumably with no effect on religion. This distinction between the ordinary and the religious was not, however, a bright line, and the nineteenth-century state courts commonly regulated matters that impinged on church governance as it regulated church property.[3]

Ninety years later, notwithstanding it being a period of dramatic expansion in the reach of the Bill of Rights, the Court decided in *Braunfeld v. Brown*[4] that the states could burden religious people so long as the burdens were merely commercial. Braunfeld was an Orthodox Jewish tailor who sought relief from Christian-inspired, state-enforced Sunday closing laws that both imposed a religious requirement on him that harmed him economically and placed an undue burden on the exercise of his own conscience, which required closing on Saturdays. The Court rejected his claim. Writing for the majority, Chief Justice Earl Warren upheld the statute, arguing that the First Amendment was not violated when the "law simply regulates a secular activity and . . . operates so as to make the practice of their religious beliefs more expensive."[5] The law was merely making religious practice more expensive, another cost in the market and not something that implicated the "abhorrence of religious persecution and intolerance [that] is a basic part of our heritage."[6]

More recently in *Burwell v. Hobby Lobby Stores, Inc.*,[7] the Court heard a challenge by for-profit businesses against a federal mandate that employee insurance include coverage of the cost of contraceptives that the religious business owners considered abortifacients. The case was ultimately decided based on the fact that the companies were owned by families whose religious commitments informed their company practices. Therefore, according to the Court majority, since corporations do not act "'separate and apart from' the human beings who own,

---

2 80 U.S. 679 (1871).
3 See Sarah Barringer Gordon, "The First Disestablishment: Limits on Church Power and Property Before the Civil War," *University of Pennsylvania Law Review* 162 (2014): 307–72.
4 366 U.S. 599 (1961).
5 Id. at 605.
6 Id. at 606.
7 573 U.S. 682 (2014).

run, and are employed by them,"[8] there is a constitutional basis for protecting the religious freedom of those human beings and the insurance mandate could not be applied. In contrast, a dissenting opinion argued that a distinction should have been retained between religious institutions and commercial ones. Justice Ginsberg wrote. "No such solicitude is traditional for commercial organizations" and all religious exemptions should be denied "the commercial profit-making world."[9] Where for Justice Alito the market was invisible in the application of religious liberty law, for Justice Ginsburg religion in the market became invisible.[10]

Thus, the free market is not merely a passive host to religion–state conflicts and collaboration. It is also a powerful site for the cultural work of secularizing religious conflict. In other words, religion and the state are shaped by the market. Though expressed as a simile—religious freedom functions *like* market freedom— "free market religion" has achieved the status of general knowledge about the nature of religion as either good or bad. Good religion operates on free market principles of private exchange (it has no formal relationship to government) and is personal (a matter of belief and conscience). As naturalized elements of historically contingent and discursively maintained beliefs about religion, these criteria have ethical and regulatory force. They make religion good: good for the faithful and good for American democracy. Thus, in culture and law, the effect of the metaphor has become instrumental, not merely descriptive. "Freedom of religion can be understood as a constitutionally prescribed free market for religious belief," write Richard Posner and Michael McConnell; "this makes economic understanding of the workings of free markets . . . pertinent to interpretation of religious cases."[11] Barak Richman argues "the First Amendment's religion clauses are best exemplified by a proverbial marketplace." Like the Sherman Antitrust Act, they are "designed to liberate individual energies and resist entrenched power, and thus both guarantee quintessential market values: personal freedom, individual expression and subjective choice."[12] The essays in this volume are an effort to extend,

---

8 Id. at 707 (Alito, J.).
9 Id. at 754 (Ginsburg, J., dissenting) (quoting Corporation of Presiding Bishop of Church of Jesus Christ of Latter-day Saints v. Amos, 483 U.S. 327, 337 (1987) (Brennan, J., concurring in judgment).
10 The unsettled nature of the intersection of law, market, and religion in this case is further highlighted by the fact that while joining most of her dissent, Justice Breyer and Justice Kagan pointedly refused to join the portion of Justice Ginsburg's opinion analyzing the question of for-profit companies.
11 Michael W. McConnell and Richard A. Posner, "An Economic Approach to Issues of Religious Freedom," *University of Chicago Law Review* 56, no. 1 (1989): 61.
12 Barak D. Richman, "Religious Freedom Through Market Freedom: The Sherman Act and the Marketplace for Religion Antitrust and the Constitutional Order Symposium," *William & Mary Law Review* 60, no. 4 (2018, 2019): 1543. See also Bernadette Meyler, "Commerce in Religion," *Notre Dame Law Review* 84 (2009): 887–912 ("Supreme Court opinions tend not to separate out religious from commercial activity per se."). In the social sciences as well, "religion is a collectively produced commodity" to be studied "within the expanding domain of economics . . . economic theory, public economics, experimental economics, macroeconomics of growth, economic history, and economic development."

analyze, and invite further analysis of this easy conflation of democracy, religion, and the market.

In her contribution to the collection, Kathryn Lofton examines the fraught relationship between religiously founded universities and their current boards of trustees to show that market-driven secularization has not robbed these universities of moral intention, but rather has shifted the grounds of their moral discernment. In the course of becoming a product in a higher education marketplace, university standards for discernment shifted to identifying their respective graduates with passing on a particular, luxury brand of socio-cultural status, not moral fitness. Thus, universities are caught, she argues, between a stated commitment to foster a more democratic society and the need to maintain financial viability and exclusive brand through profitable investments in the marketplace. The chapter concludes with a case study on market-driven secularization in the context of conflicting arguments for and against asset divestment.

Julia D. Mahoney looks to the role of the market as a mediating institution in the culture wars that so polarize American society. Rather than seeing markets as an amoral space devoted solely to the efficient allocation of resources, she argues that the market is a site of moral deliberation, one that tends to generate compromise and mutual accommodation. As the regulatory state has grown, it has displaced markets as sites of moral deliberation, moving those conflicts into administrative agencies and the courts that are supposed to serve as a check on their actions. Through a detailed account of the legal battles between the government and religious objectors to the so-called contraceptive mandate, she illustrates how government regulation has tended to exacerbate cultural divisions and suggests that a greater reliance on markets could mitigate polarization around hot button cultural fights.

Kerby Goff and Roger Finke's data analysis shows the negative effect of putatively neutral regulations on religious freedom worldwide. Examining the constitutions of countries around the world, the authors note that most countries enshrine a formal commitment to religious freedom. However, such constitutional provisions commonly coexist with regulatory restrictions on religious freedom, the authors warn. Furthermore, many otherwise mature liberal democracies have taken increasingly punitive stances towards disfavored religious groups and many countries with strong nominal protections for religious freedom strictly regulate religious minorities in practice. The authors conclude there is a modest connection between religious freedom and economic development, and a strong correlation between religious freedom, open elections, independent courts, and respect for other kinds of civil rights.

Chaim Saiman offers the Beth Din of America as a case study of a cultural fight over religious liberty that didn't happen. The Beth Din of America, one of the major rabbinical courts for the orthodox tradition, regularly arbitrates commercial disputes, offering pious Jews a forum in which such suits can be tried under halakhah (Jewish law), while at the same time offering them legally binding decisions under the Federal Arbitration Act. Saiman shows that despite points of conflict between halakhah and American arbitral and commercial law, the Beth

Din of America has chosen not to "stand on principle," thus provoking religious liberty conflict. Rather, it has accommodated itself to American legal and commercial norms so that its decisions will be respected in both the wider business and legal communities.

Samuel D. Brunson's contribution to the volume illustrates the way in which tax law has become one of the primary arenas in which public fights about the place of religion in the marketplace are fought out. Under American law, churches are granted the economic benefit of tax exemption, but they or their affiliates often engage in market activity. Brunson shows how this situation has repeatedly created conflicts in which Americans have used tax law to express their unease with religion. Ironically, this has made the IRS responsible for defining the line between religious exercise and suspect religious commerce. According to Brunson, the IRS has generally shied away from picking fights with churches over their business activities, but tax law continues to play host to expressive suits by those who wish to use the law as a way of forcing churches to conform to evolving and competing moralities.

In her chapter, Deirdre Nansen McCloskey argues that there is a connection between the liberty of the human will according to Abrahamic theology and the liberty of human action under liberal economic ideology. Thus, contrary to contemporary skepticism, core theological tenants justify economic liberalism as distinct from both democratic socialism and neo-liberalism. After an historically informed theoretical analysis of each of these competitors for ordering an ethical political economy, McCloskey argues for a third way between a coercive state and an atomistic individual. That way lies in protecting the interdependence of propertied market sellers and buyers that necessarily produces cooperation basic to a virtuous society (albeit bourgeoise) and, ultimately, provides a better basis for the Christian ideal of human equality.

Víctor M. Muñiz-Fraticelli argues that the reasons for political and legal pluralism—or its functional equivalent—should guide disputes about ecclesiastical authority. Given the permissible plurality of contemporary normative moral orders, religion should be admitted to this respected, if problematic source of legal contestants. Religious organizations are just such orders and should be recognized as such by the legal order of the state. That does not mean that the state needs to defer to religious organizations, but it means that the state can and should treat religious legal systems not as mysterious and inscrutable symbolic structures, but as legal orders akin to foreign legal jurisdictions. The paradigm for adjudicating ecclesiastical disputes should be more similar to what civilian jurists call "private international law" or common lawyers call "conflicts of law" rather than that of (mere) voluntary associations.

Christina McRorie analyzes markets as moral contexts that can influence market actors in ways that make them relevant to discussions of democracy. Markets are not sites of apolitical action or "free markets"; they are formative. Markets actively engage actors in ways that are morally formative. Applying insights from Catholic theological anthropology, she shows that markets can be a means for encouraging or inhibiting human freedom. The chapter concludes by considering the moral and political significance of how we structure the economic contexts in which Americans live. She invites engagement in markets particulars and at a granular level to properly attend to their moral complicity and power.

Nathan B. Oman argues that religious identities, like gender identities, are not merely a compound of internalized beliefs and commitments. They are forms of practice, and, more especially, they constitute a performance of identity not unlike present understanding of gender. Therefore, they should be treated as such when deciding whether they are due legal accommodation. The law has long recognized that unlawful discrimination can take the form of restrictions on the performance of gender. Oman asks what would happen if we a brought a similar approach to the application of law to religion in the marketplace? As a test case, he considers how religious tithes and offerings are treated in bankruptcy proceedings and what might change if these offerings were understood as a performance of religious identity, not merely an exercise of conscience or belief.

This collection benefited from a conference convened in 2019 and workshop hosted virtually in 2020 by the University of Virginia Department of Religion's Forum on Democracy and Religion and the Center for the Study of Law and Markets at the College of William and Mary. We are grateful to the Dean of the University of Virginia's College of Arts and Sciences and the donors to the Center for the Study of Law and Markets for their generous support. The book is not a straightforward record of the conference: papers have been revised, and a few papers were unavailable for publication here. Neither can the book capture the vitality of the conference conversation. Our hope, however, is that what is captured here will encourage more conversation on the intersection of religion, democracy, and the market.

# 1 Denominational Uncoupling in a Divestment Age
## Religion in the History of the American University

*Kathryn Lofton*

The origin of US colleges and universities is undemocratic. Into the twentieth century, higher education sifted individuals into denominational conclaves or provided vocational training in agriculture, science, and engineering to contribute to the strategic domestication of land. With few exceptions, these universities and colleges excluded women, nonwhite persons, Catholics, or Jews. Yet, the promotional account of the American university argues it is a preparatory site for democratic participation. This portrait emerged from the simultaneity of an economic boom and the reckoning with wartime grief in the period immediately following World War II. In 1947, President Truman established the Commission on Higher Education, whose report had four principal findings: the chief purpose of American higher education was the building and strengthening of democracy; institutions should expand enrollments; this growth should occur in public institutions, including community colleges; and federal financial assistance was needed and appropriate to achieve these ends. Over the subsequent years, following up on these recommendations led to an exponential access to higher education.[1]

The commission's recommendations led to a powerful sense that the university was integral to the country's fulfillment of its democratic promise. This chapter reflects on the relationship between university origins and their contemporary wrestling with issues of democratic concern. The mediating factor between the two—between where things began and where things are—is religion. Religion in two senses: religion as a metaphysics of sociality (that is, an abstract concept of how human beings organize together for the furtherance of human values) and religion as a specific, locatable claim of identity. From the beginning of the story of this country, universities have always been a religious problem in both senses: a proposition of the social good, and a molding of specific groups. They have also been a democratic problem. The 2019 college admissions bribery scandal just reiterates how much these things called "colleges and universities" represent

---

1 Roger L. Geiger, *American Higher Education Since World War II: A History* (Princeton: Princeton University Press, 2019), 10–11. See also Marvin Lazerson, "The Disappointments of Success: Higher Education After World War II," *The Annals of the American Academy of Political and Social Science* 559 (1998): 64–76.

DOI: 10.4324/9781003309291-2

something for which the word "democratic" is not exactly right. What good, then, might they be for democracy?

To narrow this large question, I ask whether what universities decide to do about particular social issues conveys principle befitting their nonprofit status. Consider, for example, reactions universities have to calls by students and faculty for fossil fuel divestment. The fossil fuel divestment campaign is part of a thirty-year effort to limit global greenhouse gas emissions. Nations have officially been discussing climate change since the signing of the United Nations Framework Convention on Climate Change (UNFCC) at the Earth Summit in Rio de Janeiro in 1992. Fossil fuel disinvestment campaigns focus their efforts on endowed universities in the hope that flipping that university's investments could have a radiating stigmatizing effect toward those large organizations that do not divest. For the universities receiving these petitions, the question is whether disinvestment in fossil fuels puts them at odds with their fiduciary responsibility to manage and indefinitely perpetuate the pool of monetary resources committed to the university's endurance. The petitioners think universities serve a social good; the administrative leadership thinks a university should protect its resources for the indefinite support of a particular identity. In the US, an organization receives tax-exempt status from the government because it furthers a social cause and provides a public benefit. The grounds for indefinite perpetuation of university endowments are justified on the grounds that those monetary resources serve a specific purpose; this purpose is determined according to the will of its founders and donors; this purpose is conceived as meritorious for nonprofit status. This purpose may serve a social good, but it is secondary to its primary intent: continuing the perpetuity of its identity.

Opponents of fossil fuel divestment argue specifically that divestment would breach the investor's fiduciary duty to its shareholders. Institutions structure endowments so that the principal value remains intact, while the investment income or a small part of the principal is available for use each year. Economists equivocate, uncertain that the benefits to the social good outweigh the losses to yearly operating budgets. A 2015 report led by Daniel Fischel argued, "Costs to investors of fossil fuel divestiture are highly likely and substantial, while the potential benefits—to the extent there are any—are ill-defined and uncertain at best."[2] Other reports follow on this one, arguing that divestment and a reduction of portfolio diversification could cost millions in lost returns annually. That the Independent Petroleum Association of America commissioned these reports should dismiss their finding out of hand. Yet, universities cite reports like these in their rejection of divestment, under the conjecture that it could hinder their financial performance and breach their fiduciary duty.[3] The irony of research

---

2 Daniel R. Fischel, "Fossil Fuel Divestment: A Costly and Ineffective Investment Strategy" (2015): 3, accessed October 1, 2020, http://divestmentfacts.com/pdf/Fischel_Report.pdf.
3 Chelsie Hunt, Olaf Weber, and Truzaar Dordi, "A Comparative Analysis of the Anti-Apartheid and Fossil Fuel Divestment Campaigns," *Journal of Sustainable Finance & Investment* 7, no. 1 (2017): 64–81.

universities using corporate-funded scholarship to serve their hoarding ends is unmissable.

Yet, here the apparent inconsistency—using corporate-sponsored data at institutions that promote rigorous free inquiry—would be rendered less so if we did not think of universities as rationalist conclaves but appreciated them instead as inheritors of religious outlooks and sectarian habitudes. Protesters think the moral weight of the environmental crisis should compel a nonprofit organization to sacrifice its profits to serve the public good. With few universities agreeing to such arguments, it suggests that the protesters' idea of the public good is not the same as the nonprofit against which they protest. How do we understand this hermeneutic gap? Remembering the religious origins of American universities allows us an opportunity to ask what universities exist to do and be for the markets they serve. At times, it can seem like universities clench and re-territorialize power better than any other activities. Thinking with the conjoined histories of universities and religion allows us to ask what other activities a university could practice. Through a description of the historic arc of university and an exploration of a particular denominational divestment, it is possible to think about what power universities have to increase democracy and resist market determination.

## Christian to Secular

In February 2019 at a special general conference meeting, the United Methodist Church passed the Traditional Plan that affirmed the church's existing bans on ordaining LGBTQ clergy and officiating at or hosting same-sex marriage and added mandatory penalties for pastors who violate these bans. Nine months later Southern Methodist University (SMU) amended its articles of incorporation to delete all references to the United Methodist Church's South Central Jurisdictional Conference (SCJC), effectively making SMU's Board of Trustees SMU's boss, not the SCJC. One month after that, the SCJC filed a lawsuit against SMU to prevent the university from so reconfiguring its relationship with the church.

This plot is familiar to students of post-Reformation Protestant sectarianism and the forging of secular power via Protestant systems. The preponderance of colleges and universities founded in the US prior to the twentieth century were Christian institutions. These college and universities had clergymen presidents; they required chapel attendance and courses in New Testament and Church Doctrine; they insisted on doctrinally confirmed content in science courses; they often required that faculty be practicing church members; they sponsored social service programs with a missionary character. What happened to change American universities from those Christian communities in the eighteenth century to largely secular institutions by the mid-twentieth century? As George Marsden explains in *The Soul of the American University* (1996), in the late nineteenth century leading American Protestant educators sought to "shape a unified national culture" committed to "freedom, science and service."[4] Those rallying university leaders succeeded in the national public culture, which was distinctively Protestant in the United States until World War II (and, some would argue, well beyond). In the process, the religious identity of their colleges and universities effectively disappeared as certain ideas of science, academic freedom, and increasingly inclusive admissions policies overtook nonsectarian Protestantism as the default moral order. Marsden details the changes that fed this transformation, including the influence of the model of the German research university.[5] He also points to the rivaling distinction drawn between scientific competence and theological commitment, as well as the establishment of religion itself as an object of scientific study. He notes the related abandonment of religious tests for professional success, and an increased emphasis on "scholarly expertise" over assessments of moral character. Finally—and most critically to the case of SCJC and SMU—he underlines the twentieth-century fight by institutions to abandon legal relationships with founding denominations and thereby be unhooked from clerical oversight. In his work on the secularization of the universities, Marsden argues that that the leaders of the American Protestant universities did not intend the secularization their institutions subsequently underwent. Indeed, they insisted that the changes they were instituting for particular short-term benefits would actually strengthen the Christian character of their institutions. For the largely Christian leadership who guided these shifts of American universities, the "methodological secularization in the universities" was not intended as secularization. It was conceived of "by most of its proponents not so much in opposition to Christianity as an extension of its liberating and uplifting spirit."[6]

In a 1931 article titled "The Denominational College" for *The Journal of Higher Education*, Clarence M. Dannelly wrote:

> Historically the denominational college has played a most important part in the field of higher education in America. It was the only college that early America knew. It was a liberal-arts college, a new institution in a new world, distinctly an American contribution to educational organization. It was established with the avowed intention of preparing Christian ministers and perpetuating Christian purposes. Under positive religious controls, it was the outstanding agency employed by church and state to assure the future of a competent leadership, both consecrated and trained. It was "the missionary of higher education in a rude land in which the State could not provide

---

4 George Marsden, *The Soul of the American University: From Protestant Establishment to Established Nonbelief* (New York: Oxford University Press, 1996), 219, 178.
5 Ibid., 124–25; 296–301; 362–66.
6 Ibid, 158 & 193. The process of secularization was not neat or simple. As recently as 2005, Yale University still worked to determine its relationship to the Congregationalist church. Alison Leigh Cowan, "Yale Ending Its Affiliation with a Church," *New York Times*, April 12, 2005, B1.

adequate culture for its youth," writes Hickman. Yale, founded in 1701, was third of these colleges in chronological order. Its charter declared its purpose to be that of preparing young men "for public employment, both in church and civic state." Specific Christian purposes were set forth in the charters of all these colleges founded before the Revolution, with the single exception of the institution that later became the University of Pennsylvania.[7]

Everything Dannelly observed in the early 1930s remains strongly true in historical appraisal. The early history of colleges and universities in the United States was bound up in Christian efforts to domesticate the land by taming and training the men who would survey, cultivate, and extract from that land. The number of colleges in the US grew steadily from the nine colonial institutions to about twenty in 1790, and at least forty-five by the mid-1820s.[8] In 1819, the Supreme Court of the United States rendered decision in the case that guaranteed the perpetuity of endowments for higher education. This gave impetus to the establishment of schools and colleges by the churches, and many Christians founded Christian colleges and universities during the period from 1820 to 1880, appropriately named "the period of great denominational effort." This is not to pretend universities were monasteries. They were specifically advertised as places for men's play and moral development under Christian supervision. As one minister preached in 1846:

> If there is any one part of education, more than another, which required to be imbued with the restraining and sanctifying influences of the gospel, it is a college education, for then passion is strongest, temptation greatest, and restraint weakest.[9]

A college education modulated by Christianity assured moral purposiveness in an epoch of Manifest Destiny violence and settler colonial ambition. Christian churches were practically the only organizations that maintained institutions of higher learning up to the Civil War. Only 17 of the 246 colleges existing in 1860 were state institutions. More than 90% of all college and university graduates came from institutions founded by the church. As late as 1870, the total enrollment in all state institutions was only about six thousand students.[10]

---

7 Clarence M. Dannelly, "The Denominational College," *The Journal of Higher Education* 2, no. 4 (April 1931): 183.
8 Donald G. Tewksbury, *The Founding of American Colleges and Universities Before the Civil War* (New York, 1932, reprinted 1965), 1; Richard Hofstadter and Wilson Smith, eds., *American Higher Education: A Documentary History* (Chicago: Chicago University Press, 1961), vol. 1, 233–34. Discussed in Paul Venable Turner, *Campus: An American Planning Tradition* (Cambridge, MA: The MIT Press, 1987), 53.
9 Rev. Thomas Smyth, *Denominational Education: Its Necessity and Its Practicability: Especially as It Regards Colleges: An Address, Delivered Before the Thalian and Phi-Delta Societies of Oglethorpe University* (Charleston, SC: B. Jenkins, 1846), iv.
10 Dannelly, "The Denominational College," 183.

## College as Sect

In 1914, the Chancellor of the University of Kansas reflected on this Christian past:

> Education was for many centuries almost wholly in the hands of the church. The development of democracy, however, as a matter of political theory and practice inevitably took the control of education out of the hands of the church. Most of us cannot reasonably complain about this, for the religious bodies to which we belong, the independent religious bodies so largely represented in America at the present time, were in the seventeenth century directly instrumental in the development of democratic ideas in England which brought about the separation of the church and state in America and handed over the control of the schools to the state.[11]

The contemporary reader might assume the chancellor of a public university in the early twentieth century would distance his work from a religious body. In this speech, we see a subtler historical claim made, namely that without "independent religious bodies" there would be no "democratic ideas," much less the "separation of church and state." It isn't that public universities exist despite a religious past. This religious past is the prerequisite for the existence of a free public. Historians of religion in the US have largely agreed with this claim.[12] What is significant is the sense that belonging to a particular religious body isn't opposed to university life but connected to it. Sectarianism becomes an instructional habit of democratization.

The original sense of "sect" is a choice based on an opinion.[13] A sect is a group of followers of a particular idea or opinion, but also it is something that chooses them: a sect is a voluntary association, but not one simply open to any volunteers. As Max Weber famously explained, a sect is restricted to those who are religiously and ethically qualified.[14] The sect itself is not an institution greater than the sum of its parts; it exists as a collection of individuals who—again, in Weber's formulation—continually engage in reciprocal acts of "probation," assessing and re-assessing one another's appropriateness for belonging.[15] The word "sectari-

---

11 Frank Strong, Chancellor, University of Kansas, "Religious Education in Universities," National Education Association of the United States, *Journal of Proceedings and Addresses of the Fifty-Second Annual Meeting Held at St. Paul, Minnesota, July 4–11, 1914* (Ann Arbor, MI: Published by the Secretary's Office of the Association), 490.
12 Sidney E. Mead, *The Lively Experiment: The Shaping of Christianity in America* (New York: Harper & Row, 1963).
13 Azmi Bishara, "Ta'ifah, Sect and Sectarianism: From the Word and Its Changing Implications to the Analytical Sociological Term," *AlMuntaqa* 1, no. 2 (August 2018): 53–67.
14 Max Weber, *Gesammelte Aufsätze zur Religionssoziologie* (Tübingen: J.C.B. Mohr, 1947), vol. 1, 211. Discussed in Peter L. Berger, "The Sociological Study of Sectarianism," *Social Research* 51, no. 1/2 (Spring/Summer 1984): 367–85.
15 Colin Loader and Jeffrey C. Alexander, "Max Weber on Churches and Sects in North America: An Alternative Path Toward Rationalization," *Sociological Theory* 3, no. 1 (Spring 1985): 3.

anism" now carries a fanatic tint, suggesting someone whose affiliation with a specific group outpaces all their other commitments. Even more: this fanaticism is itself indicating of the community's relationship to the world. Sociologists diagnose "sect" frequently as a group with tension toward other groups, as inclined toward separatism, as less *of* the world than defined by their hostility *toward* the world. Getting into a sect, and negotiating who gets to stay in, is a practice of basic disdain toward those who don't make it in, but also toward those who get in and don't make it within. This-worldly cares are so second-rate to the sect's occupants, focused as they are by each other, by judging and estimating the gates they determine through those judgments.

A sect is therefore not quite the same thing as a denomination. The term *denomination* emerged in the late seventeenth century from those groups of Christians in England who dissented from the established Church of England, considered themselves still loyal to the British state, and recognized the monarch as having rights with respect to the Church of England. In 1702, specifically, the Presbyterians, Baptists, and Congregationalists formed "the body of the Dissenting Ministers of the Three Denominations in and about the City of London." They introduced the term to distance themselves from the pejorative connotations of sect, which in popular seventeenth-century usage had the sense of deviant or undesirable practices. Denominations in plural democracies are not seen as possessing the separatism of sects, or their snobbish exclusionary regards; sociologists of religion describe denominations as generally supportive of the established social order and mutually tolerant of each other's practices. Sects start wars; denominations file their tax-exempt paperwork and create ecumenical counsels.

H. Richard Niebuhr brought the term denominationalism into the forefront of the sociology of religion in his 1929 book *The Social Sources of Denominationalism*. The central thesis of this work was that new religious organizations (which he called "sects") begin among the socially "disinherited," but in the United States, as these groups attain higher social status, their religious expressions become more "respectable" or socially accepted. Thus, there is a movement across generations from sectarian to denominational religious life—or else the sectarian group dies out. The story of the secularization of American universities told by Marsden suggests half of the plot I describe: the sectarian upstart movement becomes respectable enough to be a denomination, then—to foster that respectability—founds a college or university. That college or university facilitates higher attainments of social status by its followers, i.e., the students. Soon religious expressions incorporate into common social expectation, and whatever ghosts of the original sect are gone.

Or are they? Simply because a university is no longer denominational does not, I wager, mean it does not have aspects of a sect. Here I pull on particular elements of the voluminous sociology of religion diagnosing church-sect classifications; the elements on which I focus here charge the mind, I think, when we think about what universities do in the contemporary marketplace. Consider what sociologist Brian Wilson describes as the features of a religious sect: (1) voluntary association; (2) membership by proof to sect authorities of fitness or virtue; (3) exclusiveness emphasized and expulsion exercised; (4) elitism and the dismissal of members who do not observe its creed and morality; (5) the priesthood of all believers; and (6) hostility to, withdrawal from, or indifference to secular society.[16] What unites these six elements is, again, the sense that the sect maintains itself through an assessment, and ongoing surveillance, of fitness for membership. The relationship to the marketplace of colleges and universities is clear. Universities are discernment machines, sifting applicants and assessing their belonging as regular habits of the institution's survival. Staying in the sect, evading expulsion, not only provides a marker of fitness and virtue (the diploma) but also offers an identity marker as a market product of that particular institutional body. In putting on a hoodie with a Wisconsin Badger or a North Dakota Fighting Hawk they indicate from where they come, what priesthood is theirs.

Work on higher education in early America reiterates that the proliferation of schools in the nineteenth century was a response to competitive missionary impulses: each denomination wanted its own college in every part of the expanding country. This rivalry was criticized by some educators, such as Philip Lindsley, president of the University of Nashville, who in 1829 blamed it for "the excessive multiplication and dwarfish dimensions of western colleges," and also charged the sects with putting their schools in "small villages or retired parts of the country" in order to control their students' minds more effectively.[17] Critics attacked the emerging preponderance of colleges and their liberal arts model for its religious orientation, its elitism, its strict discipline, and the narrowness of its curriculum. Some educators, such as George Tichnor of Harvard, advocated more specialized professional training and research, as in Göttingen and other German universities; but there was only slow progress in this direction until later in the nineteenth century.[18] The traditional collegiate system remained dominant in America, symbolized by a widely hailed report issued by the faculty of Yale College in 1828, which fully endorsed the classical curriculum, the recitation method, and the college's need to substitute for "parental superintendence."[19]

As the Yale Report stated, "The parental character of college government requires that the students should be so collected together as to constitute one family."[20] Thinking about the religious past of American colleges and universities reminds us of the relational intimacy of these institutions, how their purpose

---

[16] Bryan R. Wilson, *The Social Dimensions of Sectarianism: Sects and New Religious Movements in Contemporary Society* (Oxford, New York and Toronto: Oxford University Press, 1992); Bryan R. Wilson, "An Analysis of Sect Development," in *Patterns of Sectarianism: Organization and Ideology in Social and Religious Movements*, ed. Bryan R. Wilson (London: Heinemann, 1967), 23–24; see also his treatment of the Adventists, ibid., 138–57, and his treatment of the Exclusive Brethren, ibid., 287–337; B. R. Wilson, "An Analysis of Sect Development," *American Sociological Review* 24, no. 1 (February 1959): 3–15.

[17] Paul Venable Turner, *Campus: An American Planning Tradition* (Cambridge, MA: The MIT Press, 1987), 54.

[18] Hofstadter and Smith, *American Higher Education*, Part 4.

[19] Turner, *Campus*, 54–55.

[20] Ibid., 55.

includes building up commitment to their emplacement, and the relationships built up at them to one another. As Eyal Regev, a scholar of Qumran, has written: "A sect is stereotyped as a community with spatial as well as social density—a group of people that live together."[21] Although not all college campuses are residential, the mythic sale of and historic origins for the "American" college is that they are communities in themselves, cities in microcosm where students and teachers lived and studied together in tightly regulated spaces. As Paul Venable Turner has written in his 1987 book on the campus as a physical ideal: "The romantic notion of a college in nature, removed from the corrupting forces of the city, became an American ideal."[22] After traveling in America in the 1930s, the renowned Swiss-French architect Le Corbusier observed, "Each college or university is an urban unit in itself, a small or large city. . . . The American university is a world in itself."[23]

A new Gallup report indicates that membership in religious institutions has declined nearly twice as fast as the proportion of those with no religious affiliation has risen. According to the report, since the last years of the twentieth century, "church membership" has shrunk 25%, from 69% of the population to 52%. That compares with a 14% decline in religious identification, from 90% to 77%.[24] The fortunes of college admissions are somewhat different. The higher education sector has swelled in size over the last fifty years, and now exists in a moment of possible decline. Between 1990 and 2011, college enrollment spiked by an incredible 54%. This represented a rise in total student population from 12 million to 18.5 million.[25] It also helped to drive massive hikes in tuition and a proliferation of new entrants in the marketplace. Between 2011 and 2013, enrollment in America's colleges declined by nearly one million students.[26] According to Inside Higher Ed, 2019 marked the eighth consecutive year-to-year enrollment decline. Collectively, colleges had shed 1.7% of enrollees from the prior spring. This is a loss of 300,000 students.[27]

21 Eyal Regev, "Comparing Sectarian Practice and Organization: The Qumran Sects in Light of the Regulations of the Shakers, Hutterites, Mennonites and Amish," *Numen* 51, no. 2 (2004): 171.
22 Turner, *Campus*, 4.
23 Le Corbusier, *When the Cathedrals Were White* (New York: McGraw-Hill Book Company, 1964), 135.
24 Jeffrey M. Jones, "U.S. Church Membership Down Sharply in Past Two Decades," *Gallup*, April 18, 2019, accessed October 1, 2020, https://news.gallup.com/poll/248837/church-membership-down-sharply-past-two-decades.aspx.
25 Undergraduate Enrollment, "The Condition of Education: A Letter from the Commissioner," *National Center for Education Statistics*, accessed October 1, 2020, https://nces.ed.gov/programs/coe/indicator_cha.asp.
26 Kate Gibson, "Why Is College Enrollment Declining?" *CBS News*, May 15, 2015, accessed October 1, 2020, www.cbsnews.com/news/why-is-college-enrollment-declining/.
27 Paul Fain, "College Enrollment Declines Continue," *Inside Higher Ed*, May 30, 2019, accessed October 1, 2020, www.insidehighered.com/quicktakes/2019/05/30/college-enrollment-declines-continue.

Such declines in enrollment suggest a mutable future for universities. Like denominations, their fortunes rise and fall with a variety of factors, including the political appraisal of whether education is itself of use. In a 1989 article, "How the Upstart Sects Won America: 1776–1850," sociologists of religion Roger Finke and Rodney Stark argued that the fortunes of the so-called mainline Protestant bodies declined long before contemporary statistical accounts of empty pews. Using reconstructed denominational statistics beginning in 1776, Finke and Stark show that Congregationalists, Episcopalians, and Presbyterians dominated the religious scene at the start of the American Revolution, but in less than eight decades, by 1850, they had slumped into numerical insignificance, while the Methodists and Baptists swept over the land.[28] Finke and Stark explain that the sectarian victors in the early republic reflected a shifting valuation of an educated clergy. Whereas a Congregationalist or an Episcopalian understood education as a prerequisite for clerical success, Baptists and Methodists argued formal education wasn't necessary for their leaders; at times, they intimated education was detrimental to spiritual thriving. Religious organizations launched colleges and universities in the US, but the forms of churched religions that would grow the most were not the ones with strong ties to the historic denominations that launched so many seventeenth-, eighteenth-, and nineteenth-century colleges and universities. The Christian groups and emerging sects that thrived in the nineteenth century were largely *non*denominational: not invested in the spread of a particular denominated identity but promoting a category of "Christian" as a unifying identity.

In the contemporary moment, universities are sects: they decide who is in and who is out; they control very distinct ideas of knowledge and value; they construct significant social identities for those who occupy them. Is this sectarian fact of American universities a way to understand the conflicts that take place in them? Sociologist Lorne L. Dawson, writing about cults, sects, and new religions, observes that one of the biggest problems in interpreting those groups is that it is hard to tell just really how these groups orient themselves to those outside of them. "Beliefs and practices that may appear world-rejecting from one vantage point," he writes, "may appear world-affirming or accommodating from another."[29] The problem with how we see what universities are, and whether they can be democratic, is that we forget how they began: as sites to accredit forms of authority about which we remain as ambivalent today as we were before. To consider the democratic possibilities of universities and the values they inscribe, we might do well to think about what was precisely *not* democratic in their conception and diffuse denominational flourishing.

---

28 Roger Finke and Rodney Stark, "How the Upstart Sects Won America: 1776–1850," *Journal for the Scientific Study of Religion* 28, no. 1 (March 1989): 27–44.
29 Lorne L. Dawson, "Creating 'Cult' Typologies: Some Strategic Considerations," *Journal of Contemporary Religion* 12, no. 3 (1997): 377. Quoted in Jutta M. Jokiranta, "'Sectarianism' of the Qumran 'Sect': Sociological Notes," *Revue de Qumrân* 20, no. 2 (78) (December 2001): 230.

## Secular Nonprofit as Moral Compass

Governance structures power relationships. In universities, the structuring of power relations emanates from the membership, and designation of membership, of boards of trustees. Some boards of trustees have specifically prescribed membership identities; others have a minimum number of voting members and few additional stipulations. In general, boards include figures carrying the identities of "donor" and "alumni" and "accomplished person" or "educational leader," or some combination of those roles. These boards operate collectively and through their committees, reviewing academic programs; offering strategic advice; and raising funds for the university. In notable comparison to corporate boards, academic boards of trustees usually react *to* policy rather than recommend policy. For this reason, the unifying feature of boards is not their capacity to make new profit or recruit new students; it is to protect existing profit and retain the historic idea of students. Boards rarely involve themselves in what professor teaches what class; they involve themselves in reaction to a professor's publicity. They involve themselves in the discernment of whether that publicity contributes positively or negatively to the story they tell themselves about the institution they steward through their board membership. This is a very conservative idea of power, based on preservation, not innovation.

When the South Central Jurisdictional Conference (SCJC) of the United Methodist Church sues Southern Methodist University (SMU), they do so to continue their control of SMU's Board of Trustees. When SMU moved to sever ties with the conference and denomination, it did so to have control over its Board membership. The subject of LGBT identity, and the church's relationship to that identity in liturgical practice, is the trigger that ostensibly pressed SMU to work to secularize its power structure. The specially called General Conference meeting of the United Methodist Church in February 2019 resulted in approval of the Traditional Plan, by a 438–384 vote. The Traditional Plan reinforced restrictions against same-sex unions and LGBTQ ordination.[30] The aftermath included open resistance to those policies by some US churches and conferences, and at least two plans submitted for the 2020 General Conference that call for the United Methodist Church to divide into two or more denominations, based on perspectives about homosexuality.[31] "The values of SMU remain the same, including inclusivity and respect for others," SMU president R. Gerald Turner wrote in a statement after the vote. "This commitment has not and will not change for LGBTQ individuals as well as for others." There are 13 theology schools in United States that are officially affiliated with the United Methodist

---

30 Kathy L. Gilbert, Heather Hahn, and Joey Butler, "2019 General Conference Passes Traditional Plan," *UM News*, February 26, 2019, accessed October 1, 2020, www.umnews.org/en/news/gc2019-daily-feb-26.

31 Heather Hahn, "What Comes After GC2020 Petitions Deadline," *UM News*, September 20, 2019, accessed October 1, 2020, www.umnews.org/en/news/what-comes-after-gc2020-petitions-deadline.

Church, including SMU's Perkins School of Theology. SMU is one of several Methodist universities that took steps to distance its governing body from the church after February's decision.[32] Leaders of many other United Methodist-affiliated colleges issued statements right after the 2019 General Conference, emphasizing their school's non-discriminatory policies. In April 2019, trustees of Baldwin Wallace University, in Berea, Ohio, voted to end that school's affiliation with the United Methodist Church.[33]

SMU changed its articles of incorporation to delete any mention of the General Conference in its by-laws. The proximity of this deletion to the passage of the Traditional Plan suggests SMU decided it did not want to associate with a denomination that did not affirm LGBT rights. One interpretation would argue LGBT rights often appear as a soothing frontispiece to conservative politics, a way of playing for cosmopolitan when the content of the commitment is more domesticating than divesting.[34] But this runs ahead of the specifics of what SMU did, and those particulars are our subject. In particular, SMU sought to revise the restated Articles of Incorporation filed on June 27, 1996, that confirmed the longstanding relationship between SMU and SCJC. Those restated 1996 Articles affirmed that the SCJC had specific rights, including the right to appoint SMU Trustees, the right to first approve all SMU Trustees before their appointment, the right to terminate any Trustee for cause, the right to veto any attempt to sell campus real estate, and the right to have no amendment made of these Articles of Incorporation unless first authorized and approved by SCJC.[35]

"I think this has more to do with power than with LGBTQ issues," said one SMU faculty member in a phone conversation. This is not to suggest that the SMU Board lacks LGBT-affinity. It is to suggest that a Methodist insult to LGBT rights in the General Conference is a gain for secularizing power on the SMU Board of Trustees, which isn't, necessarily, the power of queer freedom. The majority of the current Board of Trustees are on record as donating to Republican political campaigns; many openly voted for Donald Trump in the last election. Outside the school of theology, most faculty at SMU don't know what the

---

32 Audrey McClure, "South Central Jurisdictional Conference Sues SMU," *The Daily Campus*, January 22, 2020, accessed October 1, 2020, www.smudailycampus.com/news/methodist-church-sues-smu.
33 Sam Hodges, "Ohio College Severs Formal Ties with Denomination," *UM News*, April 29, 2019, accessed October 1, 2020, www.umnews.org/en/news/ohio-college-severs-formal-ties-with-denomination.
34 Jasbir K. Puar, *Terrorist Assemblages: Homonationalism in Queer Times* (Durham: Duke University Press, 2007). For an update voice on this frontier, see Greta Lafleur, "Heterosexuality Without Women," *Los Angeles Review of Books*, May 20, 2019, accessed October 1, 2020, https://blog.lareviewofbooks.org/essays/heterosexuality-without-women/.
35 Plaintiff's Original Petition, "Southern Central Jurisdictional Conference of the United Methodist Church v. Southern Methodist University," November 15, 2019, 2, accessed October 1, 2020, https://courtsportal.dallascounty.org/DALLASPROD/DocumentViewer/Embedded/uQLwR2PLSzfPBa55HUbddYHTEa5CCnj15H78RkrHfnsu0ulDRFWENZMzzcRQ8iorIVOPeOgNcTLsvljRiFNUfQ2?p=0.

word *Methodist* means. Nevertheless, its founders wove the identity of the United Methodist Church and the SCJC into its Articles of Incorporation, into specifically how they populated the Board of Trustees. Should we take the erasure of that Methodist identity from that Board as a strategic cover for internal strategic power, or should we take the erasure of that Methodist identity as a bid to become a truly secular university, more competitive with its Methodist-affiliated cousins Duke and Emory?

"By this lawsuit, the South Central Jurisdictional Conference seeks to preserve a 100-year-relationship that it or its predecessors have held with SMU," said a statement from the jurisdiction's Mission Council, which authorized the court action. SMU replied:

> SMU cherishes our history with the (United Methodist) Church, and we are committed to maintaining close connections with the church and its successors. In response to the debate regarding the future organizational structure of the church, the SMU board of trustees recently updated its governance documents to make it clear that SMU is solely maintained and controlled by its board of trustees as the ultimate authority for the university.[36]

SMU's reply says, simultaneously: *let's stay good friends* and *let's get out of business together*. SMU's November 2019 amendment to its Articles of Incorporation specifically deletes language stating that SMU was "to be forever owned, maintained and controlled by the South Central Jurisdictional Conference of The United Methodist Church."[37] This deletion is what is under dispute: did SMU have the right to do this? Or did they need to ask SCJC before they did?

The courts will decide. What interests me is to consider whether there is a value in thinking through SMU's denominational past as a component of its ethical present. The SCJC has been a governing body within SMU since the university's founding in 1911, when it gifted the campus' initial 133 acres. Prior to the opening of SMU, Vanderbilt University served as "the most potent influence in the educational awakening of the Methodist Episcopal Church, South." For forty years, its divinity school furnished just about all the professionally trained ministers of the church. Vanderbilt demonstrated that an American church's educational program was incomplete without an influential university to produce the leadership the formed establishment power. This principle led to the founding of Emory University and Southern Methodist University, both of which followed the pattern of a central school of arts and sciences surrounded by the professional schools not only of law, medicine, and theology, but also of education, agriculture, business, fine arts, and engineering. Unlike the presidents of the older

---

36 Sam Hodges, "Jurisdictional Conference Sues SMU," *UM News*, December 6, 2019, accessed October 1, 2020, www.umnews.org/en/news/jurisdictional-conference-sues-smu.
37 Elizabeth Redden, "SMU Sued for Severing Ties with Church," *Inside Higher Ed*, December 9, 2019, accessed October 1, 2020, www.insidehighered.com/news/2019/12/09/smu-sued-amending-governance-documents-separate-itself-church-authority.

Christian colleges, the leaders of this new education were not clergymen, but men defined first by a claim to a "scientific" outlook understood to be other than a "religious" one. "The complex organization," like a university, "needed men of affairs who possessed administrative skill." Eventually most boards of trustees hosted more bankers, merchants, industrialists, and railroad men rather than clergymen. "Although the new leaders of higher education were not consciously secular, their bent toward the practical considerations of life caused them to foster those aspects of the university which slowly eroded religious and sectarian influence in higher education."[38] The founders of Southern Methodist University were fully familiar with this new university movement and aspired to such status for their institution. They realized that if Methodism were to play a significant role in Texas education, it would need a university, not a Christian college.[39]

SMU was founded to be a Methodist school, but a Methodist school that *wasn't* a Christian college. It emerged in 1911 by a special educational commission of the five annual conferences of the Methodist Episcopal Church, South, in Texas. Sustaining funds by Dallas citizens were instrumental in placing SMU in Dallas. The person chosen to lead the new university was Robert Stewart Hyer (1860–1929), a native of Georgia and graduate of Emory College. He came to SMU from Southwestern University in Georgetown, Texas, where he had served as president since 1898. Hyer "immediately and significantly for all the future articulated the principle that while Southern Methodist University is denominational and cherishes the spiritual and moral values and traditions of the Church, it is by design nonsectarian." As Hyer said in 1916, "Religious denominations may properly establish institutions of higher learning, but any institution which is dedicated solely to the perpetuation of a narrow, sectarian point of view falls far short of the standards of higher learning."[40]

The original 1911 charter places ownership and control in the hands of five Texas Methodist conferences who appointed the first Board of Trustees in 1914. This was not a Methodist-affiliated school; it was, at its origins, Methodist-*owned*. As Hyer did his planning, he consulted with the presidents of Stanford and University of Chicago to think about how to build the right campus for a modern university.[41] As SMU historian Mary Martha Thomas writes,

> Hyer and Southern Methodist University did not fit into the same category as Chicago or Stanford. Instead of one enormously wealthy benefactor, SMU had to rely on the Methodists of Texas and the citizens of Dallas who

---

38 Mary Martha Hosford Thomas, *Southern Methodist University: Founding and Early Years* (Dallas: *SMU* Press, 1974), 9.
39 Ibid., 10.
40 Marshall Terry, *"From High on the Hilltop . . .": A Brief History of SMU* (Dallas: Three Forks Press and DeGolyer Library, 2008), 4.
41 "The Great Achievement of Southern Methodist University," *Texas Christian Advocate* 59, no. 47 (July 3, 1913): 1, accessed October 1, 2020, https://digitalcollections.smu.edu/digital/collection/perkins/id/9.

contributed money in relatively small amounts. Nevertheless, President Hyer designed a campus and buildings on a grand scale that would cost the kind of money Chicago and Stanford had.

Once Vanderbilt severed its connection with the Methodist Church in 1914, the Methodists sought a new "connectional institution" west of the Mississippi, meaning a university with a theology school in which to train ministers.[42] Like SMU would experience 100 years later, tensions at Vanderbilt had grown between the university administration and the General Conference of the Methodist church over the future of the school, particularly over the methods by which members of the Vanderbilt Board of Trust was chosen, and the extent to which non-Methodists could teach at the school.[43]

At its outset, SMU had an easier relationship to the church than Vanderbilt. Hyer, a physicist by training, launched the university into its early decades with a conjoined sense of scholarly and religious purpose. When he resigned in 1920, Hyer observed: "The president of a tax-supported institution must be a politician; the president of a private institution must be a financier; the president of a denominational university must be both. Since I am neither, I resign."[44] Subsequent chairmen of the Board of Trustees were bishops of the Methodist church in Texas. In 1961, observers would describe SMU as "one of the great, strong church-related universities of the United States."[45] Today SMU seeks to divest itself of formal relations with the Methodist church. I invite an analogy between divesting of religious control and control by certain financial regime. In the past fifty years, there have been calls for universities, corporations, governments, and individual investors to divest from the Sudanese government and Chinese manufacturers; from coal companies and fossil fuel industries; from companies that operate in occupied Palestinian territories and companies that operate in South Africa. Control over assets, having the right to buy or sell them, has never been a simple sovereign power of institutions. Yet institutions do move, do divest, do change through divestment and protest. The story of SMU teaches us that there is no simple cleansing of the temple.

---

42 As the legal case explained, "Then, so far as money was concerned, it was Mr. Vanderbilt, and not the church, who breathed the breath of life into this corporate body, if not dead, at least until then inert and powerless. Hence on this issue we find that Mr. Vanderbilt, and not the annual conferences or the church, was the founder and original patron of this institution." State ex rel. College of Bishops v. Board of Trust, 129 Tenn. 279, p. 22. On this legal suit, see John O. Gross, "The Bishops Versus Vanderbilt University," *Tennessee Historical Quarterly* 22 (1964): 53–65.

43 Bill Carey, *Chancellors, Commodores & Coeds: A History of Vanderbilt University* (Nashville, TN: Clearbrook Press Publishing, 2003); Daniel W. Stowell, *Rebuilding Zion: The Religious Reconstruction of the South, 1863–1877* (Oxford: Oxford University Press, 1998).

44 Terry, *From High on the Hilltop*, 9.

45 Olin W. Nail, *The History of Texas Methodism 1900–1960* (Austin: Capital, 1961), 172. Marsden takes up the specifically Methodist role in higher education in America. Marsden, *The Soul of the American University*, 276–87.

The Articles of Incorporation, original and 1996 revised, stated that SMU forever belonged to the SCJC and that the Articles couldn't be changed without the SCJC's approval. SMU says a particular part of the Texan business code supports their revision of the Articles without SCJC's approval. Now that the United Methodist Church seems to be heading back to a more moderate position on LGBT rights, the LGBT cause for SMU's divestment is gone. What is left? Nothing more, and nothing less, than the promise of sovereignty from clerical oversight. This is a familiar hope in the history of the West. And it turns out, even if you throw out the literal clerics, you don't save yourself from chauvinism and prejudice.

## Divesting the University, Divesting Ourselves

In the case of South Africa, divestment was part, and in support, of an extant political movement to end apartheid. Activists in South Africa had been using a wide array of tactics to fight for justice for decades. In the United States, the government generally ignored the call for international sanctions. Instead of heeding demands to pull out of South Africa, many companies engaged with shareholders, signed on to corporate codes of social responsibility, and changed their workplace practices. For many years, investors continued to invest in those companies while engaging with them. As repression in South Africa increased, there was a clear, understandable human cost visible every day in the struggle against apartheid.

Divestment enabled people to connect to that struggle in their own backyard by facing those invested in companies doing business in South Africa. Hundreds of companies were implicated, and the movement, of which divestment was a part, eventually succeeded in pushing the US Congress to enact strong sanctions against South Africa.[46] Divestment by itself did not end the regime in South Africa. Instead, the synergy between divestment and other aspects of the campaign eventually led to strong political action, which contributed to ending apartheid. Divestment is most successful when coordinated with a broader movement that includes multiple voices, agencies, economic, and social interests. The most compelling leaders of the anti-apartheid efforts came directly from communities suffering its worst effects; the most successful pressures place on South Africa were, finally, through financial firms.

The most popular argument in fossil fuel divestment has focused on the idea that returns will improve after an investor has removed fossil fuel stocks from his or her portfolio has played an important role in the campaign. It is based on the idea that our economy, in particular our financial markets, maintains an extraordinary overvaluation of fossil fuel reserves that at some point must burst. "Overreliance on the carbon bubble argument has the potential to undermine the clear

---

46 Daniel C. Apfel, "Exploring Divestment as a Strategy for Change: An Evaluation of the History, Success, and Challenges of Fossil Fuel Divestment," *Social Research: An International Quarterly* 82, no. 4 (Winter 2015): 919.

moral issue of investing in the destruction of the planet, yet not simultaneously promoting the financial argument may limit the number of investors willing to divest," writes Daniel C. Apfel, an expert on responsible and impact investing.[47]

What the history of Christian college secularization teaches us is that our universities have not lost their moral compass or their Protestant cohesiveness. There is no sectarian history that isn't a history of power: power within an identifiable group about who defines its authority to steward what it struggles to control. The history of the university is one about controlling communities, not about enfranchising a public outside those communities. The success of divestment programs—divestment from denomination and from certain investment patterns—requires naming the system you affirm as you elbow out someone else: a rejected application, a board member, a colleague. Although the political economy of universities is massive, the practice of their controlling interests is writ intimately, person-to-person, by—perhaps especially—those who sign divestment petitions. There is no institutional divestment without reckoning with how the reproduction of control and exclusion define the modern university more centrally than any banner about public good or moral interest. Institutions of higher education might only divest from fossil fuels when they think, too, about how hard it is for them to divest from other dependencies, integral to the system of knowledge production, necessary for their propelling of layers upon layers of sectarian power.

---

47 Ibid., 934.

# 2 Markets, Religion, and Moral Deliberation
## The Affordable Care Act's Contraceptive Mandate

*Julia D. Mahoney*

## Introduction

Deliberations about complex moral questions are a cornerstone of American democracy. These deliberations take place not only through formal, explicitly political debate but also by means of choices about whether and on what terms to participate in society, including commercial society.[1] In recent decades, the deliberative space afforded by the market sphere has shrunk as government regulation of the economy has grown. More mandates and restrictions have meant more state intrusions into areas once entrusted to individual conscience or left to ecclesial control,[2] which has in turn been accompanied by increased societal conflict. These conflicts have been particularly salient with respect to freedoms of religious conscience and exercise.[3]

The fallout from the United States Supreme Court's July 2020 decision in *Little Sisters of the Poor v. Pennsylvania*,[4] which concerned the "contraceptive mandate" for employer-provided health insurance instituted under the Affordable Care Act (ACA),[5] illustrates how combustible the intersection of commerce and religion has become. One of the most eagerly awaited rulings of the October 2019 term, *Little Sisters of the Poor* drew attention not because of the precise legal questions before the Supreme Court, which turned on technical issues of statutory interpretation and administrative law. Rather, the intense interest in *Little Sisters of the Poor* was due to its symbolism as a pitched battle in the religious "culture wars" that in recent decades have convulsed the United States.[6] On one side of the divide stands a coalition of advocacy groups and public health experts

---

1 See Julia D. Mahoney and Gil Siegal, "Beyond Nature? Genomic Modification and the Future of Humanity," *Law and Contemporary Problems* 81 (2018): 195–214.
2 See Martin E. Marty, "The Widening Gyres of Religion and Law," *DePaul Law Review* 45 (1996): 651–75.
3 See Steven D. Smith, *The Rise and Decline of American Religious Freedom* (Cambridge: Harvard University Press, 2014).
4 140 S. Ct. 2367 (2020).
5 Pub. L. No. 111–148, 124 Stat. 119 (2010).
6 See Douglas Laycock, "Religious Liberty and the Culture Wars," *University of Illinois Law Review* 2014, no. 3 (2014): 839–80.

DOI: 10.4324/9781003309291-3

that takes the position that employer-provided "cost free" contraception is essential for women's equality and well-being.[7] On the opposite side are organizations and individuals with deeply held convictions who resist—as they see it—being coerced into complicity with practices that violate their consciences.[8] What is most striking about the Supreme Court's disposition of *Little Sisters of the Poor* is how it has failed to bridge, and may even have widened, the chasm between these two groups.

The ongoing stalemate over the contraceptive mandate raises serious questions about how the United States polity will resolve (or not) tensions between fundamental values. This chapter suggests that the contraceptive mandate controversy underscores the substantial—and frequently underappreciated—costs of constricting the market sphere through heavy regulation of large chunks of the economy, including the health care sector. Decisions to transact in markets often have substantial moral components, which means that markets are key institutions for constructing and expressing moral commitments. That is, markets are spaces for working out, or at least grappling with constructively, the disagreements about moral questions that inevitably arise in any political community.

That markets can play this role in American life has ramifications for policy decisions about sensitive matters like the provision of and payment for contraceptive services. Citizens and residents of the United States hold a wide range of convictions about when human life begins,[9] how existing and potential life should be protected,[10] and what exceptions, if any, religious and moral convictions should afford their holders from laws of general applicability.[11] Consequently, rigid government rules requiring employers to cover contraception—including highly controversial methods such as hormonal therapies designed to prevent the implantation of fertilized ova—are all but guaranteed to foment anger and distrust. Private ordering, by contrast, does not compel individuals and firms to be involved in what is to them noxious activity, which means that policies that make use of voluntary transactions have the potential to avoid ill-feeling and even, in the most optimistic scenario, to foster mutual understanding.

The lesson to be drawn from an appreciation of markets as vehicles for moral deliberation is not, I emphasize, that government regulation of the economy in

---

7 See National Organization for Women, "SCOTUS Ruling on Birth Control Endangers Reproductive Health of Millions," July 8, 2020, https://now.org/media-center/press-release/scotus-ruling-on-birth-control-endangers-reproductive-health-of-millions/.
8 See Brief of Little Sisters of the Poor, Little Sisters of the Poor v. Pennsylvania (2020); Brief of Christian Business Owners Supporting Religious Freedom as *Amicus Curiae* in Support of Petitioner, Little Sisters of the Poor v. Pennsylvania (2020).
9 See Steven Andrew Jacobs, "Biologists' Consensus on 'When Life Begins'," 2018, https://papers.ssrn.com/sol3/papers.cfm?abstract_id=3211703.
10 See Michele Goodwin, *Policing the Womb: Invisible Women and the Criminalization of Motherhood* (Cambridge: Cambridge University Press, 2020).
11 See Stephanie H. Barclay, "Historical Origins of Judicial Religious Exemptions," *Notre Dame Law Review* 96, no. 1 (2020): 55–124; Micah Schwartzman, "What If Religion Is Not Special?" *University of Chicago Law Review* 79, no. 4 (Fall 2012): 1351–427.

general or health care in particular is necessarily ill advised or illegitimate. The key point, rather, is that the hard task of institutional design can be made easier by taking careful account of how Americans wrestle with moral conundrums. The failure of the political and judicial branches to settle—or even appreciably lower the temperature of—the nearly decade-long conflict over the contraceptive mandate should lead us to ask whether there might be a better way. The answer, I believe, is a clear yes, given the real promise of private ordering as an avenue for productive societal deliberation about complex moral questions of the sort implicated by the contraceptive mandate.

## The Affordable Care Act and the Administrative State

When President Barack Obama took office in January 2009, conditions looked ripe for a new "New Deal."[12] An energetic president of great personal appeal, a nation in the throes of a severe economic downturn, and substantial Democratic majorities in both the Senate and House all pointed to the possibility that the United States was on the cusp of a transformation akin to that wrought by Franklin D. Roosevelt in the 1930s. High on the list of the new administration's objectives was reforming the nation's health care system.[13]

There were good reasons for the Obama administration to focus on health care reform. Although a majority of Americans expressed satisfaction with their own medical care and health insurance coverage, the number of uninsured Americans was approaching fifty million. In addition, fears of ruinous medical costs contributed to a sense of insecurity among many Americans.[14] There were also worries about the United States' high and rapidly growing levels of health care spending.[15]

But putting together health legislation proved challenging for the Obama administration, not least because of the absence of a discernable national consensus about how best to overhaul an unwieldy system.[16] Determined not to repeat the mistakes of the Clinton administration, which had excluded powerful constituencies from the working groups that hammered out the ill-fated "HillaryCare" and then presented Congress with a completed plan,[17] the Obama administration chose to let Congress take the lead on the design of health care reform.[18]

---

12 Theda Skocpol and Lawrence R. Jacobs, *Reaching for a New Deal: Ambitious Governance, Economic Meltdown, and Polarized Politics in Obama's First Two Years* (New York: Russell Sage Foundation, 2011).
13 See Jonathan Alter, *The Promise: Obama, Year One* (New York: Simon & Schuster, 2010).
14 See Jacob S. Hacker, *The Great Risk Shift: The New Economic Insecurity and the Decline of the American Dream* (New York: Oxford University Press, 2008).
15 See Chapin White, "Health Care Spending Growth: How Different Is the United States from the Rest of the OECD?" *Health Affairs* 26, no. 1 (January–February 2007): 154–60.
16 See Paul Starr, *Remedy and Reaction: The Peculiar American Struggle Over Health Care Reform* (New Haven: Yale University Press, 2011).
17 See Paul Starr, "What Happened to Health Care Reform?" *The American Prospect* 20 (Winter 1995): 20–31.
18 See Jonathan Alter, *The Promise: Obama, Year One* (New York: Simon & Schuster, 2010).

Things soon turned ugly, even by the standards of Washington, D.C., a town accustomed to rent-seeking and partisan vitriol. What emerged from the protracted, messy legislative process was a bill of enormous complexity that was voted into law in March 2010 by narrow margins in the House and Senate and that failed to garner bipartisan support. Building on the existing system of private insurance and government programs and focusing on "coverage" (as distinct from access to care),[19] ACA imposed a plethora of additional rules on the already intensively regulated health care sector.[20] Among these new rules were an "individual mandate," which required most United States citizens and residents to maintain health insurance coverage or pay a penalty,[21] and an "employer mandate" obligating most large and medium-sized employers to offer health coverage to their full-time employees.[22]

As enacted, ACA was not just complicated but in crucial respects inchoate.[23] This was no accident. It has become standard practice for Congress not to fix the precise meaning of many statutory provisions, but instead to leave it to government agencies to fill in gaps through rulemaking and other administrative procedures.[24] This tendency of Congress to decline to make tough calls when it drafts legislation and instead devolve authority to the "administrative state" means that most of the rules Americans now live under are crafted not by elected legislators but by unelected bureaucrats, with the result that government has become less directly accountable to voters.[25]

The administrative state's critics express concerns that government agencies are now vested with legislative, executive, and judicial powers in ways that contravene—or are at the very least in profound tension with—the allocations of government power set out in the United States Constitution.[26] Defenders of a muscular administrative state counter that entrusting agencies with strong powers is not only lawful but also essential for promoting the general welfare of the

---

19 See Ezekiel J. Emanuel, *Which Country Has the World's Best Health Care?* (New York: Public Affairs, 2020), 18–26, 360–61; Jonathan Oberlander, "Unfinished Journey—A Century of Health Care Reform in the United States," *New England Journal of Medicine* 367 (2012): 585–90.
20 See Jacob S. Hacker, "The Road to Somewhere: Why Health Reform Happened, Or Why Political Scientists Who Write About Public Policy Shouldn't Assume They Know How to Shape It," *Perspectives on Politics* 8 (2010): 861–76.
21 See NFIB v. Sebelius, 567 U.S. 519 (2012).
22 See Burwell v. Hobby Lobby, 573 U.S. 682 (2014).
23 See John E. McDonough, *Inside National Health Care Reform* (Berkeley: University of California Press, 2011), 290–92.
24 See Gillian Metzger, "1930s Redux: The Administrative State Under Siege," *Harvard Law Review* 131 (2017): 1–95.
25 See Rachel Augustine Potter, *Bending the Rules: Procedural Politicking in the Bureaucracy* (Chicago, IL: University of Chicago Press, 2019).
26 See Richard A. Epstein, *The Dubious Morality of Administrative Law* (London: Rowman & Littlefield, 2020); Philip Hamburger, *Is Administrative Law Unlawful?* (Chicago: University of Chicago Press, 2014).

populace in the twenty-first century.[27] After all, or so the argument goes, it takes a substantial bureaucracy to harness the technocratic expertise needed to address the complex challenges of modern-day society.[28] As for fears that concentrating vast powers in administrative agencies threatens fundamental freedoms, administrative law has well-developed doctrines that—at least in the view of the proponents of a strong administrative state—effectively constrain agencies from abuse and overreach.[29]

## The Contraceptive Mandate: Of Politics and Experts

One of the indeterminate provisions included in ACA was the "Women's Health Amendment," which requires employers that provide health insurance to furnish their female employees with "preventive care and screenings" without "any cost sharing requirements."[30] ACA's text does not define "preventive care and screenings" for purposes of the Women's Health Amendment, instead providing that the term is to be given content "in comprehensive guidelines supported by the Health Resources and Services Administration (HRSA)," a component of the Department of Health and Human Services (HHS).[31] In discharging its duty under ACA to determine what employers must cover, HRSA sought the input of the Institute of Medicine (IOM), now known as the National Academy of Medicine (NAM). The NAM is one of three components of the National Academies of Sciences, Engineering, and Medicine, all of which are private, nonprofit organizations that operate under an 1863 Congressional charter, as the NAM's website explains, to "provide objective advice on matters of science, technology, and health."[32]

In response to HRSA's request for assistance, the IOM (as it was then) convened the Committee on Preventive Services for Women, made up of sixteen distinguished experts in medicine, public health, and health policy.[33] In July 2011, the IOM issued a report concluding that preventive services for women should include all female contraceptive methods and sterilization procedures, as well as associated services, approved by the Federal Drug Administration (FDA).[34] The list of FDA-approved contraceptive methods included "four methods that many

---

27  See Cass R. Sunstein and Adrian Vermeule, *Law & Leviathan: Redeeming the Administrative State* (Cambridge: The Belknap Press of Harvard University Press, 2020).
28  See Blake Emerson, *The Public's Law: Origins and Architecture of Progressive Democracy* (New York: Oxford University Press, 2019).
29  See Cass R. Sunstein and Adrian Vermeule, "The Morality of Administrative Law," *Harvard Law Review* 131 (2018): 1924–78.
30  ACA, 42 U.S.C. § 300gg—13(a)(4).
31  Ibid.
32  National Academy of Medicine website, https://nam.edu/about-the-nam/.
33  See Helen Alvare, "A Perfect Storm: Religion, Sex, and Administrative Law," *St. John's Law Review* 92 (2018): 697–753.
34  Institute of Medicine, *Clinical Preventive Services for Women: Closing the Gaps* (Washington, DC: The National Academies Press, 2011).

'who believe life begins at conception regard . . . as causing abortion.'"[35] The following month, HRSA issued the initial version of its "Women's Preventive Services Guidelines," which adopted the IOM report's recommendations.[36]

From one perspective, HRSA's reliance on the IOM's advice made sense. To draw on the expertise of such a distinguished body ensures—or so one might assume—that decisions about the most intimate aspects of women's lives will be grounded in scientific knowledge and shielded from partisan pressures. Yet, even as the IOM drafted the recommendations HRSA was to embrace and make legally binding, it was evident that distinguishing "science" from "politics" in the area of women's health services would be no simple task. Critics of the IOM approach argued—and have continued to argue—that the relationship between women's health and the health services recommended by IOM is at best highly attenuated, and at worst nonexistent. Far from expressing an apolitical expert conclusion, critics charge, the IOM report was a brief for a particular vision of what women need and how they should live– a vision not shared by, and indeed profoundly objectionable to, a large percentage of the electorate.[37] That IOM and HRSA saw no reason to reconsider their position on which methods the contraceptive mandate should comprise illustrates why entrusting decisions to bureaucrats can inflame the culture wars. As law and religion expert Mark Rienzi points out, administrative agencies have a pronounced tendency to "undervalue, ignore, or simply be unaware of competing interests that outside of their specialty field," a tendency that may be especially acute with respect to issues that touch on religion, as modern-day bureaucratic culture is strongly secular.[38]

HRSA did understand that a contraceptive mandate instructing employers to cover items commonly classified as abortifacients could ignite a political firestorm.[39] To address this problem, HRSA was willing to exempt a limited number of employers from the mandate's strictures. There has followed a decade-long struggle over precisely which organizations will be granted relief by the federal government. At the time of the issuance of the August 2011 guidelines, a narrow exemption was fashioned that applied mostly to houses of worship, but this "church exemption" did not quell the controversy over the contraceptive mandate. Many organizations that did not satisfy the strict eligibility requirements of the "church exemption" objected to being pressured to violate their principles, including Hobby Lobby Stores, Inc., a closely held for-profit corporation that

---

35 Brief of Little Sisters of the Poor, Little Sisters of the Poor v. Pennsylvania (2020) (quoting Burwell v. Hobby Lobby, Inc., 573 U.S. at 698 n. 7).
36 See Women's Preventive Services Guidelines, Fed. Reg. 8725.
37 See Helen Alvare, "No Compelling Interest: The 'Birth Control' Mandate and Religious Freedom," *Villanova Law Review* 58 (2013): 391–411.
38 See Mark Rienzi, "Administrative Power and Religious Liberty at the Supreme Court," *Case Western Reserve Law Review* 69 (2019): 355–94.
39 See William P. Marshall, "Bad Statutes Make Bad Law: *Burwell v. Hobby Lobby*," *Supreme Court Review* 2014, no. 1 (2015): 71–131.

operates a chain of arts and crafts stores,[40] and the Little Sisters of the Poor, an international congregation of Roman Catholic women committed to serving the elderly poor.[41]

Regulators then created an "accommodation" for certain religious nonprofit entities, most notably colleges, universities, and charitable organizations, that were ineligible for the "church exemption." This "accommodation" allowed religious entities to avoid directly covering contraception by providing notice of religious objections to some or all of the FDA-approved services.[42] After the provision of notice by the objecting nonprofit organizations, their insurers (or, in the case of self-insured health care plans, the third-party plan administrators) would take steps to provide coverage for contraceptives with no employee payment obligations at the point of service. This "accommodation," too, failed to calm the waters. Little Sisters of the Poor and other nonprofits maintained that the "accommodation" compelled them to participate, albeit indirectly, in activity they sincerely believed to be immoral or face potentially ruinous financial penalties. And for-profit firms like Hobby Lobby expressed dismay that no accommodation had been made for them.

## The Contraceptive Mandate in Court

Frustrated with the perceived failures of the federal government to adequately respect their commitments of conscience or other interests with respect to the contraceptive mandate, numerous entities have sought relief from the courts. In the past seven years, no fewer than three cases involving the contraceptive mandate have come before the United States Supreme Court: *Burwell v. Hobby Lobby Stores, Inc.*,[43] *Zubik v. Burwell*,[44] and *Little Sisters of the Poor v. Pennsylvania*.[45] All told, litigation over the contraceptive mandate has consumed staggering quantities of time, effort, and money. But none of the cases has had an appreciable impact in terms of ending, or even alleviating, the suspicions and resentments that characterize the culture war over the provision of contraception. Indeed, it is hard not to wonder whether these highly publicized court battles have not exacerbated the partisan divide.

*Burwell v. Hobby Lobby*, decided in 2014, addressed the issue of what protections the Religious Freedom Restoration Act (RFRA),[46] a 1993 federal law enacted with the stated purpose of preventing other federal laws and regulations

---

40 See James Nelson, "Conscience, Incorporated," *Michigan State Law Review* 2013, no. 5 (2013): 1565–610.
41 See Constance Veit, "Obamacare's Birth-Control 'Exemption' Still Tramples on Rights," *New York Times*, March 18, 2016.
42 78 Fed. Reg. 39,870, 39,874–39,882 (2013).
43 573 U.S. 682 (2014).
44 136 S.Ct. 1557 (2016).
45 140 S. Ct. 2367 (2020).
46 2 42 U.S.C. §§ 2000bb-1(a), (b).

from substantially burdening the free exercise of religion unless the government policy or program in question constitutes the least restrictive means to achieve a compelling government interest, affords closely held business corporations. The notion that corporations operated for profit could have religious commitments such that the contraceptive mandate should not apply to them had been soundly rejected by the Obama administration, which had declined to craft any sort of exemption or accommodation for such firms. In court, the Obama administration argued that for-profit corporations fell outside of the protections of, and thus could assert no claim under, RFRA.[47] A five-justice majority of the Supreme Court rejected the government's position. Writing for the Court, Justice Alito held that RFRA's protections extend to firms like Hobby Lobby, thus protecting the religious freedom of those who own and control them.[48] The Court further determined that the contraceptive mandate substantially burdened the religious free exercise of the closely held plaintiff corporations Conestoga Wood Specialties and Hobby Lobby, Inc., and—pointing to the accommodation offered to religious nonprofits as an indication of steps not taken—that the government had not made use of the least restrictive means when regulating. Reaction to the outcome in *Hobby Lobby* largely split along predictable ideological lines. Social conservatives heralded the Court's construction of RFRA as in accord with the statute's purpose of safeguarding religious liberty,[49] while many on the left worried that excusing compliance with government rules on the grounds of religious belief could diminish the rights of women.[50]

The contraceptive mandate returned to the Supreme Court in 2016 in *Zubik v. Burwell*, with ninety minutes of oral argument devoted to multiple cases brought by an assortment of plaintiffs, primarily religious nonprofit organizations, including the Little Sisters of the Poor. Invoking RFRA, plaintiffs argued that to submit notice of their religious objections to providing contraceptive coverage under the terms of the "accommodation" would substantially burden the exercise of their religion. Following oral argument, the Court requested additional information from the parties concerning the feasibility of a possible compromise, which would have entailed providing contraceptive coverage to the plaintiffs' employees without the need for plaintiffs to furnish the notice they so fiercely objected to. Upon

---

47 See Alan J. Meese and Nathan B. Oman, "Hobby Lobby, Corporate Law, and the Theory of the Firm: Why For-Profit Corporations Are RFRA Persons," *Harvard Law Review Forum* 127 (2014): 273–301.
48 See Elizabeth Pollman, "Corporate Law and Theory in Hobby Lobby," in *The Rise of Corporate Religious Liberty*, eds. Micah Schwartzman, Chad Flanders, and Zoë Robinson (Oxford: Oxford University Press, 2016).
49 See Kevin Walsh, "Symposium: Looking Forward from the Supreme Court's Important but Unsurprising Hobby Lobby Decision," *SCOTUSBLOG*, July 1, 2014, www.scotusblog.com/2014/07/symposium-looking-forward-from-the-supreme-courts-important-but-unsurprising-hobby-lobby-decision/.
50 See Leah Rutman, "The *Hobby Lobby* Decision: Imposing Religious Beliefs on Employees," *ACLU Washington*, August 11, 2014, https://aclu-wa.org/blog/hobby-lobby-decision-imposing-religious-beliefs-employees.

being informed that its suggested plan was in fact a possibility, the Court disposed of the case in a *per curiam* ("by the court") opinion unsigned by any of the Justices. In its brief opinion, the Court declined to express any view on "whether petitioners' religious exercise has been substantially burdened, whether the government has a compelling interest, or whether the current regulations are the least restrictive means of serving that interest."[51] The Court then remanded the cases back to the lower courts for further proceedings.

The Court's envisioned compromise plan never came to fruition. To no one's surprise, there turned out to be no clear route to modifying the applicable federal regulations so as to satisfy the various constituencies, and in any event the outcome of the 2016 presidential election led to an overhaul in federal government policy. The Trump administration revised the definition of exempt religious employer to encompass nonprofit organizations—such as the Little Sisters of the Poor—as well as for-profit firms.[52] In addition, a new "moral exemption" was created that applied to nonprofit and closely held for-profit firms with "sincerely held moral objections" to providing some or all contraceptive coverage.[53] The Commonwealth of Pennsylvania and the State of New Jersey sued, asserting that the Trump administration lacked authority under either ACA or RFRA to promulgate the revised religious and new moral exemptions. The states also claimed that the procedures by which the new regulations were put in force violated the Administrative Procedure Act,[54] the federal statute that governs the processes through which federal agencies develop and issue regulations.

The Trump administration defended its actions, and the Little Sisters of the Poor intervened in the litigation on the government's side. When the dispute over the new rules reached the United States Supreme Court, public interest ran high. Briefs were filed by not only the parties to the litigation but also a host of *amici* that included Planned Parenthood Federation of America, the American College of Obstetricians and Gynecologists, the United States Conference of Catholic Bishops, and the Foundation for Moral Law. Oral Argument in *Little Sisters of the Poor* drew extensive press coverage.

As expected, the Court's decision was controversial.[55] Also as expected, the Supreme Court's disposition of the case did not end the quarrel. Instead, *Little Sisters of the Poor* merely set the stage for yet another round of litigation. The majority opinion by Justice Thomas concludes the Trump administration acted within its statutory authority and that the rules that promulgated the exemptions at issue were "free from the procedural defects"[56] alleged by the rules' challengers. Justice Thomas' opinion also takes pains to express admiration and sympathy

---

51  136 S.Ct. 1557.
52  83 Fed. Reg. 57,536 (2018).
53  83 Fed. Reg. 57,592 (2018).
54  5 USC §551 et seq. (1946).
55  See Susannah Luhti, "Supreme Court Upholds Trump's Rollback of Birth Control Coverage Mandate," *Politico*, July 8, 2020.
56  140 S.Ct. 2367.

for the Little Sisters of the Poor, observing that for "over 150 years, the Little Sisters have engaged in faithful service and sacrifice, motivated by a religious calling to surrender all for the sake of their brother" and pointing out that

> the past seven years, they—like so many other religious objectors who have participated in the litigation and rulemakings leading up to today's decision—have had to fight for the ability to continue in their noble work without violating their sincerely held religious beliefs.[57]

Justice Kagan, joined by Justice Breyer, did not join Justice Thomas' majority opinion but did concur in the judgment of the Court. That made seven votes for the federal government and the Little Sisters of the Poor, an impressive victory. But even as Justice Kagan sided with the majority, she made it clear that the Little Sisters' victory might be short lived, for she expressed doubts that the exemptions in question "can survive administrative law's demand for reasoned decision-making."[58] As Justice Kagan observed, Pennsylvania and New Jersey might yet prevail in their fight against the exemptions on the grounds that the rules establishing them are "arbitrary and capricious."

The claim of arbitrariness and capriciousness was not before the United States Supreme Court in the *Little Sisters* case and thus remains open for lower courts to address. And, almost immediately after the decision in *Little Sisters* was handed down, Pennsylvania's Attorney General indicated the state plaintiffs plan to pursue the "arbitrary and capricious" line of argument in their ongoing efforts to persuade courts to invalidate the exemptions crafted by the Trump administration.[59] Of course, such efforts may turn out to be unnecessary, given the outcome of the 2020 presidential election. As of early 2021, it appears highly probable to knowledgeable observers that the Biden administration that took office in January 2021 will remove the "conscience" exemptions to the contraceptive mandate.[60]

## Private Ordering and the Culture Wars

For most of American history, individuals and organizations enjoyed wide latitude to determine whether and on what terms to engage in commerce. These market freedoms have been crucial components of liberties of religious conscience and exercise. That is in large measure because for many believers, religion is not a wholly separate area of life, hermetically sealed off from commercial and other

---

57 140 S. Ct. 2367.
58 Ibid. (Justice Kagan, concurring in the judgment).
59 See Josh Shapiro, "Press Release: This Fight Is Not Over," July 8, 2020.
60 See Swapna Reddy, Mary Saxon, Yeonsoo Sara Lee, and Nina Patel, "Reproductive Rights and Justice: A Critical Opportunity for the Biden Administration to Protect Hard-Fought Gains," *Health Affairs Blog*, March 31, 2021, www.healthaffairs.org/do/10.1377/hblog20210326.802027/full/.

social pursuits, but a "vital force that informs their activity in counting houses just as much as in houses of prayer."[61] The expansion of government regulation of the economy, however, has reduced these freedoms, with a concomitant decrease in the deliberative space afforded by the marketplace. As a result, many of today's most emotionally fraught controversies, including those that, like the struggle over the contraceptive mandate, arise at the intersection of commerce and religion, must be worked out—to the extent they do end up being worked out—in the political arena and in the courts. The consequences of this shift are significant and may include fueling the ideological polarization that is now such a prominent feature of American life.

It bears emphasis that there is no reason to think that amplifying partisan rancor is a goal of those who advocate or implement extensive government oversight of the economy, including the members of Congress who voted for ACA and the federal bureaucrats who promulgated the original contraceptive mandate. It is more plausible that what has gone on is a collective failure to appreciate fully the role of private ordering in societal deliberations over moral questions. After all, discussions of the benefits of markets tend not to focus—at least not explicitly—on their "social construction" aspects but instead on how markets promote economic efficiency and enhance personal autonomy.[62]

It is not that the capacity of markets to facilitate social cooperation has gone completely unrecognized. On the contrary: there is a rich literature on how commerce allows people with divergent and even inimical religious and ideological convictions to come together and transact for mutual gain without violence or strife,[63] in part by encouraging empathy, as markets reward those with a keen grasp of the minds—and hearts—of potential trading partners.[64] That said, market activity involves more than the satisfaction of needs and preferences formed outside the market realm, for markets provide both physical and metaphorical spaces for constructing moral perspectives. Many decisions to engage in or refrain from particular transactions, after all, have strong moral valences. High-profile examples include the purchase or sale of human embryos for biomedical

---

61 See Nathan B. Oman, "The Need for a Law of Church and Market," *Duke Law Journal Online* 64 (April 2015): 141–60.
62 See Roy Kreitner, "Voicing the Market: Extending the Ambition of Contract Theory," *University of Toronto Law Journal* 69, no. 3 (2019): 295–336; Hanoch Dagan, Avihay Dorfman, Roy Kreitner, and Daniel Markovits, "The Law of the Market," *Law and Contemporary Problems* 83, no. 2 (2020), i–xviii.
63 See Luigino Bruni and Robert Sugden, "Reclaiming Virtue Ethics in Economics," *Journal of Economic Perspectives* 27, no. 4 (2013): 141–64; Nathan B. Oman, *The Dignity of Commerce: Markets and the Moral Foundations of Contract Law* (Chicago: University of Chicago Press, 2016), 58.
64 See Albert O. Hirschman, *The Passions and the Interests: Political Arguments for Capitalism Before Its Triumph* (Princeton: Princeton University Press, 1977); Albert O. Hirschman, "Rival Interpretations of Market Society: Civilizing, Destructive, or Feeble?" *Journal of Economic Literature* 20, no. 4 (1982): 1463–84.

research[65] or fertility purposes;[66] dealings in "conflict minerals"[67] and "fair-trade" items;[68] preferring "local" merchants over their more geographically remote business competitors;[69] boycotting counterparties adjudged morally defective;[70] and—of course—providing health insurance that covers contraception, particularly contraceptive methods that can be plausibly classified as abortifacients. To decide whether or not to engage in such transactions and, if so, on what terms, often entails not monomaniacal attention to maximizing financial returns but identifying and weighing normative considerations.

This deliberative aspect of markets is relevant not only for the principals who must decide whether to go forward with or hold back from particular transactions. Choices of market actors may influence the attitudes and judgments of observers, for what one's fellow citizens are willing and not willing to do is strong, albeit by no means dispositive, evidence of moral acceptability. That is not to argue that verbal statements, as distinct from actions or inactions, are unimportant, much less that the giving of reasons and exchanges of views that characterize political debate and legal process are not useful for moral decision-making. Nor is it to claim that legislative, administrative, or judicial arenas are unsuitable venues for addressing disputes about issues of moral urgency. What I am suggesting is that political engagement and litigation are by no means the only vehicles through which we can arrive at and exercise moral judgments about what sort of world we aim to create.[71]

In the context of contraceptive services, reducing the scope of government regulation has the potential to scale down, if not necessarily end, the culture wars. That is because for all the fierce rhetoric that has accompanied the decade-long dispute over the terms of the contraceptive mandate, increased market freedom has something to offer both sides. A good place to start would be to consider adopting the recent recommendation of the American College of Obstetricians and Gynecologists that many hormonal contraceptives for which prescriptions are now required be available "over the counter."[72] This change promises to reduce

---

65 See Russell Korobkin, "Buying and Selling Human Tissues for Stem Cell Research," *Arizona Law Review* 49, no. 1 (2007): 45–67.
66 See I. Glenn Cohen and Eli Y. Adashi, "Made to Order Embryos for Sale—A Brave New World?" *New England Journal of Medicine* 368 (2013): 2517–19.
67 See Sy Teffel, "Towards an Ethical Electronics: Ecologies of Congolese Conflict Minerals," *Westminster Papers in Communication and Culture* 10, no. 1 (2015): 18–33.
68 See Peter Griffiths, "Ethical Objections to Fairtrade," *Journal of Business Ethics* 105 (2012): 357–73.
69 See Benjamin Ferguson and Christopher Thompson, "Why Buy Local," *Journal of Applied Philosophy* 38, no. 1 (2020): 104–20.
70 See Linda Radzik, "Boycotts and the Social Enforcement of Justice," *Social Philosophy and Policy* 34, no. 1 (2017): 102–22.
71 Cf. Seana Valentine Shiffrin, "Inducing Moral Deliberation: On the Occasional Virtues of Fog," *Harvard Law Review* 123, no. 5 (March 2010): 1214–46.
72 American College of Obstetricians and Gynecologists, "Over-the-Counter Access to Hormonal Contraception: ACOC Committee Opinion 788," *Obstetrics and Gynecology* 134 (2019): 96–105.

the prices of many of these methods, which in a number of instances have soared since the introduction of the contraception mandate.[73] More affordable prices for controversial contraceptive methods lowers the stakes of the fight over the contraceptive mandate as its existence (or not) will have significant impacts on the lives of fewer women. It is true that for some supporters of the contraceptive mandate a substantial component of the mandate's attraction may lie in its expressive value that religious and moral objections will have limited sway when it comes to women's services, and for those who feel that way, any reduction in obligations imposed on the Little Sisters of the Poor and similar groups may be experienced as a defeat. But it seems at least plausible that most of the support for the contraceptive mandate has been rooted in considerations about the importance of access to contraception for women of reproductive age, and that pressuring nuns and others to violate their consciences has not been a major aspect of the mandate's appeal. If that is correct, then an overhaul of government regulation of contraceptive methods has real promise.

Even if the cost of contraception falls, of course, some women will still struggle to afford health services. In such instances, private ordering may furnish effective, innovative solutions. For example, nonprofit organizations could step up to serve as intermediaries to purchase contraceptives to ensure that all women, including women employed by firms that have religious or moral qualms about certain forms of contraception, have available to them the full range of contraceptive services. The willingness of these nonprofit firms—which could be religious or non-religious—to traffic in contraceptive methods deemed morally problematic by a significant fraction of United States society would send a powerful message of moral acceptability with the potential to influence the moral judgments of others. This message would have particular force when delivered by religious nonprofit organizations, for throughout American history religious organizations have enjoyed high levels of public trust as they have inculcated their distinct philosophies of morality and human flourishing.[74] To meet the costs of contraceptive purchases, nonprofit firms could accept donations from individuals and organizations that believe it is important for women to have available the full range of FDA-approved contraceptive methods at zero cost to them at the time of provision. This, too, would send a moral message, one that is arguably far stronger than voting for candidates who in turn support a law that delegates the details of contraception coverage requirements to administrative agencies.

In such a world, the Little Sisters of the Poor, Hobby Lobby, and others with deep-seated objections to particular contraceptives would retain the power to communicate their negative moral judgments by standing aside and declining involvement. It is true that the message sent would be in a sense a weaker one

---

73 See Charles Silver and David Hyman, *Overcharged: Why Americans Pay Too Much for Healthcare* (Washington, DC: Cato Institute, 2019).
74 See Michael W. McConnell, "The New Establishmentarianism," *Chicago-Kent Law Review* 75 (2000): 475.

than the one Little Sisters and other objectors have been sending, for the danger of serious legal penalties would be removed, giving them less "skin in the game." Yet, even under this proposal, objectors would still shoulder a significant burden, for they would be closely identified with unpopular convictions in a society where holders of such convictions are vulnerable to "doxxing," "cancellation," and other unofficial punishments.

## Conclusion

Throughout American history, commerce and religion have been "closely intertwined."[75] Inevitably, this has led to conflict. In recent years, these conflicts have grown more numerous and protracted as government regulation of the economy has expanded. To date, debates over the scope and character of government regulation have failed to focus on how reducing the market sphere has diminished opportunities for public deliberation about crucial moral questions, with attendant negative consequences for American democracy. A more complete understanding of the deliberative function of markets could promote more thoughtfully tailored government regulations and even help build a more cohesive society.

---

75 Mark Rienzi, "God and the Profits: Is There Religious Liberty for Money-Makers?" *George Mason Law Review* 21 (2013): 59–116.

# 3 Regulating Religion in the Public Arena

## Lessons Learned from Global Data Collections

*Roger Finke and Kerby Goff*

Granting free exercise to all religions and providing formal state support to none was considered radical and potentially dangerous when proposed by Jefferson and Madison in early America.[1] It still is.

Dubbed a "lively experiment" and the "hinge upon which the history of Christianity of America really turns" by prominent historian Sidney Mead, these freedoms became an important foundation for the young democracy.[2] In his now famous *Democracy in America*, Alexis de Tocqueville commented that upon his arrival in the United States, "it was the religious atmosphere which first struck me,"[3] and he further noted that religion in America "makes full use of democratic tendencies."[4] The new freedoms resulted in an entirely new religious economy. Although religious institutions' direct influence through state channels was lost with the separation of religion and state, the new freedoms opened up new avenues for religious institutions and individuals to participate in the public arena. They quickly became institutional havens for minorities and new immigrants.[5] Rather than resulting in the demise of religion, as many had predicted, the deregulated religious market allowed all religions to compete on equal footing and resulted in what would later be called the churching of America.[6]

---

1 Various forms of religious toleration and religious diversity have existed throughout history and within many religious traditions. Contemporary non-Western initiatives for supporting religious diversity, such as the Marakesh Declaration (www.marrakeshdeclaration.org), build on these. We take the American example as a reference point simply because of its importance for contemporary global standards reflected in the UN Declaration on Human Rights.
2 Sidney Mead, *The Lively Experiment: The Shaping of Christianity in America* (New York: Harper & Row, 1976), 52.
3 Alexis de Toqueville, *Democracy in America and Two Essays on America,* trans. Gerald Bevan (London: Penguin Books, 2003), 345.
4 Ibid., 510.
5 See Jay P. Dolan, *The American Catholic Experience: A History from Colonial Times to the Present* (New York: Image Books, 1985); Fenggang Yang and Helen Rose Ebaugh, "Transformation in New Immigrant Religions and Their Global Implications," *American Sociological Review* 66, no. 2 (2001): 269–88.
6 Roger Finke, "Religious Deregulation: Origins and Consequences," *Journal of Church and State* 32, no. 3 (1990): 609–26; Roger Finke and Rodney Stark, *The Churching of America:*

Yet, the extent of religious freedom has become a source of debate in democracies and non-democracies alike. The relationship religion holds with the state and the freedoms it receives are a source of tension across the globe. Bitter and sometimes violent battles have ensued on the role of religion in the public arena. This has resulted in wide variation in how religion and state are related and little consensus on the consequences of these varied relationships.

Despite these ongoing tensions, the relationship between religion and state has received surprisingly little attention by the social sciences. Until recently, global data on the relationship was lacking, limiting our ability to document the varied relationships or to explore the consequences of these relationships. Over the past fifteen years, however, a series of cross-national data collections have documented the intensity of the debates on religious freedoms and the wide variation in the relationship religion holds with the state and larger culture. The Religion and State Project (RAS), the Association of Religion Data Archives (ARDA), and the Pew Research Center have all collected detailed measures on each nation's support, favoritism, regulation, discrimination, and persecution of religion, as well as the actions of non-state actors toward religion.[7] In addition, the RAS Project has collected the same data for individual minority groups within each nation.[8] Together, these collections have fostered a rapidly growing body of research.[9]

This chapter documents and describes the varied relationships that religion holds with the state and larger culture and how these relationships are related to religious markets, democracy, and religion's role in the public arena. Relying on the new data collections, we will review ten lessons learned from recent research. In the first three lessons, we briefly document that despite constitutional promises, religious freedoms are routinely denied across the globe, including in democracies. The next four lessons identify the motivations and sources behind the restrictions and discrimination. We find that democratic forms of governance (e.g., independent judiciary and free elections) do serve to protect religious freedoms, but societal pressures and the agencies administering government policies can remain powerful forces in reducing freedom, especially for religious

---

*Winners and Losers in Our Religious Economy*, 2nd ed. (New Brunswick: Rutgers University Press, 2005).

7 Brian J. Grim and Roger Finke, "International Religion Indexes: Governmental Regulation, Government Favoritism, and Social Regulation of Religion," *Interdisciplinary Journal of Research on Religion* 2 (2006): 1–40, www.religjournal.com/; Jonathan Fox, "Out of Sync: The Disconnect Between Constitutional Clauses and State Legislation on Religion," *Canadian Journal of Political Science* 44, no. 1 (2011): 59–81; "Global Uptick in Government Restrictions on Religion in 2016: Nationalist Parties and Organizations Played an Increasing Role in Harassment of Religious Minorities, Especially in Europe," *Pew Research Center*, accessed June 1, 2021, www.pewforum.org/2018/06/21/global-uptick-in-government-restrictions-on-religion-in-2016/.

8 Yasmine Akbaba and Jonathan Fox, "The Religion and State-Minorities Dataset," *Journal of Peace Research* 48, no. 6 (2011): 807–16.

9 All of the ARDA and RAS collections can be downloaded free of charge from theARDA.com. Select years of the Pew collections can be downloaded.

minorities. In the final three lessons, we explore the social, economic, and political consequences of placing restrictions on religions. Although less research has been devoted to understanding the consequences, the early research has documented that the consequences are many.

One final note on the data sources. Although the collections will report high levels of discrimination, regulation, and acts denying religious freedoms, the occurrences are, no doubt, much more numerous. In order for an action to be included in the collection, the act had to be reported by a trusted news or government source, and coders had to verify the credibility of the report. In most cases, the actions coded relied on multiple sources. As such, these data collections are conservative estimates of the actual levels of religious discrimination and regulation.

## The Promise and Practice of Religious Freedom

### Lesson 1

*Constitutional promises of religious freedom are the new standard.*

The radical religious freedoms granted in eighteenth-century America have gradually become the new global standard. On the record, more than nine in ten countries with populations greater than two million have constitutions modeled in part or in whole after the United Nations' Universal Declaration of Human Rights (1948), stating that "everyone has the right to freedom of thought, conscience and religion" and the freedom "to manifest [their] religion or belief in teaching, practice, worship and observance." Although debates continue on what religious freedom should mean, the Declaration of Human Rights has served as a template for many constitutions and remains a global standard.[10]

A close reading of the constitutions, however, quickly finds that the promises given in one clause of the constitution are threatened by another. Article 2 of the 2004 constitution of the Islamic Republic of Afghanistan promises that "followers of other religions are free to exercise their faith and perform their religious rites within the limits of the provisions of law," but article 3 states that "no law can be contrary to the beliefs and provisions of the sacred religion of Islam."[11]

In China's constitution, Article 36 promises "freedom of religious belief" and offers the assurance that "No state organ, public organization, or individual may compel citizens to believe in, or not to believe in, any religion; nor may they discriminate against citizens who believe in, or do not believe in, any religion." Yet,

---

10 Despite being labeled as the orphan of human rights in the 1990s, religious freedom was one of the first rights to be recognized under international law and national constitutions have followed suit (Allen D. Hertzke, *Freeing God's Children: The Unlikely Alliance for Global Human Rights* (Lanham, MD: Rowman & Littlefield, 2004), 64).
11 To review the constitutional clauses on religion for Afghanistan, see "Afghanistan," the Association of Religion Data Archives, accessed June 1, 2021, www.thearda.com/international Data/countries/Country_1_8.asp.

the same article restricts the state's protection to "normal religious activities" and activities that don't "disrupt public order . . . or interfere with the educational system of the state." What the government defines as "normal religious activities" and views as disrupting public order or interfering with the educational system has resulted in harsh restrictions being placed on the "normal" religions and other religions being defined as "superstitious," "evil cults," or in some capacity dangerous to the public order.[12]

In other cases, official government policies openly defy constitutional assurances. Article 34 promises all citizens 18 years and older the "right to vote and stand for election, regardless of . . . religious belief." Yet, the Chinese Communist Party's document addressing the "Religious Question" "insists that the CCP members must be atheists and unremittingly propagate atheism."[13]

## Lesson 2

*Despite constitutional assurances of religious freedom, there is a wide chasm between promise and practice.*

A persistent finding of the new collections is that there is a vast chasm between the promises made and actual practice of religious freedom.[14] The most recent Pew Research Center report estimates that 83% of the world's population lives in countries with high or very high levels of religious restriction.[15] The ARDA and RAS collections offer similar findings. When using the ARDA collection and limiting their attention to nations with constitutional promises of religious freedom, Grim and Finke conclude that "of the 130 countries promising religious freedom, 86% (112 countries) have at least one law denying a religious freedom and 38% have four or more such restrictions."[16]

Drawing on the RAS collection, Figure 3.1 shows that the percentage of countries violating religious freedoms is almost as high as the percentages promising religious freedoms. Some of the most common restrictions addressed the role of religion in politics, such as restricting "religious political parties" (37%), "restricting or monitoring of sermons by clergy" (27%), or restrictions on the involvement

---

12 Guobin Zhu, "Prosecuting 'Evil Cults:' A Critical Examination of Law Regarding Freedom of Religious Belief in Mainland China," *Human Rights Quarterly* 32 (2010): 471–501; Lauren B. Homer, "Registration of Chinese Protestant House Churches Under China's 2005 Regulation on Religious Affairs: Resolving the Implementation Impasse," *Journal of Church and State* 52, no. 1 (2010): 50–73; Qianfan Zhang and Zhu Yingping, "Religious Freedoms and Its Legal Restrictions in China," *Brigham Young University Law Review* 3 (2011): 783–818.
13 Fenggang Yang, "A Research Agenda on Religious Freedom in China," *The Review of Faith and International Affairs* 2, no. 2 (2013): 6–17.
14 Fox, *Out of Sync*; Dane Mataic and Roger Finke, "Compliance Gaps and the Failed Promises of Religious Freedom," *Religion, State and Society* 47, no. 1 (February 2019): 124–50.
15 "Global Uptick in Government Restrictions," *Pew Research Center*, 2018.
16 Brian J. Grim and Roger Finke, *The Price of Freedom Denied: Religious Persecution and Violence* (New York: Cambridge University Press, 2011), 28.

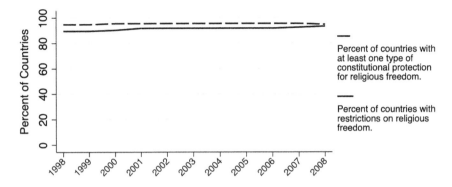

*Figure 3.1* Constitutional Protections of Religious Freedom and Legal Restrictions on Religious Freedom, 1998–2008

Note: Percentages are based on whether at least one type of constitutional protection for religious freedom and one legal restriction of religious freedom for majority or all religions exists at each year for each country or not, depending on available data. Data is from the Religion and State Collection, retrieved from the Association of Religion Data Archives. Number of countries=132.

of clergy or religious organizations in political activity (34%). The restrictions, however, go far beyond the political arena. For 23% of the countries, the government either appoints or must approve clergy appointments. As expected, most of the restrictions are far more severe for minority religions. Despite constitutional assurances that are modeled after the UN's Universal Declaration of Human Rights, religious freedoms are frequently denied, and the public expression of religion is limited.

A long list of government reports, advocacy groups, and case studies of religious freedoms reinforce the findings of the data collections. Perhaps the most convincing evidence is produced by sources that have no ties to the groups being restricted. In 2009, Asma Jahangir, the UN's Special Rapporteur on freedom of religion, concluded that "discrimination based on religion or belief preventing individuals from fully enjoying all their human rights still occurs worldwide on a daily basis."[17] This finding was confirmed and accentuated in a 2019 report by the UN's current Special Rapporteur, Ahmed Shaheed.[18]

Once again, there are many examples. Article 36 of China's constitution promises that citizens "enjoy freedom of religious belief" and that the state will not

---

17 Asma Jahangir, "Report of the Special Rapporteur on Freedom of Religion or Belief," Human Rights Council, Tenth Session, Agenda item 3, accessed July 24, 2011, https://documents-dds-ny.un.org/doc/UNDOC/GEN/G09/101/04/PDF/G0910104.pdf?OpenElement.
18 Ahmed Shaheed, "Freedom of Religion or Belief—Report of the Special Rapporteur on Freedom of Religion or Belief (Advance Unedited Version)," Human Rights Council Fortieth session, A/HRC/40/58.

"compel citizens to believe in, or not to believe in, any religion; nor may they discriminate against citizens who believe in, or do not believe in, any religion." Yet, criminal law bans groups defined as "cult organizations" and issues sentences of up to life in prison for belonging to the groups.[19] Falun Gong is the most publicized "cult organization," but many Christian and Muslim groups also fall on the list. The regulations can also vary by province. On April 1, 2017, Xinjiang defined twenty-six religious activities as illegal without government authorization. The activities included religious classes, small group studies of sacred texts, preaching, proselytizing, and ordaining clergy, as well as the publication and dissemination of religious publications and audiovisual products.[20]

Moreover, the separation of religion and state, which is often introduced to reduce the privileges and power granted to a dominant religion, is increasingly used to limit religion's presence in public spaces. Along with outlawing the open profession, practice, and proselytizing of religious beliefs, it can include the wearing of religious symbols or clothing. France, for example, has outlawed the wearing of full-face coverings in public, a law that is clearly targeted at Muslim women. The city of Lorette went further, placing a ban on the wearing of "headscarves" and prohibiting the women from wearing full-body swimwear and veils at a public outdoor swimming pool opened in 2017.[21] In France, China, and many other countries, constitutional promises of religious freedom are denied in legal codes at all levels, but the most severe restrictions and harshest discrimination are enacted through local or regional laws and ordinances.

## *Lesson 3*

*Restrictions on religion, especially for minority religions, are increasing, and are evident in all regions of the globe and for all polities.*

All the collections reveal that there is no region, world religion, or polity that is exempt from denying religious freedoms. When summarizing key findings from his most recent Religion and State collection, Jonathan Fox pointed out what seemed counter-intuitive to many: "Western democracies engage in more [government-based religion discrimination] than the Christian-majority democracies of Asia, Africa and Latin America" and "among all Christian-majority countries in Asia, Africa and Latin America, the average levels of [government-based religion discrimination]

---

19 U.S. Department of State, "International Religious Freedom Report for 2017," accessed January 30, 2019, www.state.gov/j/drl/rls/irf/2017/.
20 Ibid. To review article 36 in full, see "China," the Association of Religion Data Archives, accessed June 1, 2021, www.thearda.com/internationalData/countries/Country_52_8.asp. To review other documents published by the Chinese government addressing religion, see "Center on Religion and Chinese Society," *Purdue University*, accessed February 29, 2020, https://web.archive.org/web/20200229101245/www.purdue.edu/crcs/resources/china-docs-on-religion/.
21 U.S. Department of State, "International Religious Freedom Report."

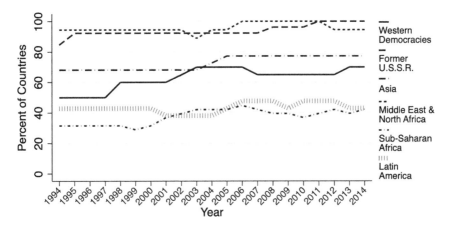

*Figure 3.2* Restrictions on Minority Religions in the Public Arena Percent of Countries by Region, 1994–2014

Note: Restrictions include accessing, leasing, and maintaining places of worship and the ability to publish religious materials, proselytize, host public worship services, and wear religious symbols and dress. Data is from the Religion and State Collection, retrieved from the Association of Religion Data Archives. Number of countries=142.

are similar between democracies and non-democracies."[22] Moreover, a consistent finding in his collection and all previous collections is that religious minorities are the most frequent targets for reductions in freedoms, increased discrimination, and open persecution in the form of physical assaults or imprisonment.[23]

The more demanding and distinctive government restrictions placed on religious minorities are many. For example, 46% of the countries have religious registration requirements that are distinctive for minority religions and 28% have distinctive restrictions on their organizations. The open expression and practice of religion also faces far more restrictions for minorities. They face restrictions on proselytizing (36%), especially if by foreign clergy (51%). Minority religions experience heavy restrictions on "building, leasing, repairing and/or maintaining places of worship" (53%) and face state surveillance of their religious activities not imposed on other religions.

Figure 3.2 graphs the percentage of countries in each region that hold additional requirements and restrictions on minority religions. Overall, there is a trend

---

22 Jonathan Fox, "Religious Discrimination in Christian-Majority Democracies from 1990 to 2014," *Politics and Religion* 13, no. 2 (2019): 285–308.
23 Grim and Finke, *The Price of Freedom Denied*, 28; *The Unfree Exercise of Religion: A World Survey of Discrimination against Religious Minorities* (New York: Cambridge University Press, 2016); Jonathan Fox, *The Unfree Exercise of Religion: A World Survey of Discrimination Against Religious Minorities* (New York: Cambridge University Press, 2016).

of gradual increase in the number of countries placing restrictions on minorities, but the sharpest increases have been among former Soviet nations and Western democracies. Just over 75% of the former Soviet nations now place additional restrictions on minority religions, a percentage that is comparable to the Middle East and North Africa. For Western democracies, the percentage of countries holding distinctive requirements for minority religions has gone from almost 15% to 33% over the past two and half decades.

Figure 3.3 offers a similar regional pattern for restrictions against all religions using a global heat map. Asia, the Middle East, and former Soviet countries have the highest rates, but no area of the globe is exempt from restricting religion. When these data are subjected to more rigorous statistical analysis, we find that neighborhood makes a difference. Even when controlling for a long list of internal characteristics of a country, the influence of bordering countries was evident.[24] When it comes to restricting religious freedoms, countries often imitate their neighbors.

Repeatedly, evidence of widespread restrictions, especially for minority religions, is confirmed by others using alternative sources and alternative research designs.[25] Moreover, these findings are not limited to the research community. When speaking to the Human Rights Council in Geneva, the UN Special Rapporteur on freedom of religion, Ahmed Shaheed, warned that "the increasing application of limits on freedom of expression . . . is having a concerning impact on freedom of religion or belief, globally," and the UN Special Rapporteur on minority issues explained that "freedom of religion or belief is at the heart of rights of minorities."[26]

## Why and How Religious Freedoms Are Restricted

### Lesson 4

*Governments seek restrictions on religion in an attempt to curb political, cultural, economic, or ethnic competitors. This often results in an alliance with a dominant religion and increased discrimination against minority religions.*

---

24 Dane R. Mataic, "Countries Mimicking Neighbors: The Spatial Diffusion of Governmental Restrictions on Religion," *Journal for the Scientific Study of Religion* 57, no. 2 (2018): 221–37.

25 James T. Richardson, ed., *Regulating Religion: Case Studies from Around the Globe* (New York: Kluwer Academic/Plenum Publishers, 2004); David M. Kirkham, ed., *State Responses to Minority Religions* (Burlington, VT: Ashgate Publishing Co., 2013); Karrie J. Koesel, *Religion and Authoritarianism: Cooperation, Conflict, and the Consequences* (New York: Cambridge University Press, 2014).

26 Ahmed Shaheed, "Religious Freedom Key to Ensuring Other Human Rights, Say UN Rapporteurs," *World Watch Monitor*, October 24, 2018, www.worldwatchmonitor.org/coe/%C2%AD%C2%AD%C2%ADreligious-freedom-key-to-ensuring-other-human-rights-say-un-rapporteurs/.

Regulating Religion in the Public Arena  47

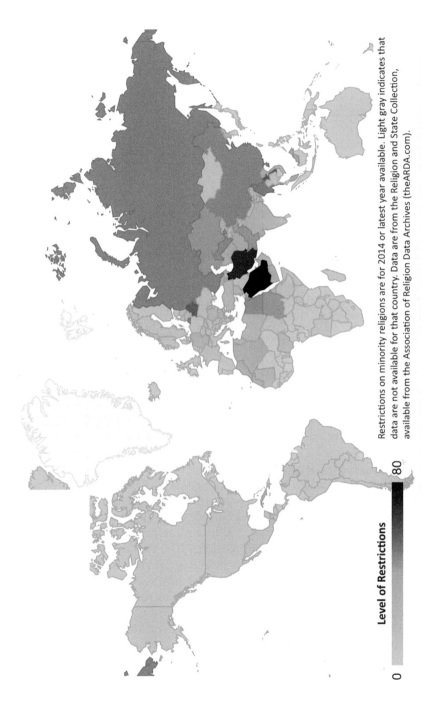

Figure 3.3 Heat Map of Government Restrictions on Minority Religions

48  *Roger Finke and Kerby Goff*

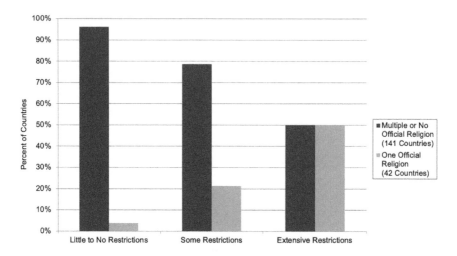

*Figure 3.4* Percentages of Countries With Restrictions on Minority Religions by Official Religion Status, 2014

Note: Percentages sum to 100% by level of restriction and are based on the level of restrictions in 2014 or latest available date. Data is from the Religion and States Collection, retrieved from the Association of Religion Data Archives. Number of countries = 183.

One of the fears for governing bodies is that religious institutions can provide organizational forms to underlying political and cultural pressures and therefore become a source of conflict. For the state, this fear is heightened when the religious group is associated with a minority that is perceived as a threat. Because religious groups can be closely aligned, and even share an identity with specific ethnic groups, political movements, and economic interests, they can provide an institutional structure for mobilizing action. Along with providing religious beliefs, symbols, and practices for the local community, religious institutions can also serve as a source of unity and division at the regional and national levels.

One option for addressing the threat of minorities and for securing the support of the religious institutions and the larger culture is for the state to hold a formal or informal alliance with the dominant religion.[27] The alliance offers the state's ruling party political stability and visible support from religion. For the dominant religion, the alliance offers increased subsidies and a favored status. For both the state and the dominant religion, the alliance serves to restrict the activities of groups posing religious or political threats.

Figure 3.4 illustrates the relationship between nations with an official dominant religion and high levels of restrictions on minority religions. Of the fifty-two

---

27 Anthony J. Gill, *The Political Origins of Religious Liberty* (New York: Cambridge University Press, 2008).

countries with little to no restrictions, 96% hold multiple or no official religion, whereas the number of countries with extensive restrictions is split evenly between those with one official religion and those with multiple or none. Hence, holding an official religion is not a necessity for supporting high restrictions on minorities. After all, half of the nations with high restrictions are not supporting an official religion. Yet, countries holding an official religion are much more likely to impose greater restrictions on religious minorities. As shown in Figure 3.4, at higher levels of restrictions, the share of countries with one official religion increases, but the share of countries with multiple or no official religion decreases. Although not shown in the graph, only 15% of the 141 nations with no official dominant religion had extensive restrictions; the percentage was 50% for the 42 nations with an official religion.

For some nations, such as Saudi Arabia, an alliance is essential for political survival because the dominant religion is so tightly integrated into all social and political institutions. For others, however, it is a mechanism for controlling majority and minority religions alike. In officially atheist China, for example, the five religions approved by the state face heavy restrictions and regulations, while other religions face a tenuous toleration from the government or are aggressively targeted for elimination.[28]

Even when alliances are weak or absent, increased discrimination and restrictions on minority religions can be justified as a necessity for the security and welfare of the larger society. When Belgium, France, and Germany compiled lists of dangerous sects and cults in the late 1990s, one of the justifications for taking actions against these groups was that they often appealed to the young and the vulnerable.[29] When the Russian Orthodox Patriarch Aleksii II wrote to then President Boris Yeltsin in the 1990s supporting more restrictive Russian laws on religious freedom and greater support for the Orthodox Church, he explained that such laws are needed for "protecting the individual from the destructive, pseudo-religious and pseudo-missionary activity that has brought obvious harm to the spiritual and physical health of people, and to stability and civic peace in Russia."[30] More recently, increased governmental discrimination and restrictions on all Muslims in Europe has been a response to perceived security threats.

---

28 Fenggang Yang, "The Red, Black, and Gray Markets of Religion in China," *The Sociological Quarterly* 47 (2006): 93–122; Fenggang Yang, *Religion in China: Survival and Revival Under Communist Rule* (New York: Oxford University Press, 2012); James T. Richardson and Bryan Edelman, "Cult Controversies and Legal Developments Concerning New Religious Movements in Japan and China," In *Regulating Religion: Case Studies from Around the Globe*, ed. James T. Richardson (New York: Kluwer Academic/Plenum Publishers, 2004), 359–80.
29 See e.g., J. Guyard and A. Gest, *Rapport fair au nom de la commission d'enquete sur les sects*, Document no. 2468 (Paris: Assemblee nationale, 1996).
30 Zoe Knox, "The Symphonic Ideal: The Moscow Patriarchat's Post-Soviet Leadership," *Europe-Asia Studies* 55, no. 4 (2003): 583.

## Lesson 5

*Governments control religious activities and groups through legal codes, physical abuse, and imprisonment, but the most pervasive tool for monitoring and controlling religion is a process for registering religions. Once again, religious minorities face the most severe restrictions.*

Governments rely on many different actions to restrict religious activities and beliefs. The most noticeable include some form of imprisonment, physical abuse, or the destruction of property. A recent study reported that from 1944 to 2018, 148 government raids on new religious movements were conducted by nineteen Western-style democracies, with France alone conducting fifty-eight.[31] Russia recently criminalized the activities of Jehovah's Witnesses, resulting in the physical abuse and imprisonment of Witnesses.[32] The Chinese government's attempt to "Sinicize" all Chinese religions has resulted in Uighur Muslims being sent to re-education camps, with the most credible estimates approaching one million.[33] In Azerbaijan, the government has a sustained record of closing and even demolishing mosques and other places of worship, as well as imprisoning and abusing religious leaders.[34]

Although these actions, and the legal codes allowing them to occur, offer a small sample of the high-profile actions taken to restrict religions, the most pervasive government tool for controlling, monitoring, and restricting religious activity is the seemingly simple request of registering with the government. The state's registration requirements can be benign, allowing all religions to register and requiring little monitoring; or, they can be used as a tool for controlling the operations of religious organizations and have strict requirements that are used to withhold or revoke a group's right to exist. Even when groups are still allowed to exist, the failure to register often limits the activities and freedom of the group, as well as any benefits the government might bestow on registered groups.

Seemingly modest requirements, such as minimum size, a minimum number of years in existence, a statement of religious doctrine, and a lack of foreign ties, can prevent a large swath of religious groups from qualifying for registration. Requirements on size and years in existence prevent any new religions from

---

31 Stuart A. Wright and Susan J. Palmer, "Countermovement Mobilization and State Raids on Minority Religious Communities," *Journal for the Scientific Study of Religion* 57, no. 3 (2018): 616–33.
32 See "Jehovah Witness gets two years in prison for possession of 'extremist literature'," *AsiaNews.it*, accessed June 1, 2021, www.asianews.it/news-en/Jehovah%E2%80%99s-Witness-gets-two-years-in-prison-for-possession-of-%E2%80%9Cextremist-literature%E2%80%9D-19529.html. See also the U.S. Department of State, 2017 Report on International Religious Freedom, accessed June 1, 2021, www.state.gov/reports/2017-report-on-international-religious-freedom/.
33 Adrian Zenz, "'Thoroughly Reforming Them Towards a Healthy Heart Attitude': China's Political Re-Education Campaign in Xinjiang," *Central Asian Survey* 38, no. 1 (2019), 102–28.
34 Forum 18 offers a long list of examples. "Oslo, Norway," *Forum 18*, accessed June 1, 2021, www.forum18.org/archive.php?country=23. See also 2017 Report on International Religious Freedom.

*Table 3.1* Trends in the Percentage of Countries With Registration Requirements of Religious Groups in 1990 and 2014

|  | 1990 | 2014 |
| --- | --- | --- |
| A registration process for religious organizations exists that is in some manner different from the registration process for other nonprofit organizations. | 48% | 60% |
| Requirement for minority religions (as opposed to all religions) to register in order to be legal or receive special tax status. | 40% | 45% |
| Registration is required but sometimes denied. | 24% | 36% |
| Groups are officially required to register; the government enforces this and discriminates against unregistered groups. | 14% | 25% |

Note: Percentage of countries with registration requirements are based on the presence of restrictions in 1990 or earliest available and 2014 or latest available. Data is from the Religion and State Collection, retrieved from the Association of Religion and Data Archives. Number of countries = 183.

arising within the country, and restrictions on foreign ties curb the proliferation of religions from other countries. Moreover, because religious registration is frequently administered by local agencies (e.g., religious bureaus), and the agencies are given substantial discretion on how to interpret laws for registering, defining, or tolerating religions, these agencies are especially vulnerable to local ordinances and social pressures.[35]

Registration requirements are often proposed as beneficial for religions (e.g., register for tax benefits); however, recent research has found a strong relationship between requiring religious groups to register and increases in governmental restrictions in subsequent years.[36] Table 3.1 documents that registration requirements are increasingly used to monitor all religions and to discriminate against unregistered religions. The percentage of all nations now relying on a registration process that is different for religious organizations than other nonprofits has increased from 48% in 1990 to 60% in 2014, and denying a required registration also increased over the same time period, rising from 24% of all nations to 36%. One of the sharpest increases, however, came in the percentage of nations discriminating against unregistered groups, from 14% in 1990 to 25% in 2014. Yet, these numbers fail to capture the full impact of the registration process. Many religious groups never attempt to register because they know they can't qualify, or they fear the state surveillance that will follow.

The rapid political changes in Russia during the 1990s illustrate the powerful impact of registration. After a flood of new religious groups entered the country

---

35 Gill, *The Political Origins of Religious Liberty*; Grim and Finke, "International Religion Indexes"; Koesel, *Region and Authoritarianism*; Ani Sarkissian, *The Varieties of Religious Repression: Why Governments Restrict Religion* (New York: Oxford University Press, 2015).
36 Roger Finke, Dane R. Mataic, and Jonathan Fox, "Assessing the Impact of Religious Registration," *Journal for the Scientific Study of Religion* 56, no. 4 (2017): 720–36.

following a 1990 law promising religious freedom, new legislation was passed in 1997 requiring a religious group to exist in a community for 15 years before they could qualify for registration. Those unable to meet the registration requirements were denied the rights to own property, publish literature, and receive tax benefits, and they faced restrictions on where worship services could be held.[37] When a 1999 amendment to the 1997 law required all groups to re-register or be dissolved, the Ministry of Justice dissolved approximately 980 groups by May 2002. Russia is not alone in making such demands.[38] In 2014, the RAS3 collection found that 32% of all countries required a "minimum number of community members" for registration.

For some countries, registration requirements effectively bar all new religions. In Egypt, for example, "non-registered religious organizations are illegal, and members of such religions are subject to detention, prosecution, and jail."[39] But no group has successfully registered since 1990. For other countries, registration requirements strongly discourage the formation and importing of new religions. In Austria, for example, religious groups applying to be recognized as religious societies are required to represent a minimum of 0.2% of the population (approximately 16,000 individuals) and to have existed for twenty years, at least ten of which were as a confessional society. Confessional societies can be recognized if they have at least 300 members but receive none of the tax benefits, legitimacy, or other government support received by religious societies.[40]

## Lesson 6

*Non-state actors impose many of the most severe restrictions on religious activities and freedoms.*

The initial ARDA collection had only a few measures on how non-state actors might restrict religious freedoms, and the RAS project had none. The handful of measures in the ARDA collection, however, soon revealed that the actions

---

37 Catherine Wanner, "Missionaries of Faith and Culture: Evangelical Encounters in Ukraine," *Slavic Review* 63, no. 4 (2004): 732–755 and Paul Froese, *The Great Secularization Experiment: What Soviet Communism Taught Us About Religion in the Modern Era* (Berkeley: University of California Press, 2008).

38 The Ministry of Justice claimed that all dissolved groups were defunct, but members of the groups claimed otherwise. See Geraldine Fagan, "Russia: Unregistered Religious Groups," *Forum 18 News Service*, April 14, 2005, www.forum18.org/Archive.php?article_id=543. Geraldine Fagan, *Believing in Russia: Religious policy after communism* (New York: Routledge, Taylor and Francis Group, 2013). "2006 Report on International Religious Freedom," U.S. Department of State, accessed June 1, 2021, https://2009-2017.state.gov/j/drl/rls/irf/2006/index.htm.

39 Jonathan Fox, *Political Secularism, Religion and the State: A Time Series Analysis of Worldwide Data* (New York: Cambridge University Press, 2015), 148.

40 Christopher J. Miner, "Losing My Religion: Austria's New Religion Law in Light of International and European Standards of Religious Freedom," *Brigham Young University Law Review* 1998, no. 2 (1998): 607–47.

of non-state actors had both an indirect and direct impact on religious freedoms.[41] Along with an indirect influence through government policies, they also took direct actions against the religious activities of religious groups, especially minority religions. Indeed, some of the most severe and violent actions taken against religious freedom are made by non-state actors. Many national and cultural identities are so closely interwoven with or against selected religions that ensuring religious freedoms for all is perceived as challenging the cultural identity as a whole.[42]

India and Egypt serve as two examples where societal pressures against select religions have resulted in extreme violence. India's Ministry of Home Affairs reported that ninety-seven deaths and 2,264 injuries resulted from "communal incidents" involving religious communities. The groups most frequently targeted were the minority Muslim and Christian groups. In Egypt, the government discriminates against many religious groups, including many Muslim groups, but the Coptic Christians have become frequent targets for kidnappings, deaths, and ongoing violence by non-government groups, violence that the government has been unable to control.[43]

India and Egypt represent two of the extremes, but this open discrimination and violence against minority religions is also evident in western democracies. In the US, the FBI reported 1,679 religious hate crime offenses in 2017,[44] and a national survey of more than 1,300 religious congregations found that nearly 40% reported they had experienced a criminal act in the past year.[45] As evidenced by the killing of eleven people at a Jewish synagogue in Pittsburgh and the burning of Muslim mosques, the social pressures go beyond minor acts of discrimination. The recent data collections all agree, however, that the level of social discrimination against minorities, especially Muslims and Jews, is even higher in Europe than the US.[46]

Figure 3.5 offers a sampling of the various forms of social discrimination and the high rate of occurrence. Some forms of societal discrimination are targeted

---

41 Grim and Finke, "International Religion Indexes."
42 Roger Finke and Robert R. Martin, "Ensuring Liberties: Understanding State Restrictions on Religious Freedoms," *Journal for the Scientific Study of Religion* 53, no. 4 (2014): 687–705.
43 U.S. Department of State, *International Religious Freedom Report for 2017* (Washington, DC: Government Printing Office, 2018) accessed January 30, 2019, www.state.gov/j/drl/rls/irf/2017/.
44 For a full report on FBI hate crime statistics, go to "Hate Crime Statistics," *Federal Bureau of Information*, accessed June 1, 2021, www.fbi.gov/services/cjis/ucr/publications#Hate-Crime%20Statistics.
45 Christopher P. Scheitle, "Religious Congregations' Experiences with, Fears of, and Preparations for Crime: Results from a National Survey," *Review of Religious Research* 60, no. 1 (2018): 95–113.
46 Jonathan Fox, Roger Finke, and Marie Eisenstein, "Examining the Causes of Government-Based Discrimination Against Religious Minorities in Western Democracies: Societal-Level Discrimination and Securitization," *Comparative European Politics* 17 (2019): 885–909.

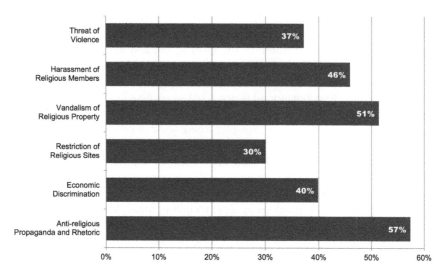

*Figure 3.5* Percent of Countries With Incidents of Societal Discrimination Against Minority Religions, 2010–2014

Note: Percentages are based on indication of incidents from 2010 through 2014. Data is from the Religion and States Collection, retrieved from the Association of Religion Data Archives. Number of countries = 183.

at the religious institutions: "vandalism of religious property" and "restriction of religious sites." Others have a direct impact on the membership: "economic discrimination" and "harassment of religious members." Still others can have an impact on both: "anti-religious propaganda" and "threat of violence." Even without formal state restrictions on religion, the societal pressures can sharply reduce religious freedoms, increase open discrimination, and lead to violence. As noted earlier, these are conservative estimates on the level of restrictions, because they rely on the event being reported in a trusted public outlet.

## Lesson 7

*The protection of religious freedoms is associated with an independent judiciary and free, fair, and open elections.*

Although democracies are not exempt from denying religious freedoms and government-based discrimination against minorities has increased sharply in western democracies since 1990, research using the new data sources has consistently found that an independent judiciary and open and free elections help to protect religious freedoms.

Because freedoms for all are inconvenient, supporting these freedoms is often conveniently overlooked. The societal pressures noted previously can result in local authorities turning a blind eye to discrimination or violence against minority religions. In Russia, minority religions frequently complain that local authorities fail to protect their freedoms, even when violence is involved.[47] Local authorities can be swayed by the social and religious pressures in their local area in whether or not they approve registrations of religious organizations. Indeed, some have concluded that local administrative action rather than national legislation often is the greater deterrent to religions meeting registration requirements.[48] Regardless of societal pressures, however, governments are often unable or unwilling to protect the freedoms promised. As a result, the governance of the nation becomes an important predictor of the freedoms protected.

The independent judiciary, in particular, has proven to be a consistent predictor of reduced discrimination and increased freedoms for minority religions.[49] Returning to the early insights of de Tocqueville in the nineteenth century, he warned of the tyranny of the majority through open and free elections and identified the judiciary as curbing this potential tyranny.[50] He explained that "the power vested in the American courts of justice of pronouncing a statute to be unconstitutional forms one of the most powerful barriers that have ever been devised against the tyranny of political assemblies."[51] Table 3.2 confirms his expectations. Whereas only 13% of the nations with an independent judiciary had extensive restrictions on religion, the percentage was 88% for nations without an independent judiciary. A similar relationship holds for nations hosting free, fair, and open elections, with restrictions being far higher in nations without free and fair elections. Both an independent judiciary and free elections remain important predictors of reduced religious restrictions even when we account for the social, economic, and political context.

## The Consequences of Freedoms Denied

### Lesson 8

*To the extent that governmental and societal forces reduce religious freedoms, social conflict related to religion will increase.*

The UN's special rapporteur on minority issues, Dr. Fernand de Varennes, has boldly stated that "infringements on freedom of religion or belief serve as

---

47 Geraldine Fagan, *Believing in Russia: Religious Policy After Communism* (New York: Routledge, Taylor and Francis Group, 2013).
48 Roman Podoprigora, "Freedom of Religion and Belief and Discretionary State Approval of Religious Activity," in *Facilitating Freedom of Religion or Belief: A Deskbook*, eds. W. Cole Durham, Jr. and Bahia G. Tahzib-Lie (Leiden, The Netherlands: Koninklijke Brill NV, 2004), 425–40.
49 Roger Finke and Robert R. Martin, "Ensuring Liberties: Understanding State Restrictions on Religious Freedoms," *Journal for the Scientific Study of Religion* 53, no. 4 (2014): 687–705; Roger Finke, Robert R. Martin, and Jonathan Fox, "Explaining Discrimination Against Religious Minorities," *Politics and Religion* 10 (2017): 389–416.
50 Toqueville, 1945 [1835], 269.
51 Ibid., 107.

*Table 3.2:* Level of Restrictions by Independent Judiciary and Free and Fair Elections, 2014

|  | Level of Restrictions | | |
|---|---|---|---|
|  | Little or None | Some | Extensive |
| **Judiciary** | | | |
| Independent | 64% | 41% | 13% |
| NOT independent | 36% | 59% | 88% |
| **Elections** | | | |
| Free and fair | 83% | 62% | 23% |
| NOT free and fair | 17% | 38% | 78% |
| # of countries | 47 | 87 | 40 |

Note: Percentage of countries with restrictions are from 2014 or latest available. Restriction data is from the Religion and State Collection, retrieved from the Association of Religion and Data Archives. Judiciary and election data is from the Varieties of Democracy data set. Number of countries = 174.

*Table 3.3* Percent of Countries With Religious Conflict by Levels of Government and Social Regulation of Religion, 2008

|  |  | Religious Conflict Is Present |
|---|---|---|
| Government regulation of religion | Low | 28% |
|  | Medium | 66% |
|  | High | 80% |
| Societal regulation of religion | Low | 30% |
|  | Medium | 71% |
|  | High | 85% |

Note: Data are taken from the 2008 International Religious Freedom data, retrieved from the Association of Religion Data Archives. Number of countries = 197.

the early warning signs of violent conflict."[52] Table 3.3 would strongly support this statement. Both governmental and societal restrictions on religious freedoms are highly associated with more religion-related conflicts. Religious conflict is reported in only 28% and 30% of the countries with low levels of governmental and societal regulation. By contracts, the percentages are 80% and over when the regulations are high.

Despite the seemingly obvious relationship between religion and social conflict, the topic has received surprisingly little research attention. Samuel Huntington

---

52 Fernand de Varennes, "UN Special Rapporteurs: Religious Freedom at the Heart of Minority Rights," *ADF International*, accessed April 9, 2019, https://adfinternational.org/news/un-special-rapporteurs-religious-freedom-at-the-heart-of-minority-rights/.

was one of the few to offer a clear and forceful argument in the early 1990s. He contended that civilization divides now "supplant ideological and other forms of conflict as the dominant global form of conflict"[53] and that religion provides the foundation for major civilizations and cultural identities. As a result, Huntington warned of social conflicts occurring along religious divides both within and across countries.

Huntington's thesis initially prompted a few scholars to explore the relationship social conflict holds with ethnicity, religion, and language.[54] Henderson and Lai found that religious similarity was associated with decreased interstate conflict, lending limited support to Huntington's claim.[55] Additional research, however, found that other elements of culture have distinct and sometimes opposing influences on conflict. For example, ethnic similarity was shown to increase conflict.[56] Further, Henderson suggested that of the three cultural components—religion, ethnicity, and language—religion possesses the most powerful influence, but his focus was primarily devoted to interstate conflict and was restricted by the measures of religion available.

Recent research using the new collections has found that the response to religious diversity is more important in explaining social conflict than the actual religious diversity.[57] As suggested by Huntington, countries harboring divides between major world religions do have higher levels of social conflict. But the research has shown that the divides are only influential to the extent that they shape the restrictions placed on other religions. In other words, when religious divides lead to a reduction in religious freedoms, the reduced freedoms will result in more conflict.[58] When religious freedoms are upheld, however, religious diversity does not fuel conflict.

Related research has found that governmental and societal restrictions on religion define the parameters for a religious group's interaction with the larger culture. This research has found that when religious groups are socially isolated, face ongoing persecution, and have effectively organized around social movements, social

---

53 Samuel P. Huntingdon, *The Clash of Civilizations and the Remaking of World Order* (New York: Simon & Schuster, 1993), 48.
54 Zeev Maoz and Bruce Russett, "Normative and Structural Causes of Democratic Peace, 1946–1986," *The American Political Science Review* 87 (1993): 624–38; Errol Henderson, "The Democratic Peace Through the Lens of Culture, 1820–1989," *International Studies Quarterly* 42 (1998): 461–84.
55 Ibid.; Errol Henderson, "Culture or Contiguity: Ethnic Conflict, the Similarity of States, and the Onset of War, 1820–1989," *Journal of Conflict Resolution* 41 (1997): 649–68; Brian Lai, "An Empirical Examination of Religion and Conflict in the Middle East, 1950–1992," *Foreign Policy Analysis* 2 (2006): 21–36.
56 Henderson, "Culture or Contiguity."
57 Brian Grim and Roger Finke, "Religious Persecution in Cross-National Context: Clashing Civilizations or Regulated Religious Economies?" *American Sociological Review* 72 (2007): 633–58.
58 Brian Grim and Roger Finke, *The Price of Freedom Denied: Religious Persecution and Violence* (New York: Cambridge University Press, 2011).

conflict increases.[59] Yet, the amount of research addressing the topic of social conflict with the new data collections remains an area that requires far more research.

## *Lesson 9*

*Religious freedoms tend to increase with an increase in other human rights. Yet, tensions occur between religious freedoms and other freedoms.*

When viewing civil rights from a distance, it appears that all boats rise together. Virtually all civil liberties hold a strong correlation with religious freedoms in cross-national research. Yet, when you take a step closer, it is equally clear that the civil liberties are often in conflict. As a result, the strength of the relationship between religious freedoms and other civil liberties shows substantial variation.

For some liberties, it is difficult to separate religious freedoms from other freedoms. Returning to the United Nations' Universal Declaration of Human Rights, we find that Article 18 on religious freedom clearly overlaps with the two articles that follow. Freedom to hold, to teach, and to change religious beliefs in public or private might be viewed as a more specific example of the freedom of opinion and expression (Article 19). The freedom to worship and observe religion publicly overlaps with the freedom of peaceful assembly and association (Article 20).[60]

Figure 3.6 offers a glimpse at the relationships religious freedoms hold with other human rights and with other economic, educational, and political measures. When looking at the freedom of expression, domestic movement, discussion, use of media, and the empowerment of women, it is evident that all boats do rise together. All of these measures hold a correlation of greater than .7 with religious freedoms, a good indication that the increase of one corresponds with the increase of another. The strong association is undeniable.

Yet, the many similarities and strong correlations can also mask some very important institutional and cultural differences. Perhaps more than any other human right, religious freedoms are intertwined with complex cultural histories and institutional ties. Religion can permeate much of the nation's culture and can hold institutional alliances with the state. Whereas all human rights seek political support and state protections, religion holds relationships that pose unique challenges for protecting religious freedoms and increased risks if the freedoms are not protected. Moreover, the religious teachings of religions can threaten other rights, such as those related to sexuality and gender.[61]

Understanding the distinctive relationships religion holds with the state and other liberties is essential for understanding the relationship religion will hold in

---

59 Roger Finke and Jaime Harris, "Wars and Rumors of Wars: Explaining Religiously Motivated Violence," in *Religion, Politics, Society and the State*, ed. Jonathan Fox (New York: Oxford University Press, 2012).
60 "The Universal Declaration of Human Rights," *United Nations*, accessed June 1, 2021, www.un.org/en/about-us/universal-declaration-of-human-rights.
61 Douglas Laycock, Anthony R. Picarello, Jr., and Robin Fretwell Wilson, *Same-Sex Marriage and Religious Liberty: Emerging Conflicts* (Lanham, MD: Rowman & Littlefield Publishers, Inc., 2008).

*Regulating Religion in the Public Arena* 59

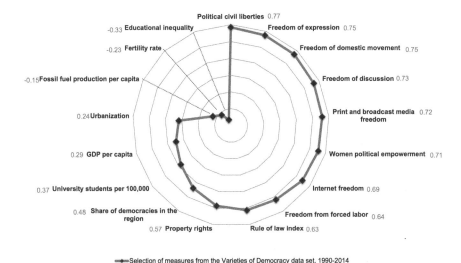

*Figure 3.6* Religious Freedom in Comparison: Correlations With Other Freedoms and Factors

the public arena and the larger culture. For example, recent research exploring the compliance gap between a nation's promise and practice of civil liberties offers some interesting and initially perplexing findings. When explaining the compliance gap between the states' promises and support for most human rights, economic development and education are typically important predictors of increased rights. When explaining the compliance gap for religious freedoms, however, an independent judiciary, open and free elections, and societal and cultural pressures have been more effective predictors.[62]

In part, the differences in predicting religious and other liberties might stem from a tension between supporting both secularism and religious freedom. This is especially evident in Western democracies where religious freedoms are consistently promised, but secularism is highly valued.[63]

## Lesson 10

*Because states often hold economic and political motives for reducing the level of restrictions on religion, religious freedoms should be associated with greater economic development and political stability.*

---

62 Dane Mataic and Roger Finke, "Compliance Gaps and the Failed Promises of Religious Freedom," *Religion, State and Society* 47, no. 1 (February 2019): 124–50.
63 Jonathan Fox, "Religious Discrimination in Christian-Majority Democracies from 1990 to 2014," *Politics and Religion* 13, no. 2 (2019): 285–308.

When support for religious freedoms offers increased revenue, economic production, or stronger political alliances, both theory and research propose that political leaders will profess more support for religious freedoms and the level of restrictions will tend to decline.[64] In the case of colonial America, toleration of religious diversity became a necessity for making many of the early colonies profitable.[65] Likewise, nations relying heavily on expatriate workers, such as the United Arab Emirates, must find ways to tolerate other religions.

Recent empirical research, however, shows a more complicated picture. Some cross-national research supports the association between religious freedom and economic development. Using data from the early 2000s, Alon and Chase find that religious freedom predicts greater economic development independently of political and economic freedom for fifty-four countries.[66] When considering the reverse association—economic development's impact on religious freedom—Fox finds that, among Christian-majority countries, developing countries exhibit more religious freedom than more economically developed countries.[67] Further, when accounting for religious, demographic, and political factors, economic development is positively associated with government religious restrictions for both Western democracies and developing countries. These findings suggest that governments may use a deregulated religious market for national development, only to increase religious restrictions with the resources and legitimacy gained from such a process. With such limited research along these lines, it is uncertain whether this generalizes beyond Christian-majority countries. China provides a good example of this instrumental joining of economic and religious freedoms during a development phase, but firm conclusions await more research.

Figure 3.7 illustrates this complicated relationship between economic development and religious freedom. While 70% of low-income countries exhibit low levels of religious restrictions, the percentage of countries with religious freedom drops dramatically at the next income level and increases with increasing levels of development. Governments must have a basic level of development or state capacity in order to enforce religious restrictions, but this increase in capacity to restrict is acted upon less at higher levels of development.[68] More research is needed to explore how this might vary within a country as it develops.

Nations also face global political pressures to respect basic civil rights. Relying on spatial analysis and the RAS collection, Dane Mataic finds that "national

---

64 Anthony J. Gill, *The Political Origins of Religious Liberty* (New York: Cambridge University Press, 2008).

65 Evert B. Greene, *Religion and the State: The Making and Testing of an American Tradition*, (New York: New York University Press, 1941); Roger Finke, "Religious Deregulation: Origins and Consequences," *Journal of Church and State* 32, no. 3 (1990): 609–26.

66 Ilan Alon and Gregory Chase, "Religious Freedom and Economic Prosperity," *Cato Journal* 25, no. 2 (2005): 399–406.

67 Fox, "Religious Discrimination."

68 Neil A. Englehart, "State Capacity, State Failure, and Human Rights," *Journal of Peace Research* 46, no. 2 (2009): 163–80.

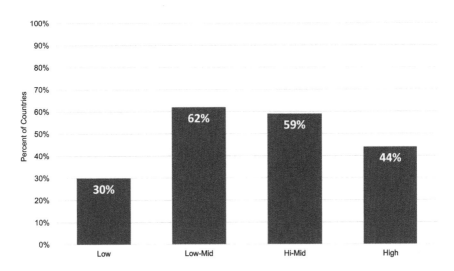

*Figure 3.7* Percent of Countries With High Government Restrictions by Economic Development, 2014

Note: Restrictions data come from the Religion and State Collection, retrieved from the Association of Religion Data Archives. Economic development categories come from the World Bank Development Indicators. Number of countries = 142.

governments mimic their neighbor's policies and practices even when accounting for internal structural characteristics."[69] These same pressures also explain why constitutional promises of religious freedom are so common (despite the lack of practice) and why the constitutional clauses so frequently mimic common global standards. When appeasing global pressures, the constitution becomes the public document for all to see.

Thus far, however, the recent data collections have provided only limited support for an association between religious freedoms and economic development. Indeed, when explaining the compliance gaps between the freedoms promised and those supported by the state, Mataic and Finke found that economic measures were important for explaining the compliance gaps of many civil liberties, but not religion. They suggested, as did Fox, that greater economic development provides more resources for monitoring religion.[70] Based on these initial tests, it remains unclear if religious freedoms and economic performance are both the product of other forces, such as national governance characteristics and stability over time.

69 Dane R. Mataic, "Countries Mimicking Neighbors: The Spatial Diffusion of Governmental Restrictions on Religion," *Journal for the Scientific Study of Religion* 57, no. 2 (2018): 221.
70 Fox, "Religious Discrimination."

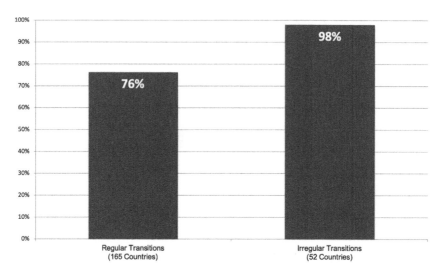

*Figure 3.8* Percent of Countries With Restrictions on Religion in 2014 by Presence of Regular vs. Irregular Transitions of Power, 1990–2013

Note: Irregular transitions of power are defined as those that do not occur according to explicit rules or established conventions, e.g., by coup, assassination, or revolution. Transition data are derived from the Archigos 4.1 data set, and restrictions come from the Religion and State Collection at the Association of Religion Data Archives, theARDA.com.

Figure 3.8 does provide initial support for a relationship between religious freedoms and political stability. Nations with an irregular transition of power for the head of state since 1990 have higher levels of religious restrictions. Yet, the relationships that political stability and economic development hold with religious freedoms remain poorly understood and are in need of far more research.

## Conclusion

Democracies, and western democracies in particular, are often viewed as bulwarks for religious freedom. Recent data collections strongly challenge this assumption. Although the democratic institutions of an independent judiciary and open and free elections are two predictors of support for religious freedoms, no single polity, world religion, or global region is exempt from denying religious freedoms.

A series of recent data collections have documented that restrictions on religious freedoms are high, increasingly and frequently targeting minority religions at the very time when constitutions are consistently promising religious freedoms for all. And, though the Middle East, former Soviet nations, and much of Asia hold the highest level of restrictions, no region of the globe is exempt. The most noticeable restrictions come in the form of social conflict, imprisonment, and forced migration, but the most pervasive restrictions result from registration requirements by the state and by the attitudes and actions of non-state actors. These subtle forms of restrictions often serve as effective controls for denying religious groups access to the public arena. Research relying on these collections finds that an independent judiciary and free and fair elections each serve to help close the compliance gap between the freedoms promised and the freedoms practiced. Unlike many other civil liberties, however, higher levels of education and improved economic standards are not strong predictors of improved religious liberties.

The consequences of freedoms denied are many. The most immediate is how it changes the marketplace of religion. The measures of the new data collection offer direct evidence of how governmental and societal restrictions are limiting how religion can be organized and expressed in the public arena. Registration requirements that are distinctive to religion, and often distinctive to specific minority religions, determine which groups can operate openly and the limits of their operation. Monitoring of clergy sermons, limiting political speech and involvement, and restricting religious speech more generally serve to limit the expression of religious belief and ideas. These restrictions limit how religious groups can both appeal for new members and serve existing members. Moreover, the restrictions limit the role of religion in the marketplace of ideas and discussion in the public arena. Whereas a single religion dominates the discussion in some nations, for others, religion is largely excluded from cultural and political discussions.

The restrictions on religion also have implications that go far beyond religion. The most immediate are the denial of other human rights. Denying freedoms of religious speech and institutional organization threatens other freedoms of expression and freedom to assemble. The restrictions can also serve to fuel social conflict. Rather than subduing tensions between religions or between religions and the state, increased restrictions are associated with higher levels of tensions and increased social conflict. Whereas states often regulate religion in an attempt to increase security and reduce violence, the consequences are increased conflict and more threats to security.

Further research is needed on the economic and political impact of religious freedoms. Cursory analysis reveals a complicated relationship suggesting that countries may use religious freedom for national development, only to shed it with increasing autonomy and state capacity. Additionally, development and state capacity are important for supporting human rights, but further research is needed to determine whether and under what conditions they might sustain religious freedoms. As religious nationalisms are waxing around the world and many developing countries are forming new alliances, religious freedoms may wane. Understanding these processes and anticipating outcomes is critical.

Despite routine constitutional assurances of religious freedom, allowing free exercise for all religions and providing formal state support for none remains a radical notion for many.

# 4 Shots Not Fired in the Culture War

## Commercial Litigation in Contemporary Rabbinical Courts

*Chaim Saiman*

This chapter offers a different perspective on this relationship. This story is anchored in the practice of contemporary beth dins (rabbinical courts; also known as *beis din, beyt din,* or *beit din*) and the civil/commercial law docket of the Beth Din of America ("BDA") in particular. Within the formal policies and unstated assumptions governing the BDA's approach to monetary disputes, we find that law (defined here as the rules and norms of the American legal system) and religion (specifically, halakhah, or Jewish law) are structured to work symbiotically.

The motivations for this approach range from the purely instrumental to the idealistic. First, there is a straightforward desire to enforce the beth din's rulings through the civil courts, which at minimum requires adherence to the basic norms of American procedural justice. Beyond this baseline, receptivity to secular law functions as a market signaling device that informs parties and their lawyers the BDA has a sophisticated understanding of secular law. This ensures the overall process and hearing will be recognizable to attorneys and that the beth din will interpret legal documents and relationships with keen awareness of how they are understood in the civil justice system.

Undergirding these practices, however, lies a more fundamental sense of what it means to serve as a traditional rabbinical forum within the milieu of contemporary American religion on one hand and commerce on the other. How should Jewish law be administered when the communities' self-understanding is constructed from both Jewish and secular norms and when business is simultaneously transacted between co-religionists and across cultural and religious divides? Prior scholarship has focused on the value of beth dins add to the American legal order.[1] Here I show the road is bi-directional. While not fully articulated, the BDA operates on the assumption that a mix of halakhah and secular norms produces the best outcomes whether measured from the perspective of either halakhah or secular law.

This practice is notable for several reasons. First, the audience for beth din commercial adjudication is typically limited to the more observant and enclavist

---

1 See Michael A. Helfand and Barak D. Richman, "The Challenge of Co-Religionist Commerce," *Duke Law Journal* 64, no. 5 (February 2015): 769–822.

DOI: 10.4324/9781003309291-5

segments of American Jewry—the segment least disposed to tailoring religious observance in light of the dominant social or legal culture. To these Americans, Judaism is an all-encompassing worldview whose cultural, legal, and political expression legitimately compete with the state.

Second, traditional sources of Jewish law contain doctrines that are in tension with American legal norms. Jewish law could potentially offer the BDA the grounds to resist or at least be skeptical over incursion of American legal norms. Yet, though its work overlaps and competes with the American legal system, the BDA and similar institutions tend to mitigate—rather than highlight—the gaps between Jewish and American law.

Finally, under contemporary religious liberty law, once an adherent asserts that a particular law or regulation substantially burdens its free exercise of religion, courts are required to credit both the description of the religious practice and the claim that complying with the state law violates it.[2] This doctrinal structure deliberately obscures the issue at the heart of this chapter—the theological-doctrinal analysis that takes place *within* religious communities as they determine how to frame their commitments in light of secular law. Is the goal to work with the secular state and harness its law towards shared aims? To preserve enclaves of religious diversity and separatism? To create flashpoints in an ongoing culture war over whether the state or religion is sovereign? While these considerations do not impact religious liberty law at the narrow doctrinal level, they are central to understanding the broader theological and socio-cultural forces that animate law and religion interactions.

Recent events have proven that Orthodox Jews are hardly reticent about using either legal or cultural/political means to fend off regulations in the name of religious freedom. In late 2020, an ultra-Orthodox umbrella group challenged some of New York State's COVID-19 restrictions on religious gatherings and were granted preliminary relief from these regulations by the US Supreme Court.[3] Orthodox groups have also used political tools to fight off New York City's attempts to regulate controversial circumcision practices,[4] as well to challenge

---

2 See, e.g., *Burwell v. Hobby Lobby Stores Inc.*, 573 U.S. 682, 724 (2014) (holding that "Federal courts have no business addressing whether the religious belief asserted in the RFRA case is reasonable . . . [This would] in effect tell the plaintiffs that their beliefs are flawed. For good reason we have repeatedly refused to take such a step."); *Emp't Div. v. Smith*, 494 U.S. 872, 887 (1990) (holding that "repeatedly and in many different contexts, we have warned that courts must not presume to determine . . . the plausibility of a religious claim").

3 *Roman Catholic Diocese of Brooklyn v. Cuomo*, 141 S.Ct. 63 (2020), 2020 WL 6948354. While the plaintiffs were ultra-Orthodox groups, the ruling was applauded by Orthodox organizations much closer to the BDA's worldview. See "Union of Orthodox Jewish Congregations of America Applauds US Supreme Court Ruling Enjoining Covid Rules That Treat Synagogues, Churches and Other Prayer Services Unfairly," *Orthodox Union Advocacy Center*, November 26, 2020, https://advocacy.ou.org/scotusruling.

4 Michael Grynbaum, "Mayor de Blasio Is Set to Ease Rules on Circumcision Ritual," *New York Times*, February 25, 2015, NY Region, www.nytimes.com/2015/02/25/nyregion/de-blasio-set-to-waive-rule-requiring-consent-form-for-circumcision-ritual.html (reporting on deal between de Blasio administration and Orthodox community to repeal Bloomberg-era restrictions on certain circumcision practices that allegedly restrict religious freedom). See also Dan

New York State's efforts to scrutinize and regulate the content of the secular studies curriculum (or lack thereof) in ultra-Orthodox primary and high schools.[5] However, by focusing on how the BDA frames and interprets relevant Jewish and American law, this chapter presents a counterexample to this narrative where mutual deference and accommodation prevail.

## The Beth Din of America and the Structure of American Arbitration Law

Blackletter halakhic doctrine prohibits Jews from litigating intra-Jewish disputes in civil courts.[6] For much of American Jewish history, however, this rule has not been rigorously abided. The large waves of Jews that migrated to America eagerly sought to integrate into the American commercial and cultural mainstream,[7] such

---

Goldberg, "De Blasio Administration Considering Starting Over on metzitzah b'peh," *Politico*, March 12, 2017, www.politico.com/states/new-york/city-hall/story/2017/03/de-blasio-administration-considering-starting-over-on-metzitzah-bpeh-110296 (discussing potential breakdown of deal).

5 Menachem Wecker, "New York State Cracks Down on Jewish Schools," *Education Next*, July 16, 2019, www.educationnext.org/new-york-state-cracks-down-jewish-schools-senator-simcha-felder-rabbi-chaim-dovid-zwiebel-joseph-hodges-choate (discussing debate over educational standards issue from a perspective that is sympathetic to status quo and is skeptical of state intervention); Valerie Strauss, "The Problem with New York's Ultra-Orthodox Jewish Schools During the Pandemic," *The Washington Post*, October 16, 2020, www.washingtonpost.com/education/2020/10/16/problem-with-new-yorks-ultra-orthodox-jewish-schools-during-pandemic (similar discussion as above from the perspective advocating for state intervention and reform to current model); Valerie Strauss, "Political Horse-Trading' by New York Mayor's Office Contributed to Delay of Report on Ultra-Orthodox Jewish Schools, City Investigators Find," *The Washington Post*, December 20, 2009, www.washingtonpost.com/education/2019/12/19/political-horse-trading-by-new-york-mayors-office-contributed-delay-report-ultra-orthodox-jewish-schools-city-investigators-find (discussing political horse-trading over release of report on educational status of Hassidic schools and other law and religion flashpoints between state authorities and Orthodox communities). While this debate mainly impacts a subset of ultra-Orthodox schools, organizations closer to the BDA also weighed in on the controversy siding against the state's guidelines. *See* Fagin, Allen and Moishe Bane, letter to Dr. Christina Coughlin, August 28, 2019, https://ouintranet.org/newsletters/files/Updated-OU-Public-Comments-on-Substantial-Equivalency.pdf (critiquing the Department of Education's proposed guidelines for nonpublic schools as "not only legally problematic, but represent[ing] bad policy . . . . ").

6 See Shulhan Arukh (hereinafter, "SA") Hoshen Mishpat (hereinafter, "HM") §26. Unless otherwise noted, all translations of original Hebrew and rabbinic sources are of the author.

7 See, e.g., David Masci and Elizabeth Lawton, "Applying God's Law: Religious Courts and Mediation in the US," *Pew Research Center Survey on Religion and Public Life*, April 8, 2013 (citing Mark Washofsky, the Solomon B. Freehof Professor of Jewish Law and Practice at Hebrew Union College-Jewish Institute of Religion, explaining that "Reform Jews typically do not rely on rabbinical courts to settle financial or other disputes between members of the movement. We don't have a problem as a movement saying to our members: 'Go to the civil authorities.'" According to Warshofsky, unlike in some countries in centuries past, Jews in the US today have the same standing under the law as other Americans and do not need to seek redress outside of the civil court system).

that even otherwise observant Jews were rarely attracted to sectarian religious courts.[8] The rule against secular court litigation was either disregarded outright or assumed as no longer relevant in the liberal-democratic American context.

Over the past two generations, as the size and wealth of America's Orthodox population has grown, there has been a dramatic increase in volume and sophistication of intra-Orthodox commerce. Further, the assimilationist trends of the early and middle decades of the twentieth century have given way to a preservationist ethos that has raised Orthodoxy's confidence in standing apart from the cultural mainstream. These shifts led to a renewed appreciation for the halakhic bar against secular court litigation and increased the demand for rabbinical adjudication of commercial disputes.

The institution known today as the Beth Din of America began as an arm of the Rabbinical Council of America, an association of Orthodox rabbis largely affiliated with Yeshiva University.[9] When it began operations in the middle decades of the twentieth century, the Beth Din primarily dealt with the ritualistic aspects of Jewish marriage, divorce, and personal status laws and stayed away from adversarial commercial disputes.[10]

In the mid-1990s, the BDA professionalized its operations and was spun off into an independent rabbinical court.[11] Its initial foray into arbitration centered on marital property disputes flowing from its work in effectuating the ritual aspects

---

8 Michael Broyde, interview by author via Zoom, December 8, 2020. Broyde, a former director and member of the BDA who was instrumental in drafting its procedures and professionalizing its operations, noted that he was unaware of any institutionalized beth din in America resolving financial disputes prior to the mid-1990s. *See also* J. David Bleich, "The Beth Din: Its Time Has Returned," *Jewish Life* (Spring 1976): 3–4. In 1976, Rabbi J. David Bleich lamented how the American Orthodox community had all but forgotten the prohibition of litigating in civil court. Bleich opens his essay noting "there is one aspect of our rich heritage which is strangely neglected by virtually all groups within our religious community" and concludes, "the *Beth Din* is an institution which has been neglected for too long and whose time has come." Bleich is well positioned to make this observation. He is a lawyer and rabbinic scholar who has written hundreds of articles on Jewish civil law and beth din matters and would later join the faculty of Cardozo law school and lead Yeshiva University's program for training rabbis specializing in halakhic civil law. *See also* Louis Bernstein, "Challenge and Mission: The Emergence of the English Speaking Orthodox Rabbinate," *Shengold* (1982): 64–71, who recounts that the creation of an institutionalized beth din in the 1950s and 1960s was motivated by concerns over marriage and personal status issues but gave little thought to providing a forum for resolving commercial law disputes.
9 See Bernstein, "Challenge and Mission," 64–71.
10 In addition to its commercial law docket that is the subject of this chapter, the BDA is involved in issuing *gittin* (Jewish bills of divorce) along with arbitrating marital property issues arising out of divorce. It is also the primary mechanism of enforcement for the Rabbinical Council of America's prenuptial agreement—a document designed to prevent husbands abusing Jewish law to "chain" their wives to a defunct marriage. The BDA is also involved in conversions and has established the protocols followed by large segments of American Orthodoxy.
11 Michael Broyde, *Sharia Tribunals, Rabbinical Courts, and Christian Panels: Religious Arbitration in America and the West* (Oxford: Oxford University Press, 2017), 139.

of Jewish divorces.[12] The docket eventually expanded to cover more business-centric monetary disputes.[13] Today, the civil docket ranges from disputes between Jewish institutions and their employers (e.g., schools and teachers, rabbis and synagogues), disputes arising out of communally focused businesses, (e.g., kosher food, restaurants, and catering; provision of ritual objects and services; religious schools and camps), and general business disputes arising between Orthodox parties. Since the early 2000s, the BDA's civil docket has grown considerably.[14]

From a cultural and ideological perspective, the BDA sits in the mainstream of American Orthodoxy. Its leading figures are closely aligned with the Rabbinical Council of America, Yeshiva University, and the Orthodox Union. Its caseload, staff, and base of communal support are drawn from the center-right to center-left of American Orthodoxy, a community hubbed in greater New York but that spans out to many major American cities. The BDA is centered in New York but hears cases from across the country.

The BDA is led by several distinguished rabbis (one of whom is also a lawyer) who establish its halakhic policies. Day-to-day operations are managed by a *menahel* or lead administrator (also a rabbi-lawyer) along with staff attorneys. In addition to its rabbinic leaders and administrator, the BDA draws from a pool of roughly two-dozen *dayanim* (rabbinical court judges) selected to arbitrate commercial cases. This group contains rabbis with special expertise in Jewish business law, lawyers with knowledge of the relevant legal fields, and individuals who possess both sets of qualifications. The BDA is governed by a board composed of rabbis and attorneys, the latter setting the course for how the BDA interacts with the American legal system.

The BDA is associated with the strand of modern Orthodoxy that is fully committed to traditional halakhic practice but also sees a value in cultural and intellectual engagement with broader society. It has earned the reputation as one of the most sophisticated rabbinical courts in the United States,[15] whose judges possess "dual system fluency" in the intricacies of Jewish and American law.[16] Indeed, few of the BDA's competitor rabbinic courts boast this combination of professionalism combined with understanding of relevant halakhic, legal, and business issues. The BDA aims for its judgments to be respected by stakeholders for whom Jewish law is important and to be compelling to an overlapping set of stakeholders for

---

12  Broyde interview, sup. note 8.
13  Ibid.
14  See Michael A. Helfand, "Arbitration's Counter-Narrative: The Religious Arbitration Paradigm," *Yale Law Journal* 124, no. 8 (June 2015): 2994, 3016 n.86 (noting growth in BDA civil docket filings from 56 in 2002, to 100 cases in 2014). In an email sent December of 2020, Rabbi Weissman updated the filings as follows: 101 cases in 2015, 115 in 2016, 112 in 2017, 147 in 2018, 167 in 2019 and 168 in 2020.
15  Michael J. Broyde, "Jewish Law Courts in America: Lessons Offered to Sharia Courts by the Beth Din of America Precedent," *New York Law School Law Review* 57, no. 2 (2012/2013): 287, 288.
16  See Broyde, *Sharia Tribunals*, 163–64.

whom secular law and norms are important. Most of the BDA's target audience prizes both competencies and expects their rabbinical court to follow suit.

These dual-system commitments make the BDA both a leader and an outlier among American rabbinical courts. In terms of operational professionalism, ensuring conformity with secular law, and demonstrating awareness of the commercial expectations of parties and their lawyers, the BDA tends to lead the field. On the other hand, because the BDA and its audience place a higher premium on dual-system fluency, the secular legal system is more present in the BDA than in parallel institutions sponsored by ultra-Orthodox communities.

In addition to internal changes in the structure of the observant Jewish community, the growth of beth din adjudication is enabled by shifts in American law that make it far more welcoming of alternative dispute resolution (ADR) and arbitration specifically.[17] Prior to the 1920s, courts were typically hostile to arbitration provisions that committed future disputes to arbitration rather than to the courts.[18] This approach shifted, resulting in Congressional passage of the Federal Arbitration Act (FAA) in 1925.[19] Under the FAA, when the parties have entered into an agreement to arbitrate, courts are required to enforce the arbitration agreement by: (1) refusing to hear the case themselves; (2) compelling the parties to submit to the arbitration as per the contact; and (3) "confirming" the arbitral award. Upon confirmation by civil court, the legal system will treat the arbitral award no differently than a judgment issued by a state-sponsored court, thus enabling recourse to the state's machinery to aid in enforcement.[20]

The best evidence suggests that Congress only intended the FAA to apply to shipping agreements and significant commercial contracts.[21] Nevertheless, in a series of controversial and closely divided decisions, the Supreme Court

---

17  See, e.g., Deborah R. Hensler, "Our Courts, Ourselves: How the Alternative Dispute Resolution Movement Is Re-shaping Our Legal System," *Penn State Law Review* 108 (2003): 165.
18  See Ian R. MacNeal, *American Arbitration Law: Reformation-Nationalization-Internationalization* (New York and Oxford: Oxford University Press 1992); Imre S. Szalai, *Outsourcing Justice: The Rise of Modern Arbitration Laws in America* (Durham, NY: Carolina Academic Press, 2013); Sophia Chua-Rubenfeld and Frank J. Costa, Jr., "The Reverse-Entanglement Principle: Why Religious Arbitration of Federal Rights Is Unconstitutional," *Yale Law Journal* 128, no. 7 (May 2019): 2087, 2089.
19  See *Gilmer v. Interstate/Johnson Lane Corp.*, 500 U.S. 20, 24 (1991).
20  9 U.S.C. §§ 2–4 (1954); 9 U.S.C. § 9 (1947); *Timmons v. Lake City Golf, Ltd.*, 293 So. 3d 596, 599 (Fla. Dist. Ct. App. 2020) (holding that "when a trial court confirms an arbitration award, it must enter judgement in conformity with the arbitration award," and "the final judgement confirmed the arbitration award and provided the relief necessary to carry out the terms of the arbitration award").
21  See 65 Cong. Rec. 1931 (1924) (remarks of Rep. Graham noting that the FAA was intended to "give an opportunity to enforce an agreement in commercial contracts and admiralty contracts"); *Bernhardt v. Polygraphic Co. of America*, 350 U.S. 198, 200 (1956) (finding that "Section 2 makes 'valid, irrevocable, and enforceable' only two types of contracts: those relating to a maritime transaction and those relating to commerce"). For an in-depth discussion of Congressional intent for the FAA, see *Circuit Stores, Inc. v. Adams*, 532 U.S. 105, 124 (2001) (Stevens, J. dissenting); see also Szalai, sup. note 18 at 191–98.

70  Chaim Saiman

expanded its reading of the statute to include arbitration provisions found in almost any contract.[22] Today, courts will enforce arbitration clauses found in standard form contracts and compel arbitration of disputes arising out employment contracts, contracts between consumers and banks, credit card companies, cell phone providers, and virtually any other contract with an arbitration provision.[23]

Contemporary arbitration law is also quite liberal in allowing parties to customize most aspects of the arbitration proceedings. In civil court, the ideology and identity of the judge is beyond the parties' control, while the rules of evidence, scope of discovery, and procedure are prescribed by state law. Pursuant to freedom of contract principles, however, parties may use the arbitration clause or agreement to customize the process. Courts have enforced clauses allowing the parties to choose the law,[24] the arbitrators,[25] the rules of discovery,[26] and the rules of evidence[27] governing the arbitration. Moving to the realm of religious arbitration, courts have enforced clauses requiring prayer during the arbitration proceedings,[28] requiring an arbitrator to be of a specific nationality or religion,[29] and those mandating the arbitration proceed in

---

22  See, e.g., *Mitsubishi Motors Corp. v. Soler Chrysler-Plymouth Inc.*, 473 U.S. 614, 628–40 (1985); *Shearson/Am. Express Inc. v. McMahon*, 482 U.S. 220, 227–42 (1987); *Circuit City Stores, Inc. v. Adams*, 532 U.S. 105 (2001); Rubenfeld, sup. note 18 at 2090 (noting that the Supreme Court has increasingly permitted arbitration for areas of the law that was traditionally adjudicated by American courts).
23  See *Gilmer v. Interstate/Johnson Lane Corp.*, 500 U.S. 20 (1991) (applying the FAA to an employment dispute); *AT&T Mobility LLC v. Concepcion*, 563 U.S. 333 (2011) (holding that an arbitration clause in a consumer contract was enforceable); *Somehow v. Citicorp Credit Services*, 253 F.Supp. 3d 197 (D.D.C. 2017) (holding an arbitration clause for a cardholder's claims against a credit card company enforceable). See also Katherine V. W. Stone and Alexander J. S. Colvin, "The Arbitration Epidemic, Mandatory Arbitration Deprives Workers and Consumers of Their Rights," *Economic Policy Institute*, December 7, 2015, www.epi.org/publication/the-arbitration-epidemic/#epi-toc-5.
24  *Volt Information Sciences v. Bd. of Trs of Stanford University*, 489 U.S. 468, 474–75 (1989) (holding that the FAA confers a right to obtain an order directing arbitration to proceed "in the manner provided for in the parties' agreement" and applying the parties' choice of law provision).
25  *Stolt-Nielsen S.A. v. AnimalFeeds Int'l Corp.*, 559 U.S. 662, 683 (2010) (holding that parties are "generally free to structure their arbitration agreements as they see fit" and can choose who will resolve specific disputes) (quoting *Mastrobuono v. Shearson Lehman Hutton, Inc.*, 514 U.S. 52, 57 (1995)).
26  See *Ridgeway v. Nabors Completion & Prod. Servs. Co.*, 725 Fed. Appx. 472, 474 (9th Cir. 2018) (upholding discovery clauses in an arbitration agreement).
27  *Am. Express Co. v. Italian Colors Rest.*, 570 U.S. 228, 233 (2013) (finding that under the FAA, courts must "vigorously enforce" arbitration agreements according to their terms, including the "rules under which that arbitration will be conducted") (citing *Volt*, 489 U.S. at 479).
28  *Spivey v. Teen Challenge of Florida, Inc.*, 122 So.3d 986, 992 (Fla. Dist. Ct. App. 2013).
29  *In re Aramco Servs. Co.*, No. 01-09-00624-CV, 2010 WL 1241525, at *2, 6 (Tex. App. March 19, 2010) (vacating the trial court's order appointing an arbitrator because the agreement gave the parties the sole authority to do so and specified that the arbitrator must be Muslim or Saudi).

a specific language.³⁰ Finally, while courts are generally reluctant to review the substantive basis of almost any arbitral award,³¹ fear of running afoul of the First and Fourteenth Amendments makes this apply with particular force to faith-based arbitrations.³² As a general rule, so long as the basics of procedural justice are maintained, civil courts will compel parties to arbitrate as per their contract and then confirm and aid in enforcing the resulting awards.³³

The *laissez faire* policies of American arbitration law along with religious autonomy doctrines potentially offer the BDA considerable leeway in limiting the influence of state law and secular legal culture on its proceedings. As a result, a rabbinical court that wanted to maximize its independence from the state and stress its Jewish law distinctiveness could go a long way towards achieving this goal.³⁴ The BDA, however, tends to move in the opposite direction. Instead of working to keep the state and its legal system at bay, the BDA uses state legal mechanisms to entwine Jewish and American law together. Four examples follow.

---

30  Ibid.
31  See Paul F. Kirgis, "Judicial Review and the Limits of Arbitral Authority: Lessons from the Law of Contract," *St. John's Law Review* 81, no. 1 (Winter 2007): 99, 104 (finding that "[awards] are almost never vacated on grounds related to the substance of an award"). See also *Hall St.*, 552 U.S. at 584 (holding that grounds explicitly stated in the FAA are the exclusive grounds for modification of an arbitration award); Richard C. Reuben, "Personal Autonomy and Vacatur After Hall Street," *Penn State Law Review* 113, no. 4 (Spring 2009): 1103, 1113–14 (noting that after *Hall St.*, courts have used non-statutory grounds such as manifest disregard of the law to vacate/modify an arbitration award, but success using those grounds is rare, and "a mere error of law or failure to apply the law does not rise to the level of manifest disregard of the law").
32  *Serbian E. Orthodox Diocese v. Milivojevich*, 426 U.S. 696, 708–09 (1976) (holding under the First and Fourteenth Amendments that civil courts must accept religious arbitration ruling barring a showing of clear bad faith on part of the tribunal).
33  See *Hall St.*, 552 U.S. at 584–86 (holding that §§10–11 are the FAA's exclusive grounds for vacatur, modification, and judicial review following arbitration).
34  The scope of this independence has been the subject of recent scholarly debate. Some scholars argue that the law should grant parties to religious arbitrations more safeguards than available under standard arbitration, see, e.g., Jeff Dasteel, "Religious Arbitration in Contracts of Adhesion," *Penn State Arbitration Law Review* 8, no. 3 (May 2016): 45–68 (arguing that since religious arbitration clauses in contracts of adhesion have the potential to violate an objecting party's religious beliefs, American law should add protections for parties in these contracts of adhesion); Chua-Rubenfeld & Costa, Jr., *The Reverse-Entanglement Principle*, 2087 (proposing to recognize novel constitutional or statutory constraints on religious arbitration because current doctrine does not contain sufficient checks on religious arbitration panels). By contrast, Michael Helfand argues that existing private law remedies are sufficient to address concerns of religious tribunals overstepping their boundaries. See Michael A. Helfand, "The Peculiar Genius of Private-Law Systems: Making Room for Religious Commerce," *Washington University Law Review* 97 (2020): 1787–832. See also *Garcia v. Church of Scientology Flag Serv. Org.*, No. 8:13-cv-220-T-27TBM, 2015 U.S. Dist. LEXIS 178033 (M.D. Fla. March 13, 2015) (compelling arbitration by former church member of claims against Church of Scientology even though arbitration clause requires arbiters to be members of good standing in the Scientology Church).

## Lawyers at the Beth Din

### Advocates in Rabbinical Courts

Courtroom advocates (differentiated from "lawyers," which refer to those licensed under state bar associations) are foreign to classical Jewish law. Mishna tractate Avot 1:8—often memorized by young schoolchildren—teaches that one "should not play the part of an advocate in court."[35] Commenting on the injunction in Exodus 23:7, *you shall veer away from falsehoods*, the tannaitic Midrash warns the judge "not to place advocates beside him" but to hear the litigants directly without intermediaries.[36] The Talmud understands Ezekiel's description of *one who did which is not good among his people* (Ez. 18:18) as referring to a person with the power of attorney to present another's claims in court.[37] Rashi's standard commentary explains that while the parties themselves can be pushed towards settlement, advocates—who are assumed to lack the legal capacity to settle for less than the demanded amount—will press the claims indefinitely.[38]

Indeed, classical rabbinic terminology has no term for a lawyer/advocate. The rabbinic canon relies on Greek loan words such as *p'raklet*, *sanegor*, and *kategor*, further emphasizing these roles are foreign to Jewish law.[39] Richard Hidary has shown that in Talmudic literature, lawyers and their equivalents *do not* appear in accounts of earthly courts but are reserved for descriptions of heavenly tribunals. While angelic prosecutors and defense advocates are appointed for souls standing trial Above, rabbinic tribunals down below function without the aid of professional advocacy.[40]

Rabbinical court advocacy nevertheless developed over the centuries and became entrenched within Jewish law. Advocates were initially required to be at least partial assignees of the claim such that representation proceeded on the theory that anyone with a financial stake could press claims on behalf of themselves

---

35 Commentaries to the Mishna debate whether this refers only to judges who must be careful not to become one of the parties' advocates or whether this applies to anyone not a party to the litigation. For a review of the various interpretations of this term, see Richard Hidary, *Rabbis and Classical Rhetoric: Sophistic Education and Oratory in the Talmud and Midrash* (Cambridge: Cambridge University Press, 2017), 225–26, n.39–43.
36 Rabbi Yishmael, Mekhilta, Mishpatim de-§20. My translation follows Hidary, *Rabbis and Rhetoric* at 222. See also discussion of *Torah Temima* to Ex. 22:8 and 23:7, *Torah Shleima* to Ex. 23:7 (found in Appendix/ Miluim #31).
37 b. Shevuot 31a.
38 Rashi to b. Shevuot 31a.
39 The etymology and use of these terms in Hellenic and Roman literature is discussed in Hidary, *Rabbis and Rhetoric*, 223–24, 240–41.
40 Hidary, *Rabbis and Rhetoric*, 240–42. For more on the role of lawyers in subsequent eras of Jewish law, see Lipkin, *Advocacy According to Torah Law*, SINAI 30 (1952), 46 [Hebrew]; Nahum Rackover, *Agency in Jewish Law* (Jerusalem: Library of Jewish Law, 1972), 308–53 [Hebrew]; Dov Frimmer, "The Role of the Lawyer in Jewish Law," *Journal of Law & Religion* 1 (1983): 297. For a discussion of the practice in contemporary beth dins, see Yona Reiss, *Kanfei Yona* (New York: Yeshiva University, 2018), 98–108 [Hebrew].

and their partners. Advocacy was thus restricted to plaintiffs and to the limited set of claims deemed assignable as choses-in-action under Jewish law.[41] Through custom and practice, the institution eventually expanded to cover all claims, and later defendants gained the ability to retain advocates.[42]

Halakhic scholars supported these innovations through reasoning familiar to lawyers of all stripes: to aid less sophisticated parties (especially women litigating with their ex-husbands), to put distance between the squabbling parties and let cooler heads prevail, and to prevent the court from having to advocate itself on behalf of unsophisticated litigants.[43] More recently, scholars have argued that since the practice has become so widespread, parties are generally free to stipulate to such arrangements even if they were not conventionally practiced.[44]

Despite these developments, beth din advocacy remains under a cloud of suspicion and has rarely received the warm reception afforded to lawyering in the Anglo-American tradition. Both Sefardic and Ashkenazic rabbis of the seventeenth century lamented how advocates one up each other "with lies, devices and deceit" to "attract higher fees,"[45] or "shout without understanding—searching the books for rules that aid their cause," while "collecting the chaff and discarding the wheat."[46] These themes go unabated in the works of some of the most significant halakhists of the nineteenth and late twentieth centuries[47] as well as in contemporary popular ultra-Orthodox discourse—the primary market for beth din adjudication.[48]

### *Beth Din's Embrace of Lawyers*

While American law places few demands on arbitration panels, it likely requires the beth din to grant parties the opportunity for legal representation by counsel of their choosing. *Kahan v. Rosner* tells of a brother and sister locked in an inheritance dispute who entered an arbitration agreement to appear before a beth din requiring that any attorney be "approved by the Rabbinical Court."[49] Kahan's selected lawyer was refused, and the beth din offered Kahan to proceed with

---

41 See Tur HM §123.
42 See Ibid. See also SA HM §§123:1 and 124:1.
43 See Eliav Shochetman, *Rabbinical Court Procedure (Jerusalem)* (Washington, DC: Government Printing Office, 2011), 172–74 [Hebrew] (Hereinafter, "*Rabbinical Court Procedure*").
44 *Rabbinical Court Procedure* at 172.
45 Statement attributed to R. Hayyim Benvenesti, as cited in *Rabbinical Court Procedure* at 168 n.232.
46 Nahalat Shiva, Shtarot § 44.
47 See, e.g. *Arukh ha-Shulhan* §§17:15 and 123:16. See also Commentary of Rabbi Yosef Shalom Elyashiv to Ketubot 52b.
48 *See* Dovid Lichtenstein, "Beis Din – Do Toanim serve a Purpose?" *Halacha Headlines Podcast*, November 16, 2019, http://podcast.headlinesbook.com. See also Dovid Lichtenstein, "Dealing with Corruption and Abuse of Toanim in Beis Din," *Halacha Headlines Podcast*, November 30, 2019, http://podcast.headlinesbook.com. This popular podcast is geared at the English speaking ultra-Orthodox world.
49 *Kahan v. Rosner*, 889 N.Y.S.2d 839 (Sup. Ct. 2009).

an approved lawyer, which Kahan in turn refused. The arbitration proceeded without Kahan having benefit of counsel and Kahan thereafter moved to vacate the award. A New York trial court held that since the right to counsel was non-waivable, the beth din's refusal to approve Kahan's chosen counsel for no articulable reason violated his rights under New York law.[50]

These secular law requirements could easily be seen as rubbing against the traditional halakhic skepticism of lawyers. This is especially so to the extent the state can mandate introducing persons who are neither Jewish nor versed in halakhah into the beth din proceedings. A tribunal seeking to limit the impact of secular law could be counseled to take aggressive legal positions and seek to restrict both the lawyer's role and perhaps the types of lawyers allowed in beth din. After all, since beth din proceedings are structured by Jewish law, it is not outlandish to assume only those who share the beth din's theological sensibilities—or even only those ordained as rabbis or Jewish law judges—should be permitted to appear.[51] A beth din could further attempt to bar lawyers from presenting substantive legal arguments to a tribunal proceeding under rabbinic law.

Steps in this direction would surely increase the chance that of the beth din's jurisdiction award being vacated or of a civil court refusing confirmation. But at the same time, demanding the state to publicly announce and justify its refusal to enforce a religious arbitral award pursued under a valid arbitration agreement would also raise the legal and political costs to the state. Nevertheless, these tactics are not typically pursued. Most institutionalized beth dins simply acknowledge the requirement of counsel as part of the background legal regime and proceed accordingly.[52]

The BDA, however, goes further. Rather than restrict access to legal counsel, BDA rules expressly permit parties to select any lawyer—including those who are not Jewish—from any jurisdiction as counsel.[53] This approach is all the more notable because the BDA prohibits a *to'en* (pl. *to'anim*; unlicensed rabbinical courts advocates) from representing clients before it. This policy is grounded both in the traditional halakhic reticence towards representation and on account

---

50 Ibid. See also *Mikel v. Scharf*, 85 A.D.2d 604 (2d Dep't 1981).
51 See *infra* note 120 for American caselaw enforcing an arbitration agreement that limits the arbitrators to persons belonging to a given religion.
52 See, e.g., Igud HaRabonim Beth Din, "Procedures of the Beth Din—Rabbinical Alliance of America," § 5, accessed June 1, 2021, www.bdigud.org/forms ("In New York, the parties have the right to retain secular legal counsel to represent them before the Beth Din. The primary parties will be required to make presentations of claims, as well as to respond to questioning, themselves . . . [Parties] may consult with such counsel in advance of the Din Torah, and at certain points during the Beth Din sessions").
53 See Beth Din of America, "Rules and Procedures," 8, § 12, accessed June 1, 2021, https://bethdin.org/wp-content/uploads/2018/04/BDA118-RulesProcedures_Bro_BW_02.pdf ("Any party shall have the right to be represented by an attorney who must be licensed to practice law in any jurisdiction in the United States"). Many of the halakhic rationales for BDA practice are set forth in an article written by one of its rabbinic leaders; see Reiss, *Kanfei Yona*, sup. note 40.

of the reputation the unlicensed *to'anim* profession has earned for raising outlandish claims and increasing the cost and acrimony of the proceedings.[54] The net result is somewhat counter-intuitive. Per American law, the BDA permits representation by secularly licensed lawyers, yet it uses its inherent halakhic power to bar advocates with ostensible Jewish law expertise from appearing before it.

### *Embracing American Legal Culture*

Perhaps the most dramatic move in this arena is that the BDA not only invites lawyers into its bar but even onto its rabbinic "bench." In commercial cases, the custom is to appoint at least one male Orthodox Jew to the panel who is also a secularly licensed attorney familiar with the practice relevant to the case.[55] In some instances, this individual is also conversant in Jewish law, while in others, that expertise is provided by co-panelists. These moves go far beyond any requirements placed by secular arbitration law, and draw the sensibilities of American law into the substantive deliberations of the beth din itself.[56]

Day-to-day workings of the beth din reveal how the presence of lawyers does more than tick the box of legal compliance. As a *dayyan* hearing cases at the BDA, I have heard lawyers claim they want to "cross-examine the other party" or that document X is "owed" in discovery. From the position of traditional halakhah, these demands ring hollow. Halakhic procedure is more akin to the civilian-inquisitorial model than the lawyer-driven process of the common law. Primarily, it is the court's job to interrogate parties[57] and witnesses,[58] and to the extent the parties maintain such rights, they are clearly secondary.[59] The same is true of documentary discovery, which is considerably narrower under Jewish law than per its American counterpart.[60]

The presence of secular lawyers and beth din judges trained in secular law invariably draws American legal assumptions into the fold, which can influence the overall tenor of the proceedings. For example, the BDA permits—and

---

54 See Reiss, *Kanfei Yona*, sup. note 40. On the reputation of *to'anim*, see Lichtenstein podcasts, sup. note 48.
55 See Broyde, *Sharia Tribunals*, 163–66 (explaining that BDA often appoints judges who are subject matter experts in the secular law or market/ social customs of a given dispute. In child custody cases, BDA often empanels a psychologist).
56 I note that this policy of the BDA is **not** generally shared by ultra-Orthodox beth dins.
57 SA HM §15:3–4.
58 See Deuteronomy 13:15; SA HM §30:1.
59 See HM §30:1 (discussing prerogatives of judges to question witnesses while recording no provisions for parties to do the same). See also *Rabbinical Court Procedure*, 1053 (parties do not generally have right to question witnesses, but discussing some later innovations in this regard) and at 1022–23 (discussing evolution of a party's right to question its counterparty).
60 See Tur and SA HM, §16. *See also Rabbinical Court Procedure*, 1063–67 (document production is only compelled when the party in possession admits that it contains evidence supporting the counter-party's claim or the demanding party is certain about the contents and relevance of the document).

sometimes even encourages—lawyers to submit briefs presenting American law arguments to the panel. These submissions do not compel the beth din to adopt American law or even to frame its decision in such terms. But they do provide an external benchmark to assess the BDA's halakhic analysis and can shape the range of considerations seen as relevant to the ultimate decision.

## Reasoned Opinions

Talmudic halakhah does not generally mandate court orders to be either reasoned or written. Following deliberation, the judges simply announce the names of the parties that came before them and issue their order.[61] This process is often understood as part of a deliberate policy to obscure internal dissent or fracture between the judges.[62] Nevertheless, over time, the practice of issuing written orders became near-universal.[63]

The history of producing *reasoned* opinions is more complex. The primary Talmudic discussion tells of X who wanted to resolve the matter locally, whereas Y wanted to litigate in a larger city before more sophisticated judges—a move that would increase costs. The Talmud rules the matter should be addressed at the local venue, but "if [the losing side] requests a document explaining the reasoning for the judgments [to show to a more learned court], the court should write it for him."[64]

This venue-driven context led most authorities to conclude reasoned decisions are only required when courts can compel parties to litigate before them or when there is a clear hierarchical system whereby superior courts review the decisions of inferior ones.[65] These conditions, however, do not typically obtain in what halakhic authorities refer to as "our days"—the exilic, post-Talmudic dispensation of the present. Other halakhists mitigate the impact of this rule by suggesting the losing party is only entitled to a document stating the facts and verdict, but not the underlying rationale.[66]

The Talmud presents another setting when a reasoned opinion may be warranted. Two partners, A and B, pooled their funds. A unilaterally withdrew his share and made a profitable investment. B then demanded half the profits. The matter was set before a Talmudic sage who ruled that since a partnership of pooled funds is subject to unilateral division at will, the profits from A's investment accrue to him alone. The following year, A and B jointly purchased wine. This time, B unilaterally moved to sell his portion and made a profitable investment, and A came to demand half the profits. The same sage ruled that since B's

---

61 See b. Sanhedrin 30a: SA HM §19:1–2. *Arukh ha-Shulhan* §19:2.
62 See SA HM, §19.
63 On the evolution of the practice of producing reasoned opinions in western legal systems, see John Dawson, *Oracles of the Law* (Ann Arbor, MI: University of Michigan School of Law, 1968).
64 b. Sanhedrin, 31b.
65 See, e.g., Tosafot Sanhedrin, 31b and b. Bava Metzia, 69b; SA HM §14; Beit Yosef to Tur HM §14:4.
66 *Hiddushie ha-Ramban on Bava Metiza*, 69b.

sale constituted an improper breach of the partnership, *A* was entitled to a share of the profits from *B*'s investment. *B* complained the sage was predisposed against him. This led the sage to respond that when there is apparent bias, a judge should explain the basis of his ruling.[67]

Most authorities conclude that while there is no general obligation to offer a reasoned opinion, a beth din should do so as a matter of best practice, especially when jurisdiction is coerced or there is some basis for questioning the result.[68] Some extend this logic to cases where litigants request a reasoned opinion.[69] Others deem it impertinent for a party to demand an explanation unless legitimate reasons to question the decision are presented.[70]

As a historical matter, it seems that most rabbinic courts did not issue reasoned opinions. Professor Jay Berkovitz published the ledger of the Metz (eastern France) beth din in the second half of the eighteenth century, when it was led by the famed halakhist R. Aryeh Leib Gunzburg (d. 1785). Gunzburg is most familiar from his book of Talmudic commentary, *Sha'agot Aryeh*, a work renowned for its erudition and analytical disquisitions on Talmudic topics. The court ledger of this same rabbi, however, is virtually free of analysis.[71] Cases are documented by presenting the names of the parties, a synopsis of the facts and claims, followed by the legal ruling. The same impression is confirmed by Edward Fram's work on parallel materials from R. Hayyim Gundersheim's beth din in Frankfurt of roughly the same period, as well as court records found in multiple other sources.[72]

The absence of legal reasoning in court opinions stands in sharp contrast to the abundance of such discourse in rabbinic *responsa*—collections of questions submitted to halakhic sages and the answers they provided.[73] This voluminous

---

67 See b. Bava Metzia, 69a–b. The Talmud reconciles the two rulings, noting that different default rules apply to partnerships of pooled assets as opposed to commodities.
68 See, e.g., Tosafot Sanhedrin, 31b and Tosafot Bava Metizia, 69b. See also *Responsa of Maharam Rothenburg* §917 (Prague Edition) and Eliav Shochetman, "The Obligation for Reasoned Opinions in Jewish Law," *The Jewish Law Annual* 6–7 (1979–80): 319, 328–31 [Hebrew].
69 *Responsa Nodeh be-Yehuda*, HM §1 (Second Edition).
70 *Responsa Hatam Sofer*, HM §12.
71 Jay Berkovitz, *Protocols of Justice: The Pinkas of the Metz Rabbinic Court, 1771–1789*, Studies in Jewish History and Culture, vol. 44 (Boston, MA: Brill, 2014), 57 ("Traditional Jewish Law, based on the Talmud and medieval/early modern codes is the legal foundation of the [court ledger]. However, no texts of the Jewish legal tradition are ever referenced by name in the rabbinical court proceedings, and even oblique references to the views of [halakhic authorities] or rabbinic *responsa* are extremely rare").
72 Edward Fram, *A Window on Their World: The Court Diaries of Rabbi Hayyim Gundersheim Frankfurt Am Main, 1773–1794* (Bristol, CT: ISD, LLC, 2012), 80 ("[Jewish] courts—at least the Frankfurt court—left almost no record of the legal reasoning that led to individual decisions . . . legal justifications—not to mention legal reasoning—are almost totally absent from Gundersheim's diary").
73 For a more complete discussion of this distinction, *see* Shochetman, *The Obligation for Reasoned Opinions*, 338–52; Shmuel Glick, *Windows to the Responsa Literature* (New York and Jerusalem: The Jewish Theological Seminary of America, 2012), 41–88 [Heb]. *See also* Fram, sup. note 72 at 68–85 (analyzing difference between responsa literature and rabbinical court documents).

literature contains detailed discussion regarding practical questions of Jewish law, including matters related to civil litigation. *Responsa* and beth din documents differ, however, in that the former is an expert opinion on an abstract question, whereas the latter reflects the more bureaucratic work of applying legal rules to the facts as determined by the judge.

More recently, the intersection of western legal systems and Jewish law has pushed some beth dins to offer reasoned opinions as a matter of course.[74] In Israel, where state-sponsored rabbinical courts are intermeshed with the legal system, the Israeli Supreme Court has mandated the state's rabbinical courts decisions must be accompanied by written halakhic reasoning.[75]

Shifting to American law, the Supreme Court has declared that "arbitrators have no obligation to the court to give their reasons for an award."[76] Courts explain that a rule requiring reasoning in an arbitral judgment will diminish the efficiency of the arbitration process.[77] As for procedural requirements, courts can only vacate arbitration awards on what is deemed an exhaustive list of reasons set forth in the FAA,[78] though some courts have vacated arbitral awards on public policy grounds or if the award evinces a "manifest disregard of the law."[79] Nevertheless, because these reasons are not expressly provided for in the FAA, the ongoing viability of vacatur on such grounds remains in doubt.[80]

Even when vacatur on public policy grounds is permitted, however, this doctrine is further limited by requiring that public policy violation be discoverable "on the face of the award," so that the court does not have to engage in extensive fact-finding to elicit the illicit decision.[81] Additionally, if these grounds for vacatur

---

74 For example, Rabbi Meir Ben-Zion Hai Ouziel, the Sephardic Chief Rabbi of pre-state Israel, wrote that rabbinical courts should be no less transparent than secular courts in articulating their reasoning and demonstrating the justness of their decisions. See *Responsa Mishpatei Ouziel*, HM §1, 13.
75 See HCJ 3914/92 *Lev v. Rabbinical Court* 48(2) at 491 (Supreme Court of Israel 1994).
76 *United Steelworkers of Am. v. Enter. Wheel & Car Corp.*, 363 U.S. 593, 598 (1960).
77 *Sobel v. Hertz, Warner & Co.*, 469 F.2d 1211, 1214–15 (2d Cir. 1972) ("[A] requirement that arbitrators explain their reasoning in every case would . . . undermine the very purpose of arbitration, which is to provide a relatively quick, efficient and informal means of private dispute settlement").
78 *Hall St.*, 552 U.S. at 578. See also 9 U.S.C. §§ 10–11 (2002).
79 See, e.g., *Sea-Land Serv., Inc. v. Int'l Longshoremen's Ass'n.*, 625 F.2d 38, 42 (5th Cir. 1980) (holding "Arbitral awards may be judicially vacated on such grounds as . . . public policy"); *Comedy Club, Inc. v. Improv W. Assocs.*, 553 F.3d 1277, 1290 (9th Cir. 2009) (holding that manifest disregard of the law remains grounds for vacatur).
80 Michael A. Helfand, "Between Law and Religion: Procedural Challenges to Religious Arbitration Awards," *Chicago-Kent Law Review* 90, no. 1 (2015), 141, 151 n.52, 153 n.63. Compare *Citigroup Global Mkts., Inc. v. Bacon*, 562 F.3d 349, 358 (5th Cir. 2009) (holding that manifest disregard of the law is no longer an independent ground for vacating arbitration awards under the FAA) with *Wachovia Securities v. Brand*, 671 F.3d 472, 483 (4th Cir. 2012) ("manifest disregard continues to exist either as an independent ground for review or as a judicial gloss on the enumerated grounds for vacatur" set forth in the statute.)
81 See e.g., *Bd. of Education v. Hershkowtiz*, 308 A.D. 2d 334, 337 (App. Div. 1st Dept. 2003) (holding that vacatur on public policy grounds must be evident from examining

are generally viable, there is even more uncertainly regarding whether they apply in the case of religious arbitrations.[82]

Placing Jewish and American law side by side, a beth din looking to conform to traditional halakhic practice *and* minimize its exposure to civil court interference would draft its orders with minimal reasoning and in rabbinic Hebrew. This would make them all but impenetrable to anyone unschooled in the intricacies of Jewish law. So long as common stock phrases of arbitration law were dutifully recited, a beth din could make it all but impossible for a party to mount a substantive challenge to its decisions.[83]

BDA practice, however, runs to the contrary. Rule 27 of its procedures obligates the beth din to issue decisions in writing and in English. As a matter of practice, most BDA decisions extend beyond this minimum and offer reasoned analysis of their conclusions. A fair number even adopt the tone and structure of judicial opinions similar to unpublished—and sometimes even published—opinions issued by sophisticated state and federal courts.

Further, while halakhic concepts are certainly cited and discussed, because the award is written with secular law and lawyers in mind, there is a tendency to frame the halakhah as relatively in sync with relevant American law. Though not every sentence can be understood by a secular lawyer or judge, the decisions often track the conceptual structure of how American-trained lawyers expect the analysis to unfold. Experienced lawyers are often able to follow the contours of the reasoning aided only by brief explanation of key halakhic concepts or the embedded social realities of American Orthodoxy. Finally, though rabbinic court judges are generally well-regarded graduates of elite yeshivot, BDA opinions are different from yeshiva-centric halakhic disquisitions. While the latter overflow with Talmudic idioms and concepts only seasoned halakhists could comprehend, the former are designed to appeal to the norms of transparency, efficiency, and justice as understood by the secular legal community.

## Jurisdiction: Inherent and Arbitral

Arbitration in American law is wholly a creature of contract law that is predicated on the consent of the parties.[84] When presented with a valid arbitration

---

the arbitration agreement or award on its face); *Cohoes Police Officer's Union Local 756 ex rel. Westfall v. City of Cohoes*, 263 A.D. 2d 652, 653 (App. Div. 3rd Dept. 2003) (holding that "before a court may intervene with an arbitration award on public policy grounds, it must be able to examine an arbitration agreement or an award on its face without engaging in extended fact-finding or legal analysis and conclude that public policy precludes enforcement").

82 Helfand, sup. note 80, at 155.
83 *Cat Charter, L.L.C. v. Schurtenberger*, 646 F.3d 836, 844 (11th Cir. 2011) (holding that "in a typical arbitration where no specific form of award is requested, arbitrators may provide a 'standard award' and simply announce a result").
84 See *Volt*, 563 U.S. at 474 (finding that "[The FAA] was designed to place [arbitration] upon the same footing as other contracts"); *Concepcion*, 563 U.S. at 351 (finding that "arbitration

agreement, American courts not only tolerate beth din decisions but also actively lend their support. Courts will compel parties to appear before a beth din, and following confirmation, use the state's mechanisms to enforce the awards.[85] In the absence of an agreement, however, in the eyes of American law a beth din is powerless to assert its jurisdiction or enforce its decisions over any party.[86]

Under Jewish law by contrast, a beth din may exert plenary civil, criminal, and religious authority on nearly every facet of Jewish life.[87] Jewish law mandates all to respect the authority of a beth din[88] and to adhere to its orders,[89] and absent beth din approval, prohibits litigating intra-Jewish claims before secular courts.[90] Should a party refuse to appear, a beth din is empowered to issue a *seruv* (akin to a contempt order) that can subject the offending party to a host of communal remedies.[91]

The anomalous status of Jews in medieval and early modern society meant that Jews were not typically conceptualized as citizens of their respective nations who were free to live and work outside designated Jewish communities and professions.[92] Particularly in Christian lands, the *kahal*—the corporate body of the Jewish community (and its constituent institutions such as the beth din)—served as the intermediary between individual Jews and the rulership. ("State" in this context is an anachronism). Though generalizations over so much time and space are bound to be imprecise, the *kahal* was often granted considerable autonomy in governing the civil and religious lives of Jewish population. In exchange, it served as a reliable conduit of the rulership's demands of the Jews, which frequently centered on taxation.[93]

The political and social power of the *kahal* and its beth din made threats of excommunication, shunning, and social shaming common and effective backstops

---

is a matter of contract"); *First Options of Chi., Inc. v. Kaplan*, 514 U.S. 938, 943 (1995) (holding that "arbitration is simply a matter of contract law"); Michael A. Helfand, "Fighting for the Debtor's Soul: Regulating Religious Commercial Conduct," *George Mason Law Review* 19, no. 1 (2011): 157, 169 (citing H.R. REP. NO. 68-96 (1924) at 1–2 (noting that arbitration is a purely a creature of contract)).

85 Helfand, sup. note 14, at 1244.
86 Michelle Greenberg-Kobrin, "Civil Enforceability of Religious Prenuptial Agreements," *Columbia Journal of Law and Social Problems* 32, no. 4 (1999): 359, 368–69.
87 See SA HM §2:1 ("A beth din that observes that the populace is flagrantly committing sins may initiate capital, corporal, criminal, and financial sanctions.").
88 See SA HM §8:4 ("the public is obligated to show reverence to the judge").
89 See SA HM §8:5 (beth din's officers must be respected and are empowered to initiate excommunication bans and administer corporal punishments towards recalcitrant parties).
90 See Tur and SA HM §26.
91 Tur and SA HM §11.
92 See, e.g., Jacob Katz, *Tradition and Crisis* (Syracuse, NY: Syracuse University Press, 2000), 13–25.
93 At times, these functions were expressly connected. Jay Berkovitz reports that in pre-revolutionary France, 50% of fines collected by the *kahal*/beth din were remitted to the secular authorities as taxes, thereby granting the rulership a financial interest in maintaining the civil authority of these institutions. See Berkovitz, *Protocols of Justice*, 53–57.

of a beth din's power.[94] Refusing beth din's authority could lead a person to be barred from sitting in his assigned seat in synagogue, from being called to the Torah, from entering the synagogue *in toto*, from having his children educated in the community, or from his wife from taking her seat in the synagogue.[95] Though less common, the halakhic and historical record is not bereft of examples of communities ensuring compliance by way of lashes, stocks, imprisonment, and pulling out of the hair.[96] The scope of a beth din's authority to effectuate such measures is a much-discussed topic in halakhic literature of the medieval and early modern periods.[97]

Due at least in part to the legal and cultural impact of American constitutionalism, most American Jewish communities never coalesced into a *kahal* framework. American law prohibits a beth din from using physically coercive force or threats of imprisonment to mandate a party to appear before it or compel anyone to obey its orders. Attempts in this direction are almost certain to land a beth din in legal jeopardy, as discovered by rabbis of a beth din who used physically coercive measures to compel Jewish men to grant their estranged wives Jewish divorce documents (known as a *get*). The rabbis found themselves in jail—though not before (unsuccessfully) raising religious freedom defenses.[98] Moreover, even if the parties signed an arbitration agreement purporting to subject themselves to the full scope of a beth din's inherent powers under Jewish law, the agreement would likely be subject to attack under claims of duress, coercion, unconscionability, and void-as-against public policy—especially if more extreme measures are attempted.[99]

---

94  See, e.g., Tur and SA to HM §2 and especially the comments of Beit Yosef. See also Tur and SA to Yoreh De'ah §334. The definitive scholarly assessment of the history and doctrine of these punishments is found in Aharon Kirschenbaum, *Jewish Penology: The Theory and Development of Criminal Punishments Among the Jews Throughout the Ages* (Jerusalem: Magnes Press, 2013), 439–64 [Hebrew]. For a historical account on the structure of the kahal and its powers of excommunication, see Katz, *Tradition and Crisis*, sup. note 92, 77–87; Jay Berkovitz, *Law's Dominion: Jewish Community, Religion, and Family in Early Modern Metz* (Boston, MA: Brill, 2020), 163–70.

95  Tur Yoreh Dea'h §334 and SA Yoreh Dea'h §334:10–11 along with Rema to §334:6. Some authorities display discomfort in applying these sanctions to the wife and children of the recalcitrant party and limit sanctions to the party himself or his minor children. See comments of *Taz* and *Be'er Heitev* to YD §334:6. See also Kirschenbaum, *Jewish Penology*, 445 n. 30; Herschel Schachter, "Synagogue Membership and School Admission," *Journal of Halacha and Contemporary Society* 12 (1986): 50, 66 (noting that "restricting [the] wife and children [of a recalcitrant party] is the single most efficacious method of forcing him to comply with Beth Din's wishes").

96  See Tur and SA HM §2 and especially the comments of Beit Yosef to Tur HM §2. See Kirschenbaum, *Jewish Penology*, 374–427.

97  See Tur and SA HM §2; and Yoreh Dea'h §334. See also Beit Yosef Yoreh Dea'h §228.

98  See, e.g., *United States v. Stimler*, 864 F.3d 253 (3d Cir. 2017), reh'g granted, and opinion vacated in part sub nom. *United States v. Goldstein*, 902 F.3d 411 (3d Cir. 2018), and on reh'g sub nom. *United States v. Goldstein*, 914 F.3d 200 (3d Cir. 2019).

99  Michael A. Helfand, "The Peculiar Genius of Private-Law Systems: Making Room for Religious Commerce," *Washington University Law Review* 97 (2020): 1787; See, e.g., *Doctor's*

Along with other beth dins, the BDA respects this constitutional settlement and refrains from asserting criminal jurisdiction over any person,[100] or from invoking its halachically sanctioned powers to enforce religious standards and observance.[101] It likewise shies away from inhabiting the quasi-executive functions frequently assigned by the *kahal* to the beth din as part of its system of internal self-governance.[102]

More interestingly, this trend even applies to less fanciful scenarios closer to the beth din's core interest in arbitrating commercial disputes. The BDA respects the automatic stay mandated by §362 of the US Bankruptcy Code, which prevents any proceeding relating to the bankruptcy estate. Notwithstanding an arguable halakhic basis, the BDA will not permit parties to use the beth din as an end-run around the bankruptcy process.[103] The BDA will also not generally assert jurisdiction in tort matters where defense and settlement duties are assigned to insurance companies, even though the named parties are Orthodox Jews.[104] The BDA is similarly cautious in limiting the issuance of *seruv*/contempt orders to observant parties situated within its religious and social matrix who can be reasonably expected to sign an agreement to arbitrate before it. The BDA also stays its hand if one of the interested parties is unlikely to recognize its authority, even if several other parties willingly agree to come before it. Finally, when it comes to determining which persons or legal entities are necessary to adjudicate a case, the BDA usually ascertains interests and ownership on the basis of secular legal principles rather than halakhah.[105]

While legal scholarship continues to debate how far a beth din could go in asserting its inherent Jewish law powers under the aegis of religious liberty law, the more important lesson is that such boundaries are not generally tested.[106] Instead, the BDA—along with a number of other institutions—structures its understanding of halakhah as functioning through the recognized channels of American arbitration law.

---

*Assocs. v. Casarotto*, 517 U.S. 681, 687 (1996) (holding that "generally applicable contract defenses, such as fraud, duress, or unconscionability, may be applied to invalidate arbitration agreements").
100 Rabbi Schlomo Weissman (Director of the Beth Din of America), in discussion with the author, June 19, 2020.
101 Ibid.
102 Ibid.
103 Ibid.
104 Ibid.
105 Ibid.
106 For an argument that in some cases a beth din may be justified in violating the automatic stay on bankruptcy law, see Helfand, sup. note 80, 157. This approach was expressly rejected in *In re Congregation Birchos Yosef*, 535 B.R. 629 (Bankr. S.D.N.Y. 2015), where a bankruptcy court held that the Mechon L'Hoyroa's beth din proceedings against a debtor's principals violated the automatic stay of §362 of the Bankruptcy Code. The beth din's rulings were thus held *void ab initio*. The court further explained why its ruling did not violate the parties' Constitutional religious liberty rights.

## Enforcement: Civil Courts or Communal Sanctions

Because beth dins are not generally subject to any specific regulatory regimes, they can generally operate outside the state's purview unless a party petitions the civil courts to become involved. A beth din intent on minimizing the incursion of secular norms would therefore follow the traditional halakhic practice and enforce its awards through internal communal means, only resorting to secular authorities if all other options failed.

In the closeknit communities that are the primary markets for beth din services, a coordinated campaign of social sanctioning sanctioned by community leaders has a reasonable chance of proving effective.[107] In addition, neither American Constitutional law or the common law of contracts and torts prevent religious institutions from applying forms of spiritual/communal pressure to encourage parties to comply with beth din rulings.[108] Religious defamation—as the law calls the practice of shaming a party into compliance with religious mandates—is not typically actionable.[109] Synagogues and religious schools are permitted to govern their membership in accord with religious law, or as one New York court put it, "the 'threat' of . . . ostracism from the religious community . . . which is prescribed as an enforcement mechanism by the religious law to which the petitioner freely adheres, cannot be deemed duress."[110] The same court held that those who feel bound to obey the laws of a religious organization or decrees of a religious court "consequently expose [themselves] to the ecclesiastical sanctions available for the enforcement of such decrees."[111] This permissive attitude includes the

---

107 Helfand, sup. note 80, 169–71. See also Caryn Litt Wolfe, "Faith-Based Arbitration: Friend or Foe? An Evaluation of Religious Arbitration System and Their Interaction with Secular Courts (Note)," *Fordham Law Review* 75, no. 1 (October 2006): 427, 438; Michael C. Grossman, "Is This Arbitration? Religious Tribunals, Judicial Review, and Due Process," *Columbia Law Review* 107, no. 1 (January 2007): 169, 177–82; Ginnine Fried, "The Collision of Church and State: A Primer to Beth Din Arbitration and the New York Secular Courts," *Fordham Urban Law Journal* 31, no. 2 (January 2004): 633.

108 See, e.g., *Grunwald v. Bornfreund*, 696 F. Supp. 838, 840–41 (E.D.N.Y. 1988) (holding that "the mere expulsion from a religious society, with the exclusion from a religious community, is not a harm for which courts can grant a remedy"); *Lieberman v. Lieberman*, 566 N.Y.S.2d 490, 494 (Sup. Ct. 1991) (holding that "while the threat of a *sirov* may constitute pressure, it cannot be said to constitute duress"); *Mikel v. Scharf*, 432 N.Y.S.2d 602, 606 (Sup. Ct. 1980) (finding that *sirov*'s religious pressure is not duress, and the parties' decision to "acquiesce to the rabbinical court's urgings was made without the coercion that would be necessary for the agreement to be void").

109 See *Klagsbrun v. Va'ad Harabonim*, 53 F. Supp. 2d 732, 742 (D.N.J. 1999) (finding that because religious defamation claims rely upon religious doctrine, they are beyond the reach of the American courts); *Abdelhak v. Jewish Press Inc.*, 985 A.2d 197 (Super. Ct. App. Div. 2009) (finding that determination of issues central to a religious defamation claim would constitute excessive entanglement with the Jewish faith in violation of the U.S. Constitution). See also Helfand, sup. note 82, 1803–04.

110 *Greenberg v. Greenberg*, 238 A.D. 2d 420 (App. Div. 2nd Dept. 1997).

111 Ibid.

revoking a party's membership and privileges within a religious organization for failing to comply with beth din orders.[112]

Despite the latitude afforded to religious courts and communities under American law, the BDA moves in the opposite direction. Rather than seek to enlist schools, synagogues, and communal organs to pressure recalcitrant parties, the BDA encourages prevailing parties in civil cases to seek recourse in secular courts.[113] In this way, the BDA functions more like a secular arbitration panel than a beth din constituted under the inherent authority of Jewish law. This scrupulous adherence to arbitration law and affinity for American legal norms are designed to ensure its verdicts are swiftly confirmed through secular courts, even as these courts are nestled within a society and profession that can be quite skeptical of religiously sectarian modes of adjudication.[114]

The tension between communal and secular-court modes of enforcement is best illustrated by two recent examples from the BDA's docket. In one case, $X$, a person entrusted to invest $Y$'s assets, was found to have embezzled and

---

112 See *Paul v. Watchtower Bible & Tract Soc'y*, 819 F.2d 875 (9th Cir. 1987) (finding that religious organizations are given great latitude in shunning and placing social sanctions on members and former members). Notably, recalcitrance can also be punished outside of an institutional setting. See e.g., *In re Pachman*, No. 09–37475, 2010 WL 1489914, at *4 (Bankr. S.D.N.Y. April 14, 2010) (finding a family's position in the Orthodox marriage market was diminished because it failed to respond to beth din summons); *In re Congregation Birchos Yosef*, 535 B.R. 629 (Bankr. S.D.N.Y. 2015) (noting social sanction placed on those who fail to respond to a beth din summons).
Interestingly this feature of American law is notably not shared across common law countries. For example, the New South Wales Court of Appeals in Australia upheld a civil order of contempt against members of the Sydney Beth Din who sought to impose communal/religious sanctions against a Jewish party who failed to appear before them. In Australia, the rabbis were held in contempt for attempting to prevent a party from accessing the civil courts. See *Ulman v. Live Group Pty Ltd*, [2018] NSWCA 338. First instance judgements at *Live Group Pty Ltd & Anor v. Rabbi Ulman*, [2018] NSWSC 393 (March 29, 2018) and *Live Group Pty. Ltd. and Anon v. Rabbi Ulman* [2017] NSWSC 1759 (December 14, 2017).
The Supreme Court of Israel likewise restricts the ability of the state-sponsored rabbinical courts to issue contempt orders against parties refusing to appear before them when the case does not implicate the rabbinical courts' statutorily granted jurisdiction. See HCJ 3269/95 *Yosef Katz v. The Jerusalem Regional Rabbinical Court*, PD 50(4) 590 (Supreme Court of Israel) *available* (in English translation) *at* https://versa.cardozo.yu.edu/sites/default/files/upload/opinions/Amir%-20v.%20Great%20Rabbinical%20Court%20in%20Jerusalem.pdf.
113 The primary exception to this approach is the BDA's cooperation with community rabbis and independent organizations to foment communal outrage against husbands who refuse to grant their (civilly divorced) wives a *get*—Jewish document of divorce. Because American law prevents a civil court from compelling a party to perform a religious act, including granting a Jewish divorce, in *get* cases communal enforcement is the only available enforcement mechanism.
114 See, e.g., Michael Corkery and Jessica Silver-Greenberg, "In Religious Arbitration, Scripture Is the Rule of Law," *New York Times*, November 2, 2015, www.nytimes.com/2015/11/03/business/dealbook/in-religious-arbitration-scripture-is-the-rule-of-law.html.

dissipated *Y*'s funds.[115] In keeping with its traditional halakhic charge of "saving the oppressed from its oppressor"[116] the BSA would certainly be within its rights to publicize *X*'s misdeeds in the community. This would both save other potential marks from *X*'s fraud and potentially encourage a campaign of communal suasion to pressure *X* to come up with the monies and return them to *Y*. The BDA, however, held itself bound by the confidentiality norms of arbitration law and did not avail itself of these public/communal remedies. Instead, it explained that *Y* may approach the SEC and other civil law authorities to report on *X*'s behavior without running afoul of the halakhic rule that may prohibit Jews from divulging illicit activities undertaken by other Jews to the civil/secular authorities.[117]

Another case involved a dispute between parties engaged in the kosher food industry. The BDA found that *A* owed money to *B*. *B*, however, was afraid that *A* would slow-walk the process and was skeptical *A* could come up with the funds to satisfy the judgment. *B* petitioned the BDA to warn *A* that kosher certification of an unrelated business in which *A* maintained an interest would be in jeopardy unless *A* quickly remitted the funds in compliance with the beth din's order. The BDA summarily rejected this motion and encouraged *B* to seek enforcement in civil court.

From the perspective of classical halakhah, *B*'s motion is not beyond the pale. While the niceties of which legal entities are parties to the arbitration agreement are of considerable importance to American law, traditional Jewish law is swayed less by complex legal structures designed to shield assets and mitigate liabilities. Jewish law places primary emphasis on individuals and their beneficial ownership of the assets.[118] In addition, beth dins and the *kahal* traditionally used whatever tools were at their disposal to enforce their authority. Because licenses to conduct business within the community were frequently controlled by the *kahal*, there is precedent for leveraging these licenses to ensure compliance with beth din orders.[119]

While the BDA does not certify kosher establishments itself, it has institutional sway with a variety of entities who do. Were the BDA to put its reputational capital behind such a request, it could prove effective by dramatically raising the social and business costs for *A* for slow-walking its compliance with the beth din orders.

---

115 See, e.g., sources cited in Beit Yosef to YD §228.
116 This phrase used across rabbinic literature encouraging judges to act courageously to correct injustices. See, e.g., *Mishne Torah*, Laws of Sanhedrin 2:7; *Netivot ha-Mishpat* to HM §7:4.
117 For an overview of this prohibition and its application in contemporary times, see Michael J. Broyde, "Informing on Others for Violating American Law: A Jewish Law View," accessed June 10, 2021, www.jlaw.com/Articles/mesiralaw2.html.
118 For a review of Jewish law approaches to corporations, see Michael J. Broyde and Steven H. Resnicoff, "Jewish Law and Modern Business Structures: The Corporate Paradigm," *Wayne Law Review* 43, no. 4 (Fall 1997): 1685.
119 See, e.g., *Responsa of Sholom Mordechai Schwadron* (Maharsham), vol. 4, § 87 (Ukraine; 1835–1911), recounting a butcher's claim that he submitted to the jurisdiction of a particular beth din for fear that his kosher status would otherwise be discredited.

Such a move, however, raise complications with arbitration law. Despite common beneficial ownership, because the unrelated business was not a party to the initial arbitration agreement, it probably lies beyond the reach of the beth din's jurisdiction as conceived by the agreement.[120] Such a remedy could therefore complicate the parties' efforts to confirm and enforce the arbitration award in the civil courts.

Notwithstanding the risk of vacatur or non-confirmation by the courts, if the beth din decided to opt for communal enforcement, it would be very hard for the state to sanction this approach. Determining whether a given establishment is kosher is squarely a matter of Jewish law that is unreviewable.[121] Further, courts cannot compel certifying agencies to grant kosher status to an establishment even if the certification was withdrawn as a pretext to secure enforcement of a beth din order on another business.[122] A beth din could even withdraw certification merely because a party attempted to contravene religious law by involving secular courts in the dispute.

The upshot is that a beth din proceeding with sufficient legal sophistication could effectively enforce its orders via traditional halakhic communal remedies even under the constraints imposed by American law. But though it has access to sophisticated lawyering, the BDA does not usually attempt these tactics and eschews communal enforcement in favor of those prescribed by the Federal Arbitration Act.

## Conclusion: Shots Not Fired

The confluence of prevailing secular law and norms, their potential conflict with Jewish law and its historical practice, the enclavist tendencies of the underlying religious communities, and potentially expansive religious liberty rights would seem to set the stage for sharp-edged fights between beth dins, religiously observant litigants, and state law. Yet, these institutions for the most part peacefully coexist. Three reasons explain why.

The first relates to general trends in arbitration law. For reasons that have more to do with the interests of business than religions, American law has become

---

120 See *United Steelworkers*, 363 U.S. at 582 (finding that "arbitration is a matter of contract and a party cannot be required to submit to arbitration any dispute which he has not agreed so to submit"); see also *Freyr Holdings, LLC v. Legacy Life Advisors, LLC*, No. CV 10-9446 GAF (Ex), 2014 WL 293649 (C.D. Cal. Jan 24, 2014) (finding that when the complaint in a case named the wrong entity, the judgment must be entered in favor of the entity sued).

121 *United Kosher Butchers Ass'n v. Associated Synagogues of Greater Bos.*, Inc., 349 Mass. 595, 211 N.E.2d 332 (1965) (declining on Constitutional grounds to determine whether one party must accept the kosher certification of another party). See also Kent Greenawalt, "Religious Law and Civil Law: Using Secular Law to Assure Observance of Practices with Religious Significance," *Southern California Law Review* 71, no. 4 (May 1998): 781, 791–810.

122 Ibid.

dramatically more permissive of arbitration.[123] So long as beth dins ground their actions in formally consensual arbitration agreements and commit to rudimentary standards of procedural justice, American law places few restrictions on how a beth din's commercial adjudication can unfold. Further, while American due-process norms are not indigenous to Jewish law, they are not contrary to it either, making the cost of compliance relatively low. As strategic use of contract and arbitration law allows beth dins to accomplish many of their objectives with the active support of the American legal system, it is probably not worth rocking the boat.

The second aspect relates to enforceability. Though communal enforcement can be a more powerful tool than measures available through the courts, that will not always be the case. Communal enforcement is largely ineffective against those who have become indifferent to their reputation within the community or who have sufficient socio-political standing to draw important rabbis and institutions to their cause. The Orthodox world is diverse enough for its members—especially wealthy and influential ones—to establish bases of support enabling them to withstand communal pressure or prevent such pressure from forming. This dynamic is well known to beth dins and their constituencies, who therefore endeavor to ensure that secular law enforcement can serve at least a back-up means of enforcement.[124] Doing so requires a beth din to comply with relevant state law.

Moreover, owing to the suspicion of religious tribunals within some quarters of the general and legal culture,[125] enforcement is most assured when the legal community trusts—rather than is merely ordered to tolerate—the institution of beth din. This trust is built by moving beyond the bare requirements demanded by American law, but also by adopting certain American legal norms into the beth din's internal dialogue. These same conditions caution beth dins from testing the outer limits of their ability to depart from the established norms of American legal practice.

The desire for secular law respectability is similarly driven by competition between beth dins. Justified or not, beth dins do not all have the strongest

---

123 See, e.g., Jessica Silver-Greenberg and Robert Gebeloff, "Arbitration Everywhere, Stacking the Deck of Justice," *New York Times*, November 1, 2015, www.nytimes.com/2015/11/01/business/dealbook/arbitration-everywhere-stacking-the-deck-of-justice.html. See also Jessica Silver-Greenberg and Michael Corkery, "In Arbitration, a 'Privitization of the Justice System'," *The New York Times*, www.nytimes.com/2015/11/02/business/dealbook/in-arbitration-a-privatization-of-the-justice-system.html.
124 See, e.g., "About the Bais Din," *Vaad Hadin V'Horaah, Rabbinical Court of New City*, accessed June 10, 2021, https://vaadhadinvhoraah.org/about. The "About" page of the ultra-Orthodox beth din of New City, known as the Vaad Hadin V'Horaah, touts that it works with lawyers to ensure that its rulings are enforceable via civil court. In addition, the website of the Beth Din of the Rabbinical Alliance of America (Iggud HaRabonim) includes an arbitration agreement that is materially similar to the one offered by the BDA and clearly drafted with enforceability in civil courts in mind. See *Forms*, Igud Beth Din Harabonim, accessed June 10, 2021, www.bdigud.org/forms.
125 See e.g., *In Religious Arbitration, Scripture Is the Rule of Law*, sup. note 114.

reputation for predictability, professionalism, attentiveness to the nuances of commercial reality, or secular law implicated in complex business relationships. In broad strokes, the market for beth din services can be seen as structured as a choice between institutions that stress a religious insularity that is more removed from secular law but perceived (by some) as more religiously authentic, and those priding themselves on dual-system fluency but seen (by some) as too compromising of their halakhic autonomy. The BDA's niche is squarely in the latter category and its processes are designed to appeal to both the religious convictions of observant parties and the professional convictions of their (often) non-observant or non-Jewish lawyers. This establishes its place in the market by making its process intelligible to those unschooled in Jewish law and by ensuring broad conformity with secular understandings and expectations.

Dovetailing on these instrumentalist concerns, however, is a more foundational commitment to how religion and modernity ought to ideally relate to each other. Though not directly stated, there is a sense that—at least in the current American context—reading halakhah through American norms produces the best law measured from either an American or Jewish perspective.

The BDA's rabbis and communities pride themselves on strict adherence to Jewish law in all its classical rigor. But they also live, and especially do business, within an American framework, where deal documents are drawn up under American law and intended to work within the broader market economy. These communities have come to internalize the value of these norms and interpret Jewish law in a way that welcomes them into a rabbinic adjudication. This rests on a theological orientation that while Jews may need to fight the state when their core principles are challenged, they should otherwise begin with the presumption of working within the state and its legal order. Translated into adjudicative practice, this fosters an environment where Jewish law is read through American law, not as an abdication of a beth din's halakhic mission, but as fulfilling its responsibility of providing a rabbinic forum for a community enmeshed within the business norms of general commercial society.

Finally, it is not surprising that these accommodationist tendencies are heavily concentrated where the interaction between law and religion is mediated by the market. Matters often thought of as "religious"—specific rituals, canonized theology, adherence to conservative sexual mores—tends to draw believers inwards. Markets, by contrast, require participants to establish a framework that crosses religio-cultural divides drawing religious communities outwards and towards a more integrationist posture.[126] There is a long tradition in Jewish law of both allowing parties to contract around Talmudic rules and interpreting Talmudic commercial law in light of market practices. The BDA expands on this tradition and structures its procedural apparatus accordingly.

---

126 See e.g., Nathan B. Oman, *The Dignity of Commerce: Markets and the Moral Foundations of Contract Law* (Chicago, IL: University of Chicago Press, 2017).

This case study illustrates that law and religion disputes are not formed by inexorable clashes between conflicting normative systems but are the product of deliberate choices—by the state, on the one hand, and by religious communities, on the other. Jewish religious parties are constantly negotiating questions about how to frame their traditions in light of both state law and the range of norms found across society. When a religious group wants to challenge the state, it will present its practices as irreconcilably conflicting with the state and its laws. By contrast, when it wants to live symbiotically with the state, it will structure its religious doctrines to work within the state and achieve objectives neither is capable of accomplishing on its own.

# 5 Go Tell It [to the IRS]

## American Suspicions Around Religious Profit-Making

*Samuel D. Brunson*

On December 17, 2019, the *Washington Post* broke an enormous religion story: according to a self-styled whistleblower, the Mormon church had stockpiled a $100 billion war chest. The $100 billion endowment was made up of surplus donations from members—allegedly the church received about $1 billion a year more than it needed to cover its operational expenses—and the return on the church's investments.[1]

A month earlier, David Nielson, a former member of the Mormon church, had filed a complaint with the IRS, detailing allegations of wrongdoing related to the church's $100 billion. Nielson had worked as a senior portfolio manager at Ensign Peak Advisors, an investment company owned by the church, until September 2019.

The whistleblower complaint shined a light on one corner of the generally opaque finances of the Mormon church. (In addition to financial drama, the story ended up providing familial drama: Nielson's twin brother Lars, a health care consultant in Minnesota, helped him prepare and file the complaint. Ultimately, Lars released the complaint to the press not only without his brother's permission, but also against his brother's wishes.[2])

---

1 Jon Swaine, Douglas MacMillan, and Michelle Boorstein, "Mormon Church Has Misled Members On $100 Billion Tax-Exempt Investment Fund, Whistleblower Alleges," *Washington Post*, December 17, 2019, www.washingtonpost.com/investigations/mormon-church-has-misled-members-on-100-billion-tax-exempt-investment-fund-whistleblower-alleges/2019/12/16/e3619bd2-2004-11ea-86f3-3b5019d451db_story.html [https://perma.cc/3CPF-CFEN]. It is worth noting that, while the *Washington Post* was the first major press to release a story on the Mormon church's $100 billion endowment, *Religion Unplugged* published a story on the whistleblower complaint a day earlier. Paul Glader, "Whistleblower Alleges $100 Billion Secret Stockpile by Mormon Church," *Religion Unplugged*, December 16, 2019, https://religionunplugged.com/news/2019/12/16/whistleblower-exposes-100-billion-stockpile-by-mormon-church [https://perma.cc/J7PJ-FBSP].

2 When *Religion Unplugged* ultimately reached David Nielson to ask about his whistleblower complaint, he responded that "no one has been authorized to speak for me, including my brother, Lars Nielsen. Any public disclosure of information that has been in my possession was unauthorized by me. Repeated attempts to dissuade my brother, Lars Nielsen, from making public disclosures have been ignored. I will have no further comment on this matter." Paul Glader and Emma Penrod, "Mormon Whistleblower Denounces Brother's Media Leaks

DOI: 10.4324/9781003309291-6

Nielson largely built his whistleblower complaint around the enormity of the Mormon church's accumulated investment wealth. He asked rhetorically whether "any tax-exempt religious institution [can] hoard contributions into the hundred billions—or even trillions by the time Jesus might come again—making no charitable contributions along the way?"[3]

It turns out that US tax law does not prevent churches from accumulating hundreds of billions, or even trillions, of dollars. So while the headline number—$100 billion!—certainly catches the eye, Nielson also had to allege that Ensign Peak Advisors had committed tax violations. Fundamental to his complaint was his allegation that Ensign Peak Advisors had never made a single charitable distribution with the money. Over the life of the fund, the only two outflows were to buoy for-profit companies owned by the church.

(Though the technical tax rules governing churches are beyond the scope of this chapter, it is worth noting that, had the Mormon church kept its investments in-house, there would be no tax issue with accumulating $100 billion or with not making charitable expenditures with the money. Ensign Peak Advisors is an entity separate from the church, though, and investing money is not a tax-exempt purpose. Ensign Peak Advisors' tax exemption thus depends on its relationship with the Mormon church, but that exemption may require it to make charitable distributions "commensurate in scope with its financial resources."[4] If Ensign Peak Advisors were subject to the *commensurate-in-scope* requirement and it had made no distributions, it would clearly fail the test.[5])

Over the subsequent several weeks, the story made significant rounds in the press and on the internet. Few of the stories focused on whether Ensign Peak Advisors had violated the tax law. That discussion, while important, was a technical and esoteric one and one, ultimately, that probably did not matter. The chances that the IRS would investigate, much less sanction, either Ensign Peak Advisors or the Mormon church were astronomically low.[6]

---

as Church Responds to $100 Billion Tithing Controversy," *Newsweek*, December 21, 2019, www.newsweek.com/mormon-whistleblower-denounces-brothers-media-leaks-church-re sponds-100-billion-tithing-1478647 [https://perma.cc/PWF3-6Z34].

3 Lars Nielson, "Letter to an IRS Director," December 11, 2019, 9–10, www.scribd.com/document/439385879/Letter-to-an-IRS-Director.

4 IRS Rev. Rul. 64–182, 1964–1 C.B. 186.

5 For a more in-depth look at the tax questions here, including why the question of whether Ensign Peak Advisors is subject to the commensurate-in-scope test, see Sam Brunson, "Some Thoughts About Ensign Peak Advisors and the Church," *By Common Consent*, December 17, 2019, https://bycommonconsent.com/2019/12/17/some-thoughts-about-ensign-peak-advisers-and-the-church/ [https://perma.cc/V5T7-4F6V].

6 Even for clear-cut violations of the tax law, the IRS rarely revokes a church's tax-exempt status. For instance, since 2008, the Alliance Defending Freedom has sponsored "Pulpit Freedom Sunday." Over the years, thousands of clergy members have preached sermons endorsing or opposing candidates for office, in direct violation of the tax law. And not one of those churches has lost its tax-exempt status. Samuel D. Brunson, "Dear IRS, It Is Time to Enforce the Campaigning Prohibition. Even Against Churches," *University of Colorado Law Review* 87, no. 1 (2016): 143–204. 145–46.

Ultimately, for reasons discussed in the remainder of this chapter, the whistleblower's complaint rests on a weak basis and a poor understanding of the tax law.[7] But although the complaint is framed in a legal context, it is best understood not as a legal, but as a performative, document. Its lack of legal basis does not mean we can or should be entirely disregard it. In its performative nature, it evinces a strong distrust of religious wealth and religious participation in business. That distrust has roots in the history of the United States and is far more widespread than merely one individual or one religious tradition. This strong distrust of church wealth has historically reflected two main concerns: worry that churches engaged in business are unfairly competing with for-profit businesses and worry about churches accumulating wealth. The whistleblower complaint embodies both of these concerns.

## Competing

In the 1920s, US courts heard a pair of cases dealing with Hutterite communities. The Hutterites trace their roots directly to the Anabaptism movement in the sixteenth century. They believed in strictly following biblical principles. From the beginning, they followed Jesus' exhortations from the Sermon on the Mount, which meant they did not retaliate, swear oaths, or take people to court. And, critically, they adopted the early Apostolic economic system.

According to the New Testament, shortly after Jesus' death and resurrection, the early Christian community "had all things in common" (Acts 2:44). The Hutterite concept of *Gelassenheit*, derived in part from this Apostolic economic arrangement, demands that Christians yield their will to God and simultaneously to members of the church. As a practical matter, *Gelassenheit* means that Hutterites give up their material goods to community, practicing a type of Apostolic Christian communism.

Heretical in their beliefs, the Hutterites faced significant—and sometimes violent—opposition throughout Europe.[8] Hutterite communities began to move to North America in 1874, originally settling in North Dakota. From there the Hutterites spread, largely to South Dakota, Montana, and Western Canada.[9] Today, most Hutterites live in North America.[10]

---

7  For instance, while it is not relevant to the topic of this chapter, it is stunning how the complaint misunderstands the difference between the distribution requirements applicable to private foundations and the lack of any such distribution requirements for public charities such as churches.
8  Rod Janzen and Max Stanton, *The Hutterites in North America* (Baltimore: The Johns Hopkins University Press, 2010), 12–20.
9  William L. Smith, "Are the Old Order Amish Becoming More Like the Hutterites?" *Michigan Sociological Review*, no. 10 (Fall 1996): 68–86. 70.
10 Karl Peter, Edward D. Boldt, Ian Whitaker, and Lance W. Roberts, "The Dynamics of Religious Defection Among Hutterites," *Journal for the Scientific Study of Religion* 21, no. 4 (December 1982): 327–37. 327.

Their communitarian economic beliefs have not prevented Hutterites from participating in the American capitalist marketplace. While they eschew individual accumulation of property, their beliefs and practices allow them to collectively accumulate wealth. Hutterite colonies generally consist of around 100 people; once they reach a population of 130, colonies split into *mother* and *daughter* colonies.[11] Because their revenue comes primarily from agriculture, a daughter colony needs to immediately invest in production to pay back the loans it takes out from both banks and other Hutterite colonies. Once a colony has paid back its debt, it often buys additional land and equipment to provide additional jobs for its population and, ultimately, to fund a new daughter colony.[12]

In their expansion, the Hutterites have not shied away from profit-making. In fact, they have historically diversified their production. They produced "basic agricultural products as efficiently as possible," then used the grain they produced to feed livestock, which offered higher profits. To hedge the risks associated with high-profit livestock, they sold surplus grain on the market.[13]

Although the Hutterites participated in the capitalistic economy of the United States (albeit with a communitarian bent), the country was skeptical of the religion's dual religious and profit-making ethos. In the 1920s, two Hutterite colonies appeared before federal courts to defend their tax exemptions. In both cases, the courts found that they did not qualify as exempt.

The first case addressed the Hutterische Bruder Gemeinde. Incorporated in South Dakota in 1905, the Hutterische Bruder Gemeinde's purpose, according to its articles of incorporation, was to engage in and carry on

> the Christian religion, Christian worship, and religious education and teachings, according to our religious belief that all members should act together as one being, and have, hold, use, possess and enjoy all things in common, we all being of one mind, heart and soul, according to the word of God revealed to us.[14]

Members' religious beliefs required them to renounce their personal property to join the Hutterite community and, upon joining, to work on behalf of the Hutterische Bruder Gemeinde. (The work requirement applied not only to members—according to the court, members' spouses and children could live with them and the community would educate and support them, but even non-member family members had to perform services on behalf of the Hutterische Bruder Gemeinde.)

---

11 Donald W. Huffman, "Life in a Hutterite Colony: An Outsider's Experience and Reflections on a Forgotten People in Our Midst," *The American Journal of Economics and Sociology* 59, no. 4 (October 2000): 549–71. 558.
12 Hanna Kienzler, "Communal Longevity: The Hutterite Case," *Anthropos*, Bd. 100, H. 1. (2005): 193–210. 197.
13 Karl Peter and Ian Whitaker, "The Hutterite Economy: Recent Changes and Their Social Correlates," *Anthropos*, Bd. 78, H. 3/4 (1983): 535–46. 536.
14 Appeal of Hutterische Bruder Gemeinde, 1 B.T.A. 1208, 1208 (1925).

If a corporation—including an incorporated Hutterite community—wanted to qualify for federal income tax exemption, the corporation had to be "organized and operated exclusively for religious . . . purposes, . . . no part of the net earnings of which inures to the benefit of any private stockholder or individual."[15] The Hutterische Bruder Gemeinde claimed that, because it was organized for religious purposes and because it had no equity owners (meaning its net earnings did not inure to the benefit of a private shareholder), it met the requirements for exemption.

The Commissioner of Internal Revenue disagreed. So did the Board of Tax Appeals (the tax court to which the Hutterische Bruder Gemeinde appealed the Bureau of Internal Revenue's decision). In determining that the Hutterische Bruder Gemeinde did not qualify for exemption, the Board pointed to the corporation's economic activity. It pointed out that the Hutterische Bruder Gemeinde owned 10,000 acres of farmland, on which it produced far more than its members needed. It sold its surplus to the general public at market prices.

In addition to agriculture, the religious corporation operated a ferry, a machine shop, and a carpenter shop. The profits it earned in its market activities exceeded the members' needs and were not applied to fund proselyting beyond the boundaries of the colony itself. Moreover, the court said, its businesses competed with other people who engaged in agriculture, ferrying, machining, and carpentry.

The Board found that the extensive business activities of Hutterische Bruder Gemeinde, combined with the uses to which it put its profits, belied its assertion that it qualified for a tax exemption. The Board of Tax Appeals explained that the tax law assumed that exempt organizations would use their tax-exempt income for the benefit of the public. The Hutterische Bruder Gemeinde's profits, by contrast, solely benefited the members of the religion. The general public did not benefit from the group's profits. While the Hutterites had every right to "lead a communistic life," the Board of Tax Appeals decided that they did not have the right to earn a profit at the expense of the federal tax system.[16]

Three years later, the United States Court of Claims adjudicated a similar case dealing with a different Hutterite colony. Like the Hutterische Bruder Gemeinde, the Hutterische Gemeinde Elspring engaged in the business of agriculture. During the year in controversy, Hutterische Gemeinde Elspring consisted of four colonies and owned 17,940 acres of land. The Court of Claims described the breadth of its agricultural pursuits: it raised "wheat, rye, oats, corn, cattle, hogs, horses, sheep, poultry, and garden truck." Hutterische Gemeinde Elspring also ran blacksmith shops, harness and shoe shops, a bakery, and a broomworks.[17]

In 1917, Hutterische Gemeinde Elspring received gross income of almost $228,000 on its sales to the public. (According to the Bureau of Labor Statistic's CPI calculator, that would have about the same purchasing power as

---

15 Revenue Act of 1918, ch. 18, § 231(6), 40 Stat. 1057, 1076 (1919).
16 Appeal of Hutterische Bruder Gemeinde.
17 Hofer v. United States, 64 Ct. Cl. 672, 673 (1928).

$5 million in 2020.) Applying the relevant deductions, the Bureau of Internal Revenue assessed corporate and excess profits taxes of about $14,000. Hutterische Gemeinde Elspring paid the assessment then sued for a refund, claiming that as a religious corporation it was exempt from federal taxes.[18]

The Court of Claims acknowledged that earning income does not disqualify a religious organization from federal income tax exemption. The exemption provision of the federal tax law "recognizes that a corporation may be organized and operated exclusively for religious, charitable, scientific or educational purposes, and yet have a net income."[19]

While acknowledging that exempt religious organizations *can* earn income, the Court of Claims found that this Hutterite corporation did not qualify as exempt. It its opinion, the court provided two bases for its conclusion. The first was that the income went to support Hutterites, and the survivors of deceased Hutterites. There was, therefore, private inurement. In addition, the court cryptically noted that it cannot "be said that such a corporation was operated exclusively for a religious purpose within the meaning of the exemption clause."

The court does not explain why Hutterische Gemeinde Elspring's actions prevented it from being operated exclusively for a religious purpose. The tax law's exclusivity requirement did not require an exempt religious organization to do nothing but religious activities. As the Supreme Court said, an organization could be organized *exclusively* for religious purposes and, at the same time, earn a profit. Effectively, then, "exclusively" meant something like "principally."

But the Court of Claims apparently believed that Hutterische Gemeinde Elspring's commercial activities were so extensive that the corporation was not principally engaged in religious activities. While it did not draw a precise line, its holding demonstrates skepticism about the ability of a religious organization to engage in commerce. Effectively, while it did not lay out where the line falls, the court suggested that at a certain point, commercial activities overwhelm religious activities. The court's opinion underscored its skepticism that a truly religious organization could also participate in commerce.

Concerns about tax-exempt organizations unfairly competing with for-profit businesses came to a head in the late 1940s and early 1950s. The primary flashpoint in this concern was not a church, but a university. During the 1940s, a group of alumni donated all of the stock of the C.F. Mueller Company to NYU. C.F. Mueller was, at the time, the largest manufacturer of macaroni in the United States.[20] While C.F. Mueller had paid taxes on its profits prior to its acquisition by NYU, once it was wholly owned by NYU, it claimed to be exempt from taxes. While making and selling macaroni does not qualify as a charitable purpose, the Third

---

18 Ibid.
19 Trinidad v. Sagrada Orden de Predicadores, etc., 263 U.S. 578, 581, 44 S. Ct. 204, 205, 68 L. Ed. 458 (1924).
20 Samuel D. Brunson, "Repatriating Tax-Exempt Investments: Tax Havens, Blocker Corporations, and Unrelated Debt-Financed Income," *Northwestern University Law Review* 106, no. 1 (2012): 225–72. 230.

Circuit Court of Appeals decided that historically, organizations had qualified as tax-exempt where funds went toward qualifying charitable purposes, irrespective of how the organization raised those funds. (It did not explain how the Hutterite cases fit into its proffered history.) Because profits from the sale and manufacture of macaroni went solely to NYU's law school, which qualified as exempt, the court held that the C.F. Mueller Company did not have to pay taxes on its income.[21]

Before the Third Circuit's decision came out, Congress had changed the rule. In hearings, Representative Noah Mason complained that a macaroni company in his district was "now being forced to the wall by the competition from this macaroni factory of the New York University that is gradually getting out into the Middle West with their product."[22] A handful of other taxpayers also complained about unfair competition from tax-exempt businesses, albeit largely in the abstract.[23]

In response to these abstract and tangible worries about unfair competition from tax-exempt businesses, Congress enacted the unrelated business income tax.[24] The initial unrelated business income tax required tax-exempt organizations that engaged in a business unrelated to its charitable purpose to pay ordinary corporate income tax on income from that business. Economically, the unrelated business income tax assuages concerns about unfair competition because to the extent a tax-exempt organization engages in business, it must pay taxes on that income.

Unless the tax-exempt organization was a church. When Congress enacted the unrelated business income tax, it exempted churches and associations of churches from the tax.[25] And for the next almost twenty years, churches could compete with for-profit businesses without having to pay taxes.

By 1969, Congress had started to have the same concerns about churches that had motivated it to create the unrelated business income tax two decades earlier. In Congressional testimony, Rep. John Rarick of Louisiana highlighted the Vatican's then-recent announcement that it would sell some of its assets—including the Watergate Hotel—to "Rockefeller interests." The Vatican, Rep. Rarick pointed out, would owe Italian taxes on its earnings.

Rep. Rarick contrasted those Italian taxes to how the United States treated religious profits. He mentioned the vast property wealth of US churches, contrasting it with the amount churches paid for services to people outside the churches, which amounted to "only 41 cents a month for everyone who belong (sic) to a church in America." But Rep. Rarick found it "even more striking" than

---

21 C.F. Mueller Co. v. Comm'r, 190 F.2d 120, 121–22 (3d Cir. 1951).
22 Revenue Revision of 1950: Hearing Before the H. Comm. on Ways and Means, 81st Cong. 380 (1950). [https://heinonline.org/HOL/P?h=hein.cbhear/cblhaetg0001&i=626&a=bHVjLmVkdQ].
23 Ethan G. Stone, "Adhering to the Old Line: Uncovering the History and Political Function of the Unrelated Business Income Tax," *Emory Law Journal* 54, no. 4 (2005): 1475–556. 1512.
24 Ibid., 1479.
25 Revenue Act of 1950 § 301, 64 Stat. 906, 948 (1950).

churches' accumulated wealth the degree to which churches engaged in for-profit businesses. "Almost every field now has church-owned components."

Rep. Rarick went on to list various church-owned businesses. California's Christ's Church of the Golden Rule owned and ran a $500,000 motel. Utah's Mormon church owned a newspaper, radio station, television station, and Hawaii tourist attraction. The Self-Realization Fellowship owned a chain of Mushroomburger restaurants. The Vatican, he said, was allegedly a controlling shareholder in a company financing a $70 million shopping center/hotel/apartment project. And Ohio's Cathedral of Tomorrow owned what Rep. Rarick characterized as the "most ecumenical portfolio": a shopping center, an apartment building, an electronics company, a wire and plastics company, and even (to the Representative's apparent shock) the Real Form Girdle Company.

Beyond the extensive active businesses owned by churches, Rep. Rarick underscored churches' massive passive stock portfolios. And why were churches suddenly interested in the business of business? Rep. Rarick believed that the tax laws played a significant role. Although non-church tax-exempt organizations had to pay taxes on their unrelated business income, churches remained "exempt from federal tax on *any* income property or business—*even if totally unrelated to their sacerdotal functions.*"[26]

Rep. Rarick was not alone in his concern about churches' involvement in business. The National Council of Churches of Christ and the United States Catholic Conference issued a joint statement calling for Congress to extend the unrelated business income tax to all exempt organizations, including churches. Exempting churches from the unrelated business income tax, the statement said, provided churches with "a potential advantage over tax-paying organizations engaged in commercial business activities" and allowed them to act as counterparties in tax shelter transactions.[27]

Similarly, Rev. D. James Kennedy of the Coral Ridge Presbyterian Church testified about the business activities of churches in front of the House Committee on Ways and Means. Rev. Kennedy ran a broadcast ministry but said that he believed that churches should pay taxes on income they earned from non-religious broadcasts. He testified that he did

> not believe that churches ought to go into business unrelated to the mission of the church in which they compete with private enterprise and do so with tax exemption. I think that is an unfair advantage which they should not have.[28]

---

26  115 Cong. Rec. 17,678–79 (June 27, 1969).
27  Tax reform act of 1969, H.R. 13270 at 139: Part A, testimony to be received Wednesday, September 17, 1969: Part B, additional statements: (topic: charitable contributions). Washington, U.S. G.P.O.
28  Federal Tax Rules Applicable to Tax-Exempt Organizations Involving Television Ministries, Hearing Before the Subcommittee on Oversight of the Committee on Ways and Means, One Hundredth Congress, first session, October 6, 1987. (1988): 74.

Ultimately, a majority of Congress agreed with Rep. Rarick and others who pushed to include churches within the unrelated business income tax. As part of the Tax Reform Act of 1969, churches lost their exemption from the unrelated business income tax.[29] Going forward, churches could continue to engage in for-profit business, but would pay taxes on their income from those businesses.

If Americans' only issue with churches being involved in business was unfair competition, this change should have quieted their concerns. While there was little evidence that nonprofits were in fact competing unfairly with for-profit businesses, it was nonetheless possible that they did. Not paying taxes reduced the tax-exempt organizations' cost of capital.[30] As long as churches have to pay taxes on their income from businesses that they engage in, though, their cost of capital is essentially the same as the cost to for-profit businesses. In addition, including churches and other religious organizations within the unrelated business income tax represents an explicit acknowledgment by the federal government that engaging in business is not antithetical to religious purposes. If unfair competition were the only concern, then, any concern about religious business should have disappeared in 1969.

## The Church Should Not Be Wealthy

The concern has not disappeared, as evidenced by the whistleblower complaint against the Mormon church. In fact, the whistleblower complaint only referred to for-profit businesses twice. It alleged that Ensign Peak Advisors' only outflows were to prop up the Beneficial Financial Group, a church-owned insurance company, and to meet cost overruns from the City Creek Mall, a church-owned shopping center.[31] Rather than alleging inappropriate business dealings by the Mormon church, the whistleblower complaint focused on the net asset value of the church's investment portfolio.

Concern about religious wealth runs the gamut, from individuals to religious institutions to Congress itself. For the magazine *Christianity Today*, the problem lies with the incongruity of a focus on business and a focus on God. The magazine argues repeatedly that churches should not be run like businesses. In part, it differentiates the individual ownership of business from the divine ownership of the church. "A church does not belong to the pastor. Or the church members. Or the denominational officials. It belongs to Jesus."[32] It acknowledges that running a church can benefit from applying some business principles. Still, while the Bible uses "many colorful words to describe the church," it does not use the word "business."[33]

---

29 Tax Reform Act of 1969, Public Law 91-172 § 121, 91 Congress, 83 Stat. 487, 537 (1969).
30 Stone, "Adhering to the Old Line," 1489.
31 Letter to an IRS Director, 7.
32 Karl Vaters, "Why It's a Bad Idea to Run a Church Like a Business," *Pivot* (July 6, 2017), www.christianitytoday.com/karl-vaters/2017/july/why-its-bad-idea-to-run-church-like-business.html?paging=off [https://perma.cc/NFP3-SS35].
33 Karl Vaters, "3 Big Problems with Running a Church Like a Business," *Pivot* (July 10, 2017), www.christianitytoday.com/karl-vaters/2017/july/3-big-problems-with-running-church-like-business.html?paging=off [https://perma.cc/6DCB-X86K].

Others have warned that churches trying to adopt the clothing of the corporate world creates a "bad deal for churches" as they try to pursue their distinctly religious mission. Churches, they argue, should pursue "discipleship [rather] than market share," and when they become comfortable shedding market values, they will be more authentically religious.[34]

The government has also expressed concern about religious wealth. In 2017, IRS agents raided the offices of prosperity gospel preacher Benny Hinn.[35] Almost a decade earlier, Senator Chuck Grassley and his staff launched an investigation of several televangelists, including Hinn. Each of the televangelists' ministries had for- and nonprofit related entities. Sen. Grassley's staff was concerned, though, by the "number and types of entities, including private airports and aircraft leasing companies." The existence of some of these entities suggested that some of these ministries were using their tax-exempt status to shield for-profit businesses from paying taxes.[36]

Concern about prosperity gospel preachers' focus on wealth, in contrast to a focus on religion, is not limited to legal and congressional spheres. In 2015, John Oliver's *Last Week Tonight* broadcast a segment specifically about televangelists. In his introduction, Oliver acknowledged that the 350,000 churches in the United States were a "cornerstone of American life," and that many made positive contributions to society. "This is about the churches that exploit people's faith for monetary gain."[37]

Objection to churches' wealth *qua* wealth is not new, of course. In the 1520s, Lutheran rulers in what is now Germany began to seize Catholic property.[38] Still during the sixteenth century, Henry VIII of England rejected the Catholic Church's political authority and also seized ecclesiastical land.[39] In the nineteenth century, Spain seized and sold more than 80% of property belonging to religious orders, while France nationalized church property during the French Revolution.[40]

While these and other seizures of church property suggest discomfort with church wealth, these moves were not primarily motivated by that discomfort.

---

34 Michael L. Budde and Robert Brimlow, *Christianity Incorporated: How Big Business Is Buying the Church* (Eugene, OR: Wipf and Stock Publishers, 2007), 7–8.
35 Jack Jenkins, "IRS Raids Offices of 'Prosperity Gospel' Preacher Benny Hinn," *ThinkProgress*, April 27, 2017, https://archive.thinkprogress.org/irs-raids-prosperity-gospel-preacher-5ea1e94fd434/ [https://perma.cc/PYJ6-S2E6].
36 Senate Finance Committee Staff Memo to Senator Chuck Grassley, January 6, 2011, www.finance.senate.gov/imo/media/doc/SFC%20Staff%20Memo%20to%20Grassley%20re%20Ministries%2001-06-11%20FINAL.pdf [https://perma.cc/4CG9-946C].
37 "Televangelists," *Last Week Tonight with John Oliver* (August 16, 2015), www.youtube.com/watch?v=7y1xJAVZxXg.
38 John M. Owen IV, *The Clash of Ideas in World Politics* (Princeton: Princeton University Press, 2010), 92.
39 Philip Benedict, *Christ's Churches Purely Reformed: A Social History of Calvinism* (New Haven: Yale University Press, 2002), 231.
40 David Blackbourn, "The Catholic Church in Europe Since the French Revolution: A Review," *Comparative Studies in Society and History* 33, no. 4 (October 1991): 778–90.

Rather, they were political moves, meant to break the political control and authority of the Catholic Church and replace it with Protestant or non-religious control. Political seizure of religious property also provided additional revenue for new states and heads of state.

In the United States, no broad seizure of religious property ever occurred. But even in its founding years, the country worried about religious wealth and worked to limit it. By 1830, every state in the young country had formally disestablished. As part of that disestablishment, the states had all put explicit limitations on the financial capacity of religious societies. For example, most states limited the amount of real property a religion could hold (two acres in some states, four or five in others). Similarly, states limited the amount of annual income a church could receive.

Professor Sarah Barringer Gordon explains that states hoped to accomplish two things through these limitations on church property and income: they sought to limit religious authority and to protect individual conscience.[41]

Today, US law still retains a small handful of vestigial remains of these early limitations on church property. While no state substantively limits the amount of property a religious organization can hold, some limit the amount of church-owned property they will exempt from their property tax. For instance, the majority of US states exempt parsonages from their state property tax, but several limit the size of an exempt parsonage. In Washington, D.C., for instance, any given church can only own one exempt parsonage. In New Jersey, a church can own two, but the parsonages cannot sit on more than five acres of land. Texas and Rhode Island limit tax-exempt parsonages to a single acre.[42]

Concerns about church wealth are distinct and separate from concerns about unfair competition. After all, a church's ownership of a parsonage, available solely to house that church's clergy, does not compete with private for-profit business. Similarly, as we have seen earlier, as Rep. Rarick argued for including churches within the ambit of the unrelated business income tax, he mentioned the size of church investment portfolios.

Even today, this concern with church wealth as wealth, not as competition, continues. The whistleblower complaint does not characterize the problem of a large church-owned investment portfolio as being one of unfair competition with for-profit investors. Rather, it asserts that the problem with Ensign Peak Advisors is threefold: it "exists 1) to avoid taxes, 2) to obscure the enormity and absurdity of mining millions of mites from its membership, and 3) to hide that it apparently can't come up with anything good to do with the money."[43]

---

41 Sarah Barringer Gordon, "The First Disestablishment: Limits on Church Power and Property Before the Civil War," *University of Pennsylvania Law Review* 162, no. 2 (2014): 307–72.

42 Samuel D. Brunson, "God Is My Roommate? Tax Exemptions for Parsonages Yesterday, Today, and (If Constitutional) Tomorrow," *Indiana Law Journal* 96 (2021), https://papers.ssrn.com/sol3/papers.cfm?abstract_id=3536524.

43 Letter to an IRS Director, 8.

As a legal matter, none of these complaints has any substance. Tax exemption explicitly exists to allow some entities to avoid taxes. The structure of having a tax-exempt investment fund organized as a "supporting organization" and an "integrated auxiliary" may be uncommon,[44] but if the Mormon church had held the investments in-house, there would be no question about returns being exempt from taxes.[45]

Similarly, US law no longer places any impediment on the wealth that a religious organization can hold. The tax law has no cap on an entity's wealth above which it no longer qualifies for tax exemption. Tax-exempt organizations in the United States range from holding very few assets to holding billions of dollars of assets. On the small side, the IRS created a special form for tax-exempt organizations with less than $50,000 in gross receipts.[46] On the opposite side of the spectrum, Yale University ended 2016 with almost $37 billion in gross assets.[47] And the Bill and Melinda Gates Foundation ended 2017 with nearly $52 billion of assets.[48] Neither Yale University nor the Bill and Melinda Gates Foundation is a religious organization, though. Does the tax law prevent religions from acquiring tens (or hundreds) of billions of dollars?

It does not. In fact, Congress has deliberately avoided making any legal judgments about religious wealth. At the same time it applied the unrelated business income tax to churches, Congress declined to extend to churches the filing requirements that apply to most tax-exempt organizations. Senator Russell Long of Louisiana explained that "the Committee agreed to exempt churches from the requirement of filing annual information returns in view of the traditional separation of church and state."[49] The intersection of this exemption from annual filing and the fact that churches do not have to apply for federal tax exemption[50] means that the IRS has no information about churches' finances (including their wealth)

---

44 Anecdotally, I have spoken with a handful of tax attorneys who say that many churches have separate investment companies organized as supporting organizations, albeit not with the same level of assets as the Mormon church.
45 Moreover, it is not clear from the whistleblower complaint how much Ensign Peak Advisors would have owed in taxes had it not been exempt. Even if Ensign Peak Advisors had been a taxable entity, it would not have owed taxes on the church's initial investment, or on the $1 billion annual surplus that the church had allegedly added to the amount. It also would not have owed taxes on any appreciation in its portfolio assets. Assuming it had a passive portfolio (and that its foreign investments were not controlled foreign corporations or passive foreign investment companies), Its only taxable income would have been dividends and interest it received. The whistleblower complaint did not quantify how much of the appreciation came from additional capital investments, how much from appreciation in value, and how much represented the reinvestment of dividends and interest.
46 IRS, Annual Electronic Filing Requirement for Small Exempt Organizations—Form 990-N (e-Postcard), www.irs.gov/charities-non-profits/annual-electronic-filing-requirement-for-small-exempt-organizations-form-990-n-e-postcard [https://perma.cc/6UKC-LEBU].
47 Yale University, IRS Form 990 (2016).
48 Bill and Melinda Gates Foundation, IRS Form 990 (2017).
49 115 Cong. Rec. 32148 (1969).
50 I.R.C. § 508(c)(1)(A) (2018).

unless a church voluntarily provides that information. As a result, not only does the government avoid directly regulating church wealth, but it cannot even play a role in a church's qualifying for tax-exempt status.

Along the same lines, the tax law does not require churches to spend their money in any particular way. That is not to say that the law completely ignores church spending: it imposes some limitations on how tax-exempt organizations—including churches—spend their money. For instance, the benefit of its expenditures cannot inure to a private individual or group of individuals.[51] And all but an insubstantial part of its activities must further one or more exempt purposes.[52] The law does not contain an affirmative requirement that churches spend down their assets, however.

If Congress wanted to require churches to spend money in particular ways, it has the ability to enact laws mandating its desired expenditures.[53] The tax law requires private foundations (essentially tax-exempt organizations that fund other charities rather than engaging in charitable work themselves and that are generally funded by an individual or small group of individuals rather than the public at large) to distribute 5% of the value of their net assets annually. If a private foundation fails to make the minimum distribution, it has to pay a penalty to the IRS.[54] The law contains no similar distribution requirement for active charities, including churches. Whether or not the Mormon church could come up with something to do with its $100 billion, it would have faced no legal infirmity in doing nothing with that money.

Ultimately, then, this distrust of religious wealth has no legal consequences. True, churches are organized as nonprofit entities. But *nonprofit* does not mean that an organization cannot earn a profit. Rather, a nonprofit organization cannot distribute that profit to shareholders or other individuals. As long as a church keeps its money or uses it in pursuit of charitable gains, however, it is legally allowed to earn—and to stockpile—a profit.[55]

## The IRS as Regulator

As we have seen, one response to allegations of wrongdoing by a church is to request that the IRS revoke the church's tax-exempt status. But this response raises at least two questions. The first question is a relatively general one: why

---

51 I.R.C. § 501(c)(3) (2018).
52 Treas. Reg. § 1.501(c)(3)-1(c)(1) (as amended in 2017). The law is unclear on what constitutions more than an "insubstantial" part of an organization's activities. Brian Galle, "The LDS Church, Proposition 8, and the Federal Law of Charities," *Northwestern University Law Review Colloquy* (2009): 372, https://scholarlycommons.law.northwestern.edu/nulr_online/159.
53 Whether such required spending would violate the Constitution's religion clauses is a separate question.
54 I.R.C. § 4942 (2018).
55 Henry B. Hansmann, "Reforming Nonprofit Corporation Law," *University of Pennsylvania Law Review* 129, no. 3 (1981): 497–623. 501.

would a complainant go to the IRS? The second is why complain at all, given that there is no law against churches accumulating wealth or engaging in business?

The first question has an easy answer: the IRS has become the primary regulator of churches and other tax-exempt organizations. True, churches potentially face regulation both at the federal and the state levels. Churches generally incorporate as nonprofit entities.[56] Incorporation occurs under state law and, as a result, the state in which an organization incorporates has the legal right to regulate the nonprofit. State-level regulation of nonprofits is often cursory, though, with "many states devot[ing] very few personnel or resources to nonprofit oversight."[57] First Amendment concerns complicate even this cursory regulation. State regulation could potentially force religion to choose between its religious convictions and state requirements.[58] As a result, states may sensibly regulate religion with a light touch.

As a result, the federal government has taken states' place as the primary regulator of the charitable sector. And more specifically, the federal government regulates nonprofits through the tax law. "The most significant development of the last half century has been the emergence of the federal government through the IRS as the primary regulator of charitable nonprofits."[59]

As it regulates churches, the IRS faces many of the same challenges that state governments face. It cannot impinge on the religious liberty of churches and it cannot become overly entangled in questions of religious belief. On top of these general constitutional impediments, the IRS faces some unique problems. One significant impediment the IRS faces in regulating churches is its ambit—the IRS administers the tax law. It can only regulate a church to the extent the church's actions implicate the tax law.

Even where the tax law comes into play, the IRS does not have free rein to ensure churches' compliance with the tax law. Congress has enacted special rules limiting the IRS' ability to audit churches. Among other things, before the IRS can initiate a church audit, a high-level Treasury official must sign off on the audit. The IRS must provide the church with a detailed description of its concerns with advance notice. It has limited time to complete the audit, and, once it completes the audit of a church, it cannot initiate a new audit for five years.[60]

It is important to understand that even where the IRS *could* regulate a church's behavior, taxpayers cannot force it to take enforcement action if it chooses not to.

---

56 See, e.g., Stephen M. Bainbridge and Aaron H. Cole, "The Bishop's Alter Ego: Enterprise Liability and the Catholic Priest Sex Abuse Scandal," *Journal of Catholic Legal Studies* 46, no. 1 (2007): 65–106. 75.
57 Norman I. Silber, *A Corporate Form of Freedom: The Emergence of the Nonprofit Sector* (Boulder: Westview Press, 2001), 2.
58 Forest Hills Early Learning Ctr., Inc. v. Grace Baptist Church, 846 F.2d 260, 263 (4th Cir. 1988).
59 James J. Fishman, "Wrong Way Corrigan and Recent Developments in the Nonprofit Landscape: A Need for New Legal Approaches," *Fordham Law Review* 76 (2007): 567, 574.
60 I.R.C. § 7611 (2018).

104  *Samuel D. Brunson*

The tax law, as well as general administrative law principles, shield the IRS from pressure to act.

The Tax Anti-Injunction Act prevents taxpayers from suing over the assessment or collection of any federal tax.[61] While the scope and contours of the Anti-Injunction Act are not entirely clear, it prevents courts from telling the IRS it cannot revoke an organization's tax exemption.[62] It likely restrains a taxpayer from objecting to another's tax exemption as well.[63]

Even if a court held that the Tax Anti-Injunction Act did not bar such a challenge, a complainant would have to get past a second hurdle: constitutional standing. For a court to hear a case, a plaintiff must demonstrate that they have suffered an "injury in fact, i.e., a concrete and particularized, actual or imminent invasion of a legally protected interest."[64] In the 1960s, the Supreme Court loosened the contours of standing slightly in cases where a taxpayer challenges government support of religion, permitting so-called Establishment Clause standing to create justiciability.[65] But in 2011, the Supreme Court narrowed those expanded contours, only allowing litigants to invoke Establishment Clause standing where the government expended money. Tax breaks do not represent literal government expenditures, and therefore tax breaks—including tax exemptions—do not create standing for a suit challenging an organization's tax-exempt status.[66]

Finally, even if a taxpayer could get past the Anti-Injunction Act hurdle and the standing hurdle, they would still lack the ability to force the IRS' hand. The IRS' decision to not enforce a provision of the tax law is shielded by its administrative discretion. The Supreme Court has recognized that the executive branch of the federal government (of which the IRS is part) has the "administrative discretion" to decline to enforce laws, and that courts cannot force the IRS—or any other executive agency—to enforce a particular law. The Supreme Court grounded its recognition of administrative discretion in three main considerations. First, agencies have finite resources, and need the flexibility to decide how to deploy those resources. Second, in refusing to enforce a particular provision of the law, an

---

61  I.R.C. § 7421(a) (2018).
62  Bob Jones Univ. v. Simon, 416 U.S. 725, 727, 94 S. Ct. 2038, 2041, 40 L. Ed. 2d 496 (1974).
63  Almost forty years ago, a district court in New York held that applying the Tax Anti-Injunction Act to prevent a taxpayer from *challenging* an organization's tax exemption read the Tax Anti-Injunction Act too broadly. To read it that broadly, the court held, would be to entirely foreclose a taxpayer from receiving relief if the IRS wrongly granted an exemption. Abortion Rights Mobilization, Inc. v. Regan, 544 F. Supp. 471, 489–90 (S.D.N.Y. 1982). Another similarly situated district court narrowed that holding significantly, though, requiring a cognizable injury for a taxpayer to challenge an organization's tax exemption. Dalton Farms Assocs. v. Baker, 704 F. Supp. 460, 464 (S.D.N.Y. 1989).
64  Lujan v. Defs. of Wildlife, 504 U.S. 555, 112 S. Ct. 2130, 2134, 119 L. Ed. 2d 351 (1992).
65  Linda Sugin, "The Great and Mighty Tax Law: How the Roberts Court Has Reduced Constitutional Scrutiny of Taxes and Tax Expenditures," *Brooklyn Law Review* 78, no. 3 (2013): 777–834. 798.
66  Arizona Christian Sch. Tuition Org. v. Winn, 563 U.S. 125, 142, 131 S. Ct. 1436, 1447, 179 L. Ed. 2d 523 (2011).

agency does not exercise potentially suspect coercive power. Third, the refusal to enforce is similar to a prosecutor's refusal to indict, a power the executive branch has long enjoyed.[67]

## Performative Complaints

The whistleblower's complain has two significant deficiencies, then. First, it does not describe any legal wrongdoing by the Mormon church. Second, even if it did, the whistleblower could not force the IRS to act. So why did the whistleblower file a complaint with the IRS? In large part, the complaint is performative. And by "performative," I mean it does two related things. First, it allows the whistleblower to actively participate in the process of governance. And second, it punctuates the seriousness of the breach the whistleblower believes the Mormon church's wealth represents.

The concept of performative legal actions is not new, though it has been recognized more frequently in the litigation context. For example, Professor Alexandra D. Lahav laid out a theory of performative litigation in 2016. Professor Lahav explained that even where a particular lawsuit has no chance of success, that lawsuit nonetheless can be a democracy-forcing activity. Among other things, litigation forces governmental response, and often a response from a powerful adversary, neither of which would otherwise respond to a plaintiff who lacks power. It provides an aggrieved party a forum in which they can both explain and defend their position. It also increases transparency. Because legal filings and opinions are (generally) public information, a lawsuit can broadly provide the public with information it would not otherwise have, information that can allow the public to make better decisions. Ultimately, Professor Lahav says, this type of performative litigation, repeated by various people, enhances democracy. But it does more than merely enhance democracy: it cements a collective identity among those who engage in it.[68]

In many ways, this description of performative litigation also resonates with complaints to the IRS. Filing a whistleblower complaint allowed the whistleblower to take an official action and to engage with the government. Even if Ensign Peak Advisors' actions did not violate the tax law, the whistleblower had a forum in which he could articulate a reasoned allegation of wrongdoing and explain why the Mormon church's business dealings were bad. Moreover, even though the Mormon church is under no legal obligation to respond, the complaint nonetheless proved information-forcing. While there has been no formal adjudication of its allegations, it made significant waves in the court of public opinion. Journalists, experts, and the public at large have engaged with its

---

67 Samuel D. Brunson and David J. Herzig, "A Diachronic Approach to *Bob Jones*: Religious Tax Exemptions After *Obergefell*," *Indiana Law Journal* 92, no. 3 (2017): 1175–220. 1195–96.
68 Alexandra D. Lahav, "The Roles of Litigation in American Democracy," *Emory Law Journal* 65, no. 6 (2016): 1657–704.

allegations, and the Mormon church ultimately chose to respond.[69] As a result of the whistleblower complaint's release, the public has more information with which it can consider the benefits and detriments of allowing churches to engage in the financial world.

Which leads to a second type of performative legal action: lawsuits that are truly performative, in the sense that they both are not going to win *and* the plaintiff knows (or, at the very least, does not care) that they will lose. Sometimes these types of performative suits are filed to harass the target of the litigation, forcing the defendant to incur the emotional, temporal, and financial costs that litigation entails. So-called *strategic lawsuits against public participation* ("SLAPP") have attempted to weaponize these costs to prevent people from speaking out. SLAPP lawsuits "are not initiated with the intention of winning on the merits, but rather to harass, threaten, and intimidate the opposing citizens" into silence.[70]

But this second type of performative litigation is not always intended to harass. Non-SLAPP performative litigation can be significantly less insidious. Rather than attempt to harass the target, the plaintiff in this type of performative legal action intends to underscore the seriousness of the defendant's alleged bad act. For example, in 2006, Amanda Blackhorse filed a suit to cancel the trademark registration of the Washington Redskins on the basis that the trademark violated the Lanham Act's proscription on disparaging marks.[71] In spite of some early success, in 2017 the Supreme Court ruled that the disparagement clause of the Lanham Act violated the First Amendment.[72] That ruling effectively negated Blackhorse's win. Still, the following year, she said that her suit had been successful: "To cancel the R-word and the Washington logo was a symbolic move by Native people using legal tactics to shift the paradigm."[73]

Even if she could not win as a legal matter, filing and pursuing the suit emphasized how serious the disparaging use of Native American stereotypes was. While the courts could not remedy the wrong—a wrong that did not, after the Supreme Court's decision, violate any law—social norms could shift to recognize the wrong, and could pressure the wrongdoer into fixing their behavior.[74]

---

69 First Presidency Statement on Church Finances, December 17, 2019, https://newsroom.churchofjesuschrist.org/article/first-presidency-statement-church-finances [https://perma.cc/N42H-ME32].
70 "Recent Developments in Utah Law," *Utah Law Review* 2005, no. 4 (2005): 1291–465. 1384.
71 Pro-Football, Inc. v. Blackhorse, 112 F. Supp. 3d 439, 451 (E.D. Va. 2015), vacated, 709 F. App'x 182 (4th Cir. 2018).
72 Matal v. Tam, 137 S. Ct. 1744, 1751, 198 L. Ed. 2d 366 (2017).
73 Sarah Burstein, Twitter post, May 21, 2018, 12:31 pm, https://twitter.com/design_law/status/998617238495084544?s=20 [https://perma.cc/T4H4-S9KF].
74 In fact, public opinion shifted enough that the team has announced that it will change its name, though, as of the writing of this chapter, it had announced that it would go by "Washington Football Team" for the 2020 season and come up with a new name subsequent to that. Les Carpenter and Mark Maske, "NFL Franchise to Go By 'Washington Football Team' This Season, Delaying Permanent Name Change," *Washington Post*, July 23, 2020,

Publicly asserting that a church should lose its tax exemption for engaging in business seems largely to serve this same purpose. It is not, as we have seen, a winning argument. But it is a deeply salient argument. In 2021, the internet turned against famous pastor Joel Osteen for allegedly owning a Ferrari. To the internet, his alleged ownership of a luxury sports car felt incompatible with his being Christian clergy and, in response, the hashtag #TaxTheChurches began trending on Twitter.[75] There is no reason to believe that Osteen did not pay taxes on his income, and there is absolutely no connection between the tax exemption for religious organizations an Osteen's ownership of a Ferrari. From a substantive legal perspective, this hashtag makes no sense. While there may be arguments for taxing churches, that they and their leaders engage in business and make money has no legal relevance.

But while the tweets lack substantive legal heft, they reflect a deep salient view of both the role of churches and the role of tax exemption. Although the tax law clearly permits churches to engage in business, courts continue to separate religion from business, at least rhetorically. For example, in 2007, the Texas Supreme Court reiterated a previous court ruling pointing out that the relationship created by church membership differs from other relationships, including those in "other voluntary societies formed for business."[76] Another Texas court wrote that the core of church government "pertains not to business but rather to the mysteries of faith."[77]

A Florida court denied a church's request for business damages in an eminent domain case, holding that "because the promotion of religion, not its own livelihood, is the primary purpose of a church, and because the business damages statute is to be construed strictly in favor of the state, we conclude a church is not a business as that term is used" in the eminent domain statute.[78] A California court questioned whether a woman engaged in fortunetelling as part of her religion or as a business and ultimately concluded this as well, because "her religion did not require her to do fortunetelling as a business."[79]

Ultimately, then, although the law technically does not preclude religious organizations from engaging in business, courts, like ordinary people, view business and religion as separate spheres. In both the popular mind and the legal sphere, the two endeavors are viewed as incompatible and at odds with one another.

---

www.washingtonpost.com/sports/2020/07/23/washington-redskins-new-team-name-washington-football-team/ [https://perma.cc/UA6Q-RDTQ].
75 Juliana Caplan, "Joel Osteen's Taxes: What's Probably True and What Isn't," *Insider* (July 19, 2021), www.businessinsider.com/joel-osteen-rich-taxes-wealth-ferrari-twitter-2021-7 [https://perma.cc/P6XY-S7ET].
76 C.L. Westbrook, Jr. v. Penley, 231 S.W.3d 389, 398 (Tex. 2007).
77 The Episcopal Church v. Salazar, 547 S.W.3d 353, 393 (Tex. App. 2018), review granted (August 30, 2019), aff'd in part, rev'd in part sub nom. The Episcopal Diocese of Fort Worth v. The Episcopal Church, No. 18-0438, 2020 WL 2610207 (Tex. May 22, 2020).
78 Trinity Temple Church of God in Christ, Inc. v. Orange Cty., 681 So. 2d 765, 766 (Fla. Dist. Ct. App. 1996).
79 In re Bartha, 63 Cal. App. 3d 584, 590, 134 Cal. Rptr. 39, 42 (Ct. App. 1976).

Similarly, the popular view of tax exemption differs from the its technical legal version. As a legal matter, an entity qualifies as tax exempt if it meets certain largely technical requirements. To qualify, an entity must have an appropriate charitable purpose, it must ensure that profits it earns do not inure to the benefit of any private individual, no substantial part of its activities can include non-charitable or lobbying activities, and it must not endorse or oppose candidates for office.[80] In determining whether a tax-exempt entity is a church, the IRS has developed a 14-point checklist; if an entity checks enough of the boxes, the IRS will recognize it as a church.[81]

The popular view of tax exemption is far more expansive than simply a series of checked boxes. Both supporters and critics of religion view tax exemption as an official government endorsement. Perhaps most famously, when the IRS finally granted a tax exemption to the Church of Scientology, David Miscavige, the head of the church, announced that the "magnitude" of becoming exempt "is greater than you may imagine." The Church of Scientology used this apparent imprimatur of legitimacy from the US government to argue in other countries that it was a true religion and deserved recognition in those countries, too.[82]

Other new religions have also used tax exemption to bolster their claim of legitimacy. Indiana's First Church of Cannabis was approved as a church by the Indiana Secretary of State. More important than the "state law approval, the church has even been granted tax-exempt status by the IRS."[83] Upon receiving the church's exempt status, the church posted on its Facebook page:

> What a GLORIOUS DAY it is folks ... Absolutely BEAUTIFUL ... HAPPY TUESDAY! Our NOT FOR PROFIT 501 C3 status came in today ... WE ARE 100 % a LEGAL CHURCH ... All say HALLELUJAH and SMILE REAL BIG! ... We are OFFICIAL![84]

While the IRS' recognition of an entity as a tax-exempt church has no bearing on whether that entity is, in truth, a church, the public nonetheless views its technical approval as carrying more weight. If the IRS says an entity is a church, that entity is a church.

---

80 I.R.C. § 501(c)(3).
81 IRS, "'Churches' Defined," www.irs.gov/charities-non-profits/churches-religious-organi zations/churches-defined [https://perma.cc/9FA2-H35J].
82 Samuel D. Brunson, *God and the IRS: Accommodating Religious Practice in United States Tax Law* (New York: Cambridge University Press, 2018), 125.
83 Robert W. Wood, "IRS Approves First Church of Cannabis. What's Next for Marijuana?" *Forbes* (June 1, 2015), www.forbes.com/sites/robertwood/2015/06/01/irs-approves-first-church-of-cannabis-whats-next-for-marijuana/#45d321b315a3 [https://perma.cc/CH28-XC97].
84 "Tune in, Toke Up, Smile Big: Introducing the First Church of Cannabis," *Yahoo! News* (June 6, 2015), www.yahoo.com/entertainment/s/tune-in-toke-up-smile-big-introducing-the-first-church-of-cannabis-155421770.html [https://perma.cc/8KA3-L3AH].

## Conclusion

These performative complaints about churches' tax exemptions are unlikely to effect substantive change. For both constitutional and practical reasons, neither Congress nor state governments are likely to prevent churches from amassing wealth and are equally unlikely to mandate that churches spend it in any particular way. Churches, like other for- and nonprofit entities, are part of American capitalism and must engage with the economic world to survive.

It is certainly possible, though, that performative complaints will lead Congress to make minor changes. Churches may lose some of their exceptional benefits. Almost twenty years after creating an unrelated business income tax that exempted churches, Congress pulled churches into the regime. Similarly, it may someday require churches to apply for tax-exempt status and to file information returns in the same way other tax-exempt organizations must. In fact, outrage against churches amassing wealth opaquely may speed up the change.

Whatever changes it result (or fail to result) from the whistleblower's complaint, it needs to be taken seriously. The complaint reflects real discomfort with religion engaging in business and acquiring wealth. That discomfort exists at the individual level, but it also exists in the courts and in the halls of Congress. While the law does not exclude churches from the world of business, the makers and interpreters of the law are not as certain that they belong.

Performative complaints will not cause the Mormon church—or any other religious entity—to lose its tax exemption. Performative complaints will not change the law to prohibit churches from earning or stockpiling money. But performative complaints may well accelerate the process of treating religious wealth the same way any other nonprofit's wealth is treated.

# 6 The Liberty of the Will in Theology Permits the Liberated Markets of Liberalism[1]

*Deirdre Nansen McCloskey*

There is an intimate, and perhaps desirable, connection between liberty of the human will under Abrahamic theology and the liberty of human action under liberal economic ideology. The theology does not require a liberal economy, but a Christian conviction allows it. The proposal is not original. After all, a specifically Christian conviction about the efficacy of works of a liberated will coexisted in, say, the Italian city states with a specifically "capitalist" conviction about the efficacy of liberated markets. Not all the businessmen of Florence ended up in one of Dante's circles of hell.

But in the past century or so, liberal ideology has been under suspicion in theological circles. In 1919 Paul Tillich, then a 33-year-old Protestant pastor in Germany, wrote with Carl Richard Wegener an *Answer to an Inquiry of the Protestant Consistory of Brandenburg*:

> The spirit of Christian love accuses a social order which consciously and in principle is built upon economic and political egoism, and it demands a new order in which the feeling of community is the foundation of the social structure. It accuses the deliberate egoism of an economy . . . in which each is the enemy of the other, because his advantage is conditioned by the disadvantage or ruin of the other, and it demands an economy of solidarity of all, and of joy in work rather than in profit.[2]

"Egoism" is a mischaracterization of "capitalism," as Max Weber had argued in 1905. Greed, he wrote, is "not in the least identical with capitalism, and still less with its spirit. . . . It should be taught in the kindergarten of cultural history that this naïve idea of capitalism must be given up once and for all."[3] The lust for

---

1 This chapter was originally published as an article in *Journal of Economics, Theology and Religion* 1, no. 1 (2021): 81–108. Reproduced here with permission from the journal.
2 Paul Tillich and Carl Richard Wegener, "Answer to an Inquiry of the Protestant Consistory of Brandenburg," trans. Mrs. Douglas Stange, *Metanoia* 3, no. 3 (1971).
3 Max Weber, *Die protestantische Ethik und der Geist des Kapitalismus* (The Protestant Ethic and the Spirit of Capitalism), trans. T. Parsons, 1930, from the 1920 German edition (New York: Scribner's, 1958), 17. In his *General Economic History*, he writes, "The notion that our

sacred gold "has been common to all sorts and conditions of men at all times and in all countries of the earth." Love is in fact the foundation of a market economy, as even some recent economists have argued, and as old Adam Smith certainly did.[4] And "an economy of solidarity" and a top-down propaganda for a "feeling of community"—as communism and then fascism were about to show—yielded evil fruit. Yet, economic theories similar to those of the two pastors, sweetly intended but decidedly non-liberal, are increasingly common.

By "liberal," I do not mean the use of the term in the United States since about 1933, namely, "advocating a tentative democratic socialism." Nor do I mean the cruelty of what the political left has come to call "neo-liberalism," as in many of Margaret Thatcher's policies. I mean its use internationally, as on the Continent of Europe now, and its use originally, when in the late eighteenth century, the word was coined—that is, a society of adults liberated from coercive hierarchies. Liberals admitted excerptions for great externalities such as a plague, which cannot be solved any other way than by state action, though they recommended it be exercised with temperance and humility, not with the envy and anger of state-sponsored solidarity. Otherwise, no one was to impose on another a religious faith or way of life.

As a sober proposal for a non-policy of policy, *laissez nouis faire*, it was a new idea, though with a long if somewhat thin tradition of radical egalitarianism behind it. Spartacus died in battle for it in 71 BCE, and in 1381 CE the defrocked priest John Ball was drawn and quartered for asking, "When Adam delved and Eve span,/Who was then the gentleman?" In 1685 the Leveler Richard Rumbold, facing his hanging, declared, "I am sure there was no man born marked of God above another; for none comes into the world with a saddle on his back, neither any booted and spurred to ride him."[1] Few in the crowd gathered for the entertainment would have agreed with such anti-hierarchical sentiments. A century later, many more would have. By 1985 virtually everyone would, at any rate in official theory.

In the *Oxford English Dictionary on Historical Principles*, "Liberal*ism* 5a. Supporting or advocating individual rights, civil liberties, and political and social reform tending towards individual freedom or democracy with little state intervention" is first recorded in 1761 in David Hume's *History of England to Henry VIII*.[5] Under the phrase "at liberty," the earliest quotation in the *OED* is from 1503, "That euery freman be at liberte to bye and selle eueri w$^t$ other," which is the point here—that liberalism is the permission to participate at liberty in, say, the economy, as in the polity or in the church, equally if a "freeman." The

---

rationalistic and capitalistic age is characterized by a stronger economic interest than other periods is childish." Max Weber, *General Economic History*, trans. Frank Knight (New York: Greenberg, 1927), 355.
4 Adam Smith, *The Theory of Moral Sentiments*, Glasgow ed., eds. D. D. Raphael and A. L. Macfie (1790; repr., Indianapolis: Liberty Classics, 1982).
5 *Oxford English Dictionary Online*, s.v., "liberalism, n," accessed December 1, 2020, www.oed.com/view/Entry/107864?redirectedFrom=liberalism.

novelty in the eighteenth century and beyond was that *everyone* was to be equally at liberty. The priesthood of all believers anticipated a governorship of all citizens.

An old idea in many theologies, of course, such as the Christian one, was that souls are created equal in dignity. But the secular extension in liberalism, peculiar at first to northwestern Europe, was an equality in permissions of all sorts, from religious to economic. The case is sometimes made that Western Christianity had been long preparing for such liberty, but it is weak.[6] The extension came rather suddenly in the eighteenth century, without anticipation in a decidedly illiberal Europe.

The *OED* again speaks of liberty, sense 3a: "Freedom to do a specified thing; *permission*, leave" (my italics). In the opinion of radical liberals in the late eighteenth century such as Thomas Paine and Mary Wollstonecraft, the lord-and-servant and priest-and-parishioner hierarchies natural to an agricultural society were to be overturned, to make the world anew. They imagined a liberal utopia, with no slaves or serfs, no beaten wives, no beaten protestors, no select permission granted in a special charter to petitioners following on a humble appeal to the noble lord, or to the bishop, or to a state functionary. Harmless permissions for the generality were to be laid on in all directions.

The extreme of the theory was literal anarchism, *an-archos*, no ruler, a theory animating among the Russians Count Tolstoy in traditional Christian form and Prince Kropotkin in secular evolutionary form, and among southern Europeans the numberless Italian and Spanish anarchists. But a broad-church liberalism can admit that some limited coercion and hierarchy in the form of laws against force and fraud, and taxes for a few common purposes, are desirable. It says merely that the realm of human coercion should be small, and the realm of human autonomy large. On "liberty" sense 3, the *OED* quotes John Stuart Mill (who admittedly had a hint of social democracy about him), in 1841: "The modern spirit of liberty is the love of individual independence."[7]

Note the word "individual," Kant's "autotomy" of a rational being. The social cooperation that supplies our daily bread is to be achieved mainly not by coercive commands from human lords but by voluntary agreements among equal souls. The cooperation is individual, not collective. It contrasts with "ancient liberty," as defined in 1819 by the Swiss philosopher Benjamin Constant, namely, the right to have a voice, to carry a shield in the phalanx.[8] Modern liberty was the right to be left alone by a coercive state. The turn in England in the late nineteenth century to a "*New* Liberalism" re-focused on ancient liberty and its coercions.

---

6 Dierdre Nansen McCloskey, "Christianity Did Not Cause Liberalism: A Comment on Klein Out of Siedentop," *Svensk Tidskrift*, September 11, 2020, www.svensktidskrift.se/christianity-did-not-cause-liberalism-a-comment-on-klein-out-of-siedentop/.
7 On Mill's double role, as the height of liberalism and the beginnings of social democracy, see Joseph Persky, *The Political Economy of Progress: John Stuart Mill and Modern Radicalism* (Oxford and New York: Oxford University Press, 2020).
8 Benjamin Constant, "De l'esprit de conquête et de 'l'usupation," trans. Biancamaria Fontana, in *Political Writings: Cambridge Texts in the History of Political Thought* (Cambridge: Cambridge University Press, 1988), 45–167.

You are privileged to carry the shield, said philosophers such as T. H. Green and subsequently politicians such as David Lloyd George and Theodore Roosevelt, and you must. Such an anti-liberal and coercive "liberalism" is what most modern leftists recommend. Social liberalism and then democratic socialism are usually seen as a natural evolution, the obvious next step. It will unify us in collective projects, projects for which the majority of us, after all, have voted. But a society of non-slaves able to pursue their varied individual projects without approval by a majority seems to liberals to be a better end of history, more suited to humans.[9]

In medieval English, the plural "liberties" meant *in*equality of permissions, as in the English Magna Carta of "*Liberatum*" (liberties) in 1215 affirming baronial privileges against the king. Compare the southern Dutch *Groot Privilegie* in 1477 affirming local privileges against Burgundian centralization.[10] This person or that city was to have certain named and limited privileges, to run a market with specified frequency or to be exempted from specified taxes. The *OED* speaks of liberty sense 2c, "chiefly in plural, the entitlement of all members of a community." The lexicographers note that in such a plural form it is "in early use not always distinguishable from sense 6a, now chiefly historical," as in "the liberty" of the City of London granted to a specified person, and not at all to *hoi polloi*.

The liberal turn in the eighteenth century was, so to speak, from "liberties" to "liberty," from unequal privileges to equal ones, ideally for all (though in fact at first only for free males with property). The core of modern liberalism, in other words, is equality of permissions. And so is the core of Christian theology, the equal permission granted to all to sin or not. In the early church and in the Radical Reformation bent on re-establishing the early church, the equality was extended to all believers—though not in the Magisterial Reformation that came to dominate northern Europe.

Such a liberalism promised an equality, note, of *permissions*. It is not an equality of initial opportunity or of final outcome, to be expressed in material command over goods and services, which has been the socialist utopia since 1762 and Rousseau. The *OED*, in the entry on liberalism, quotes H. G. Wells in 1920 offering liberalism's epitaph, at a time when the British Liberal Party was dying, and collectivisms such as Wells supported were beginning to seem lovely: "The dominant liberal ideas were freedom and a certain vague equalitarianism." By "vague," he means that it did not legislate equality of outcome. But equal permission to worship or to trade is not "vague." To be at liberty to gather as two or three in Christ's name, or to be at liberty to buy or sell with every other, are as concrete as can be, and related.

§

---

9 Francis Fukuyama, *The End of History and the Last Man* (New York: Free Press, 1992); Dierdre Nansen McCloskey, "Fukuyama Was Correct: Liberalism *Is* the Telos of History," *Journal of Contextual Economics – Schmollers Jahrbuch* 139, no. 2–4 (2019): 285–303.

10 Thus sense 6a in the *Oxford English Dictionary's* entry on 'liberty': "Chiefly in plural. A privilege, immunity, or right enjoyed by prescription or grant. . . . Now chiefly historical."

True, a socialist utopia of equality of outcome echoed the early Christian one of equality in the face of an imminent *eskhaton*. But in its modern and secular form, especially in a society larger than a family or a monastery, such an equality entails subordination to a human master elevated in a hierarchy. If we are to rob Peter to pay Paul, in order to achieve end

> state equality of goods, some lordly coercion is necessarily involved, whether aristocratic or democratic. And needless to say even families and monasteries have not usually been equal in permissions, not really. The *pater familias*, or the abbot, or the mother superior, was tempted, as recorded in numberless complaints in ancient and medieval literature and folklore, to take selfish advantage of superiority. Agamemnon took Briseis from Achilles, with known results. Equality of permissions by contrast opposes any coerced hierarchy of gender or status or race or office. It, too, of course, has an early Christian lineage: "there can be neither Judaean nor Greek, there can be neither slave nor freeman, there cannot be male and female, for you are all one in the Anointed One Jesus" (Gal 3: 28).[11]

Coerced end-state equality in goods and services, from Rousseau to central planning communism, an economist would note, distorts the messages we send by demand and supply to each other about our material priorities. To be sure, before God the two souls are equal. The liberal democrats of the nineteenth century extended such an equality to political dignities, the franchise and the assurance of equality before the law, to achieve a nation of the people, by the people, for the people. Yet we should, the liberal economist says, pay a brain surgeon more than a waiter, because (to give the usual utilitarian reasoning, as in John Rawls) in that case both of them in the end will be better off, putting aside in the short run any indulging of the sin of envy. If they were paid the same, the services of surgeons would be grossly under-supplied, the services of waiters over-supplied. Forcing an equality of wages leads to lower income in total.

The argument for such a justified differential in pay is not so much the incentive to effort, though for learning to do brain surgery as against learning to wait tables it is a part of the story (a quite small part for Jeff Bezos incentivized to earn another billion). It is much more about sending the correct signals as to what in this vale of tears needs urgent augmentation. The economy is saying, "More brain surgeons, please. More re-inventions of the mail-order consolidators of a century ago in Sears, Roebuck, or Montgomery Ward, please."

Comprehensive equality of opportunity or of outcome is anyway not achievable. We are diverse in graces and can benefit from accepting them so to speak

---

11 I will use throughout David Bentley Hart's translation in 2017. Hart makes a persuasive case in his Postscript that the New Testament leans socialist. Using his translation therefore will not bias the case in a liberal direction. David Bentley Hart, *The New Testament: A Translation* (New Haven: Yale University Press, 2017).

gracefully, and then exchanging them: "There are differences in the graces bestowed. . . . To each is given the Spirit's manifestation for some benefit. . . . [To one] realizations of deeds of power, to another prophecy, to another the discernment of spirits" (1 Cor 12:4,7,10). Shakespeare lamented that he could not be "like to one more rich in hope, / Featured like him, like him with friends possessed, / [Having] this man's art and that man's scope."[12] The equality in goods and services imagined by Rousseau and the rest of the European socialist tradition does not make us equal in the God-given graces of height or beauty or intelligence or natural optimism or entrepreneurship or skill with a scalpel or luck of birth or length of life. By denying what the economists call "comparative advantage," a coerced equality of wages diminishes even the material riches of us all. A coerced equality of human heights or intelligence, likewise, would reduce the collective gains from such graces, by a Procrustean trimming of feet or by pounding nails into the heads of the gifted, to bring all to full equality. Coerced equality makes the poor poorer, thus violating Rawls' collectivist concession to liberalism: that a further enrichment of the rich can be justified if the poor are thereby also enriched.[13] For social policy, then, the pursuit of equality of opportunity or of outcome, as against comprehensive permission to work as a lawyer or to braid hair for a living, is a mistake.

For a Christian, further, equality of wages, at the beginning or at the denouement, seems oddly materialistic. Trying to achieve end-state equality of wages tempts us to the sins of envy and then anger against the brain surgeon, envying this man's art and that man's scope, as in the recent wave of populism. And in fact, contrary to the zero-sum ethic of the world in which Jesus and St. Paul lived, and contrary to its secular echo in recent claims about inequality, liberalism and its economic ideology of "innovism" (a more economically and historically accurate word than the misleading "capitalism") have resulted in fact in massive equalizing of real human comforts, materialistically speaking.[14] The American economist John Bates Clark predicted in 1901 that

> the typical laborer will increase his wages [in real terms, allowing for inflation] from one dollar a day to two, from two to four and from four to eight.

---

12 William Shakespeare, "Sonnet 29: When, in Disgrace with Fortune and Men's Eyes," lines 5–7," accessed June 7, 2021, www.poetryfoundation.org/poems/45090/sonnet-29-when-in-disgrace-with-fortune-and-mens-eyes.
13 Aa argued in John Rawls, *A Theory of Justice* (Cambridge: Harvard University Press, 1971).
14 Two economists report on the basis of detailed study of the individual distribution of income—as against comparing distributions nation by nation—that "world poverty is falling. Between 1970 and 2006, the global poverty rate [defined in absolute, not relative, terms] has been cut by nearly three quarters. The percentage of the world population living on less than $1 a day (in PPP-adjusted 2000 dollars) went from 26.8% in 1970 to 5.4% in 2006." Sala-i-Martin and Pinovsky 2010; Sala-i-Martin 2006. "PPP-adjusted" means allowing for the actual purchasing power of local prices compared with, say, U.S. prices. It has become the standard, an improvement over using exchange rates (which are largely influenced by financial markets).

Such gains will mean infinitely more to him than any possible increase of capital can mean to the rich. . . . This very change will bring with it a continual approach to equality of genuine comfort.[15]

The prediction was accurate.

It is the illiberal hierarchies of coercion, not uncoerced exchanges—or so the Christian liberal claims—that tempt fallen humans to arrange unfair advantages in order to overturn the core equality of permissions. The American state enforces monopolies of doctors and electricians by licensure preventing a free entry that would make the rest of us better off. The Dutch state keeps out new pharmacies that would reduce drug prices in the neighborhood. All states prevent consumers from being at liberty to buy and sell, everyone with another. States choose winners (though in fact regularly losers) in pursuit of industrial and innovation policy. In most places, with the exception of a handful of Swedens and New Zealands and Minnesotas, the state regularly takes from poor Peter to subsidize rich Paul. Most states are in this respect like China or Russia or, at best, the US in Illinois and Louisiana.

Illiberalism re-establishes the hierarchy that once upon a time liberalism proposed to overturn. The fictional pig/commissar in Orwell's *Animal Farm* declared that all animals are equal, but some animals are more equal than others.[16] The literary critic Tzvetan Todorov reports that Margarete Buber-Neumann (Martin Buber's daughter-in-law),

> a sharp-eyed observer of Soviet realities in the 1930s, was astonished to discover that the holiday resorts for ministry employees were divided into no less than five different levels of "luxury" for the different ranks of the communist hierarchy. A few years later she found the same stratification in her prison camp.[17]

The very word "liberalism" contains the program. "Liberal" is of course from classical Latin *liber*, understood by the slave-holding Romans as (in the words of the *Oxford Latin Dictionary*) "possessing the social and legal status of a free man (as opp. to slave)," and then *libertas* as "the civil status of a free man, freedom."[18]

As is so often the case in English, however, there are paired words, the Latin-origin "liberty" and the Germanic-origin "freedom." The two have relatively recently acquired slightly different connotations, and it is desirable to distinguish them if we are not to become muddled. "Liberty" retains the political connotation of all people being non-slaves to other humans. "Freedom" in English,

---

15 John Bates Clark, "The Society of the Future," *The Independent* 53, no. 2746 (July 18, 1901): 1649–51.
16 George Orwell, *Animal Farm* (London: Secker and Warburg, 1945), last page.
17 Todorov 2000 (2003), p. 83.
18 P. G. W. Glare, ed., *Oxford Latin Dictionary*, 2nd ed. (Oxford: Oxford University Press, 2012), 1025–25.

though, has increasingly come to mean not subject to constraint by physics or, in particular, by wages. Thus, Franklin Roosevelt in his Four Freedoms speech in 1941 numbered as third a freedom from want, and the economist Amartya Sen wrote in 1999 of economic development as freedom.[19] The trouble is that we already have words for such lack of want, or for economic development, namely, income, wealth, riches, capabilities, adequacies. To push together, as the modern English usage of "freedom" does, the politics-word of non-enslavement to others (liberty) and the wage-word of ability to buy things from others (wages, wealth) leads only to confusion. The liberal claim, to be sure, is that liberty does result in an increased ability to buy things—and so it has done over the past two centuries. But for the claim to be meaningful, its alleged truth needs to come from the evidence, not from a mis-definition of development as being freedom, *simpliciter*.

Classical Latin does not conceive of liberty as the choice to do what is morally good. Such is a Christian concept and may be seen in medieval Latin, as a step to somehow making human liberty consistent with obedience to God's will. It is the issue between liberty of the will and determinism. But the issue is not to be resolved by merely redefining the will of humans to be exactly the will of God, as tempting as such a resolution is in the less liberal Christian traditions. Nor is Latin *libertas* simply "choice," as modern economists see it, *arbitrium*, the license to follow one's impulses, be they good or evil.[20] It is the condition of non-slavery, which is the point in liberalism—celebrating even poor people being, as illiberal early moderns in England put it (terrified by the very thought), "masterless."

The slave societies in which Christianity grew up did not admire masterlessness, and waxed eloquent in favor of everyone having a master. St. Paul appears to have thought that slavery was unavoidable, even natural—for God made some slaves and other free. In the Letter to Philemon, he sends a fugitive slave back to his master, though asking the master to liberate him, considering the services (he uses commercial language) that the slave had rendered to Paul. In the long run, as it were, God values both slave and master equally. But the modern liberal message is that the here and now also matters. Nowhere does the Apostle reflect on literal slavery, except when he says, repeatedly, that we are all, slaves and masters, one in Christ.

Yet that is the point. People didn't object to the system of secular slavery, right up to the liberal abolition movements of the late eighteenth and especially the early nineteenth century. The Pope in 1537 deemed native Americans to have human souls, and therefore, when converted to Christianity, were not to be directly enslaved; yet Africans were another matter. It is not true that Christians early or late were opposed to slavery as a system (which is one among many reasons it does not make sense to attribute liberalism itself to Western Christianity).

A slave did not have the moral luck to be virtuous. He was coerced to good, at any rate "good" in the eyes of his master. (Thomas Carlyle in 1849 called

---

19 Franklin D. Roosevelt, "Four Freedoms," *State of the Union Address*, January 6, 1941. Amartya Sen, *Development as Freedom* (Oxford: Oxford University Press, 1999).
20 Glare, *Oxford Latin Dictionary*, 160.

economics the "dismal science" because his friend John Stuart Mill, among other liberals, dared to oppose slavery—which, like medieval serfdom, Carlyle reckoned was a good, un-dismal discipline for the numerous people slavish by nature.[21]) But in an age of non-slavery in political and economic ideology, and the resulting gigantic positive sum in the economy, it is not obvious from Christian theology that a masterful state should be enforcing the virtues. It should not at least if a liberated will—a choice between virtues and vices—is to be meaningful, which God so evidently wishes.

One can be a slave in a metaphorical sense, to lust, say, or to other disordered passions (among which natural-law theologians have often placed homosexuality). But, among the numerous sub-definitions and quotations in the three pages of the *Oxford Latin Dictionary* concerning *liber* and its derivatives, none so much as hints at such an ethical as against political/social notion. The word is about literal slavery to another human, as one might expect from pagan Romans with many slaves. Yet, the *Oxford* English *Dictionary* does give as the earliest use of the French-origin "liberty" in Middle English the theological definition, namely, "Freedom from the bondage . . . of sin," quoting Wycliffe's bible of c.1384, 2 Cor 3:17 (verse 18 in Wycliffe's numbering): "Forsoth where is the spirit of God, there is liberte." The *OED*'s last quotation on this score, as recently as 2007 from the theologian Glenn Tinder, speaks plainly that "an inner liberty—from sin . . . —renders outer liberty a secondary, or even unimportant, consideration." Well, not for an eighteenth-century liberal.

By 1776, among advanced intellectuals in northwestern Europe (fluent, needless to say, in classical Latin, and often hostile to and ignorant of medieval Latin or of the substance of medieval theology), such a liberalism had become fashionable, as for example in the novel and highly non-classical opposition to literal, chattel slavery. Consider, as the most well-known example, the declaration by the conflicted Virginia slave-owner and deist, based on John Locke's formulation in the 1690s, that all men are created equal, and are endowed by their Creator with certain unalienable rights, among which are life, liberty, and the pursuit of happiness.

§

That year 1776 saw also the publication of Adam Smith's *An Inquiry into the Nature and Causes of the Wealth of Nations*. Smith was a permission-egalitarian, opposed to slavery and to "protection" in commerce, which are respectively the private and the public subjugation of one human to another, backed by the state's coercion. To call Smith, and his liberalism, "egalitarian" is mildly controversial, but not mistaken. True, Smith's two books—the other, *The Theory of Moral Sentiments* [1759, 1790], is the one he loved the most—are rich and subtle enough, and very occasionally (it must be conceded) confused enough, that his words can be marshaled for the political left as much as for liberalism (though never for the political

---

21 Joseph Persky, "A Dismal Romantic," *Journal of Economic Perspectives* 4, no. 4 (1990): 165–72.

right). They have been so marshaled recently for example by the brilliant Smith scholar, the philosopher Samuel Fleischacker.[22] But other brilliant Smith scholars, in particular Sandra Peart and David Levy, attribute to him a modest "analytical egalitarianism" so characteristic of eighteenth-century social thought in Scotland.[23] The analyst and the human subject are to be seen as equal, contrary to—masterful French schemes of top-down. "It is the highest impertinence and presumption . . . in kings and ministers," Smith wrote, "to pretend to watch over the economy of private people."[24] And the private people are to be equal in permissions.

Smith advocated in all his writings "the obvious and simple system of natural liberty."[25] In Smith, the word "natural" and his much less frequent locution (three times only in all his surviving wirings) "the invisible hand" are stand-ins for "the Christian doctrine of divine providential care for humanity," as the economist and theologian Paul Oslington has argued.[26] In line with British natural theology of the Newtonian sort, a theology in which Smith was immersed (whatever his personal faith, about which we have to speculate), God's "other book," of nature, reveals the truths of the heavens, and of humanity, too. Like his children, the other so-called classical economists down to Marx and Mill, Smith had no real conception of what an obvious and simple system of natural liberty would in fact yield in the two centuries after his death. But he did sketch a reason it would yield a continual approach to equality of genuine comfort, as Oslington also argues.

If God-given, in view of the Christian equality of souls, Smith was recommending a society that was, at any rate by the standard of his age, radically egalitarian—in permission, I repeat, not in initial or end-state material capabilities expressed in money. Smith was particularly indignant about restrictions on a worker's right to use his labor as he saw fit. The English (not Scottish) Settlement and Removal Acts, which attempted to prevent poor people from overwhelming local systems of poor relief, would force the poor back to the parishes of their birth—literally removing and resettling them, a cleansing by social class. There is doubt whether it actually happened on a large scale. But never mind: Smith's indignation at the trespass on a poor man's liberty was aroused.

> To remove a man who has committed no misdemeanor from the parish where he chooses to reside is an evident violation of natural liberty and justice. . . . There is scarce a poor man in England of forty years of age, I will

---

22 Samuel Fleischacker, *A Short History of Distributive Justice* (Cambridge, MA: Harvard University Press, 2004).

23 Sandra J. Peart and David M. Levy, eds., *The Street Porter and the Philosopher: Conversations in Analytical Egalitarianism* (Ann Arbor, MI: University of Michigan Press, 2008), 84–85; Adam Smith, *An Inquiry into the Nature and Causes of the Wealth of Nations*, Glasgow ed., eds. R. H. Campbell, A. S. Skinner, and W. B. Todd, 2 vols (1776; Indianapolis: Liberty Classics, 1981).

24 Smith, *Wealth of Nations*, 346.

25 Ibid., 687.

26 Paul Oslington, "God and the Market: Adam Smith's Invisible Hand," *Journal of Business Ethics* 108, no. 4 (July 2012): 429–38.

venture to say, who has not in some part of his life felt himself most cruelly oppressed by this ill-contrived law.[27]

He is not requiring that the laborer be paid the same as the landlord, merely that an executive committee of the landed classes does not deny him permission to live and work where he wishes, "at liberty." It is Smith's "liberal plan of [social equality, [economic] liberty, and [legal] justice."[28]

In the line of Smith's predecessors Locke and Voltaire, he at length acquired political allies for such novel opinions, though it took some decades after 1790 to bring liberal policies to ascendancy in Europe. Liberalism's hour, that is, came recently. It is not anciently implied by the European character. Yet, the timing of liberalism's coming is not an entire mystery. From 1517 to 1789, the north and especially the northwest of Europe and its offshoots witnessed, *Dei gratia*, successful reformations and revolts and revolutions, which could easily have gone in an unsuccessful and illiberal direction. Two among many such happy turning points for a nascent liberalism a-borning were the Sunfish army's failure at the Siege of Alkmaar in 1573, and then in 1588 the failure of another portion of the best army in Europe to land in England. At length around the North Sea a liberalism against hierarchy was (always partially) victorious.[29]

Until liberalism came to Europe, the equal immortal souls of Christianity were to take up in this life, uncomplainingly, their highly unequal crosses, and not to whine about hierarchies of permissions enforced by guild or *Graf* or government. The pre-liberal theory was, as the Swedish-American radical Joe Hill expressed it in 1911 with anti-clerical sarcasm, "Work and pray, live on hay. / You'll get pie in the sky when you die."[30]

Liberalism is sometimes construed by its enemies, and sometimes even by its less wise friends, as an amoral Prudence Only, Greed is Good, a social Darwinism of egoism in the style of Ayn Rand. It need not be so. Think of John Stuart Mill or Ramon Aron. Ethical constraints are surely needed against Greed is Good. I myself wrote a book in 2006 on the constraints on sheer selfish will, if such a will is seen as "maximize profit regardless" or some other encomiastic fantasy encouraging sin. Prudence is a virtue, but it is decidedly not the only virtue relevant to a liberal society—again contrary to the less wise opinions of my economist colleagues. Greed is a great sin, and is to be resisted, I affirmed, by the constraints of other virtues in attendance on buying and selling, and non-slavery: temperance, justice, courage, faith, hope, and love.

One may ask who fashions such constants on greed. Most of them are ethical habits learned at one's mother's knee, if one pays attention, and then they are

---

27 Smith, *Wealth of Nations*, 4.5.55.
28 Ibid., 664, 687.
29 Deridre Nansen McCloskey, *Bourgeois Equality: How Ideas, Not Capital or Institutions, Enriched the World* (Chicago: University of Chicago Press, 2016).
30 Joe Hill, "The Preacher and the Slave," in *International Workers of the World, Little Red Songbook* (Spokan, Washington: Lumber Workers' Industrial Union No. 500, 1911).

molded by churches, communities, friends, novels, movies. The notion expressed by communitarians of the left such as Michael Sandel or of the right such as Patrick Deneen that liberalism must leave community to one side is mistaken.[31] And even in the agora (which is a commune, too, argued the Dutch economist Arjo Klamer), the ethical schooling is not derisory, being what the liberals among the French in the eighteenth century called *doux commerce*.[32] Contrary to an illiberal rhetoric elevating the state with its coercions as an ethical model, a life in private business is nothing like automatically corrupting.

In a collection of mini-essays asking "Does the free market corrode moral character?" the political philosopher Michael Walzer replied "Of course it does." But then he wisely added that *any* social system can corrode one or another virtue. That the Bourgeois Era has tempted people into thinking that greed is good, wrote Walzer,

> isn't itself an argument against the free market. Think about the ways democratic politics also corrodes moral character. Competition for political power puts people under great pressure . . . to shout lies at public meeting, to make promises they can't keep.[33]

Fallen humans are to be expected to be like that. Or think about the ways even a mild socialism puts people under great pressure to commit the sins of state-enforced envy or class hatred—or in the non-mild case the environmental crimes such as draining the Aral Sea. Or think about the ways, before the progressive historian Charles C. Sellers' alleged "commercial revolution" in the early United States (which he claimed damaged an alleged "affective and altruistic relations of social reproduction in traditional societies") put people under great pressure to obey their husbands in all things and to hang troublesome Quakers and Anabaptists.[34]

That is to say, any social system, if it is not to dissolve into a Hobbesian war of all against all, needs ethics adopted by its participants. It must have some device—taboos, preaching, coyote tales, songs, movies, the press, child raising, or in a pinch the state (as in a Prohibition of alcohol advocated by the New Liberals)—to slow down the corrosion of moral character, to maintain what

---

31 For the case against them, see Deirdre Nansen McCloskey, "What Michael Sandel Can't Buy: Review of Sandel's What Money Can't Buy," *Claremont Review of Books* 12 (Fall): 57–59. A longer version (in English) is in the German journal *ORDO* Band 64 (Spring 2013): 538–43. Deirdre Nansen McCloskey, "Why the Enemies of Liberalism Fail" [A Review Essay on Patrick Deneen, *Why Liberalism Failed*], *Modern Age* 60, no. 3 (Summer 2018): 15–23.
32 Arjo Klamer, *Doing the Right Thing: A Value Based Economy* (London: Ubiquity Press, 2017).
33 Michael Walzer, "Of Course It Does," in "A Templeton Conversation: Does the Free Market Corrode Moral Character?" *John Templeton Foundation Big Questions*, 2008 www.templeton.org/market/
34 Charles G. Sellers, "Capitalism and Democracy in American Historical Mythology," in *The Market Revolution in America: Social, Political, and Religious Expressions, 1800–1880*, eds. Melvyn Stokes and Stephen Conway (Charlottesville: University of Virginia Press, 1996), 311–29.

standard the society adopts, good or bad. The Bourgeois Era has in many ways set a higher ethical standard than others—abolishing slavery and giving votes to women and the poor; taking profit from its astounding innovations, yes, but a profit soon competed away by others rushing forward, and yielding therefore gigantic progress for the wretched of the earth. One can put a number on it, as the Nobel economist William Nordhaus did.[35] He calculated that since World War II only 2% of the social gain in the US from innovations such as bar codes (this Walmart and Amazon) or the computer (Gates and Jobs) or containerization (Malcom McLean) has stayed with the innovators. The 2% made them to be sure immensely rich, but it left the 98% of gain from cheaper retail or better computers or more goods shipped from China to the rest of us.

For further progress, Walzer, who is another communitarian, puts his trust in an old conservative trope of ethical education arising from good-intentioned laws enforced by the police. One might doubt that a state strong enough to enforce such laws would remain uncorrupted for long. Power tends to corrupt. Look at the results of Prohibition and the War on Drugs. The state is regularly a poor instructor in ethics. People speak of the state's courts as the "ultimate" or "foundational" protection, but such metaphors slip in a factual supposition that is false. Most protections against force and fraud, such as locks on doors and prudence in the agora and cooperatively enforced practices in businesses and religious exclusion if a diamond merchant in Brooklyn who cheats his orthodox Jewish colleagues, are not in fact provided by the state. They do not appeal to a gentile court.

§

Such a liberal economy, I claim, is consistent with a Christian life, employing a liberated will constrained by ethical treatment of others and oneself and God.

True, the Orthodox theologian David Bentley Hart notes in the postscript to his recent translation of the New Testament that the Christian testament has numerous passages in which God's word interpreted by humans demands, literally or in effect, that the rich give away their goods and follow Jesus.[36] The Christian gospels and many a Christian theologian early and late attack accumulated wealth, surprisingly harshly by the standards of the rest of the world's religious canon. In *A Passage to England* (1959), Indian professor of English Nirad C. Chaudhuri noted the contrast between the Lord's Prayer requesting one's daily bread and the Hindu prayer to Durga, the Mother Goddess, "Give me wealth, long life, sons, and all things desirable."[37] One prays as a Hindu to the elephant-headed god Ganesh for overcoming obstacles at the outset of a project, to obtain longevity, desired powers, and prosperity. The Vedic hymns are filled with passages like this one in a hymn to Agni the god of fire: "I pray to

---

35 William D. Nordhaus, "Schumpeterian Profits in the American Economy: Theory and Measurement" (working paper W10433, National Bureau of Economic Research, 2004).
36 Hart, *The New Testament*.
37 Nirad C. Chaudhuri, *A Passage to England* (London: Macmillan, 1959), 178. Compare chapter V, "Money and the Englishman."

Agni ... who ... brings most treasure.... Through Agni one may win wealth, and growth from day to day, glorious and most abounding in heroic sons."[38] It makes the Prosperity Gospel in its promises look stingy.

Thus, too, in Zoroastrianism a prayer of blessing (Afrinagan Dahman) reads "May these blessings of the Asha-sanctified come into this house, namely, rewards, compensation, and hospitality; and may there now come to this community Asha, possessions, prosperity, good fortune, and easeful life."[39] Like all the faiths of the Axial Age, Zoroastrianism recommends charity to the poor. But it does not condemn fortunes honestly made and devoutly spent (which may have something to do with the unusual recent prosperity under "capitalism" of the tiny group of Zoroastrian Parsis in Pakistan, northwest India, and England). Likewise, Jewish herders and traders viewed herding and trading as ethically acceptable. The Israeli economist Meir Tamari argues that there are few anti-commercial traditions in Judaism. In the thirteenth century, Rabbenu Bachya, like Aquinas and certain other Christian theorists at the time, as town life revived, declared that "active participation of man in the creation of his own wealth is a sign of spiritual greatness. In this respect we are, as it were, imitators of God."[40] *Imago Dei.* Nor is it surprising that the religion sprung from a merchant of Mecca "protects and endorses the personal right to own what one may freely gain, through legitimate means, such as gifts and the fruits of one's hand or intellect. It is a sacred right."[41]

What is surprising is that a Christendom so unusually hostile to commerce, profit, trade, wealth, and gain would in the nineteenth century commence admiring the bourgeois versions of the seven principle virtues and encouraging, out of liberalism, a universally enriching "innovism" (a word for the modern system much to be preferred, by the way, to the deeply misleading word "capitalism"). Yet, what is *not* surprising in view of the ancient hostility of Christianity to the accumulation of wealth is that also, and immediately, a bourgeois but still seriously Christian Europe in the nineteenth century invented the ideal of socialism, at first in an explicitly Christian form. True, Marx and Engels in 1848 sneered at it: "Nothing is easier than to give Christian asceticism a Socialist tinge. Has not Christianity declaimed against private property? Christian Socialism is but the holy water with which the priest consecrates the heart-burnings of the aristocrat."[42] Yet, most non-Marxists of the left down the to present retain an economic faith tinctured by Christian socialism.

---

38 Kim Knott, *Hindusim: A Very Short Introduction* (New York: Oxford University Press, 1998), 15. Compare another translation in Ainslee Embree, ed., *Sources of Indian Tradition. Vol. 1, From the Beginning to 1800*, 2nd ed. (New York: Columbia University Press, 1988), 9.
39 "Afrinagan-I Dahman," accessed June 7, 2021; http://avesta.org/ka/a1.htm.
40 Quoted in Jonathan Sacks, *The Dignity of Difference: How to Avoid the Clash of Civilizations* (London and New York: Continuum, 2002), 87.
41 Both of these are mottoes to Chapter 2 in Michael Novak, *Catholic Social Thought and Liberal Institutions: Freedom with Justice*, 2nd ed. (New Brunswick: Transaction, 1996), 41.
42 Karl Marx and Friedrich Engels, *The Communist Manifesto*, English trans. (Chicago: Charles H. Kerr & Co., 1888), 77.

Socialism, too, contains its program in its very word, from Latin *socius*, "ally," and as an adjective, "sharing." The closest allies in a traditional society are of course members of one's family. We are to have a family (of 330 million souls, say) making decisions socially, not individually, at any rate in mailers of Mammon. Erasmus in the 1508 and later editions of his collection of Latin tags always placed as the first item *Amicorum communia omnia*, among friends all [is held] in common.[43] What made such a lovely (if approximate) truth in a family or in a small group of friends into a social theory was its rigorous application increasingly after 1848 to societies of 330 million strangers, or even of 6 million, such as Sweden in 1927. A famous speech then to the Swedish parliament introduced the term *folkhemmet*, the people's home. It was inspired by an alliance characteristic of the era, of conservative corporatists and progressive socialists (thus the New Deal in the United States), consecrated by the holy waters of Christian socialism or the social gospel or Catholic social teaching. It emphasized not Marx's class struggle but, in a liberal echo, a sweet society of (often formerly) Christian friends, such as advocated by the American theologian Walter Rauschenbusch's grandson, the philosopher Richard Rorty. In the United States, the co-founder with Dorothy Day of the Catholic Worker movement, the French peasant and priest Peter Maurin, used to wander the streets declaring, "The world would be better off / if people tried to become better. / And people would become better / if they stopped trying to be better off."[44] Do good by doing poorly.

I am giving the word "socialism," note, a baggy definition, ranging from housing regulations up to communism-with-gulags. A housing regulation, even if mild and reasonable, is of course necessarily backed by physical coercion, however seldom in ordinary circumstances the coercion is applied. Otherwise, the intended regulation by society is a dead letter. Public coercion, not private agreement, is the method. If you violate the building code, you will be fined. If you don't pay the fine, you will be jailed. If you try to escape, you will be shot.

The intent in the baggy definition is not to tar social democrats with Stalinism, or with the new Maoism of Xi Jinping. It is to persuade the social democrats to stop supposing that there exists an easily attained third position between coercion and persuasion, between state action and non-coerced interaction. There is a bright line, as English Puritans c. 1642 could affirm, between being physically coerced to attend Anglican services by state action, on the one hand, and being amiably persuaded to do so, on the other.

Let us stipulate, for the sake of argument, that social democracy is stable and does not devolve into East-German tyranny and a rule by the *Stasi*. That is, stipulate that mere housing regulations, say, do not lead inevitably to a larger and

---

43 Desiderius Erasmus of Rotterdam, *The Adages of Erasmus*, selected by William Barker (Toronto: University of Toronto Press, 2001).
44 Roberts Ellsberg, "Introduction," in *Dorothy Day, Selected Writings*, ed. R. Ellsberg (Maryknoll, NY: Orbis, 1983), xxv.

larger state, on the road to serfdom.[45] (On the other hand, it is only prudent to worry about such a devolution, as some social democrats do not worry enough, supposing the state to be a sweet bunch of wise folk.) Yet, the true liberals since Voltaire and Smith and Wollstonecraft have recommended a restrained state, and the wide practice of persuasion in voluntary exchange. Thus in 1776 Paine, who was a free trader, declared that "government even in its best state is but a necessary evil, in its worst state an intolerable one."[46] In 1849, the American naturalist and essayist Henry David Thoreau, who in aid of innovism had improved the machinery in his father's pencil manufactory, agreed: "I heartily accept the motto, 'That government is best which governs least'; and I should like to see it acted up to more rapidly and systematically."[47] Modern social democrats and US "High Liberals" attack such notions, and yearn for *folkhemmet*.

Hostility to an imagined "capitalism," and enthusiasm for some version of socialism, became in the early twentieth century a commonplace among intellectual Christians. "By the late 19th century," notes the historian Jürgen Kocka, "capitalism was no longer thought to be a carrier of progress."[48] The case against "capitalism" was summarized in 1910 by the Reverend H. H. Williams of Oxford, writing on "Ethics" in the 11th edition of the *Encyclopædia Britannica*: "The failure of 'laissez-faire' individualism in politics to produce that common prosperity and happiness which its advocates hoped for caused men to question the egoistic basis upon which its ethical counterpart was constructed."[49]

Even in 1910, the Reverend Williams was mistaken factually, and as the twentieth century proceeded, the facts became less and less supportive of the anti-innovism view. As early even as 1910, a commercially tested betterment and the creativity of steam and steel had yielded unprecedentedly common prosperity and happiness, at any rate by historical standards. The prosperity of British working people had doubled since 1848, and at least had not fallen in the face of rapid British population growth in the half century before 1848. Then, in the century after 1910, it redoubled and redoubled again and yet again redoubled, for a factor since 1848 of sixteen at least, even in a United Kingdom that in 1800 vied with the Netherlands as the richest country per person in the world.

Yet, in 1800 even the average person in the United Kingdom was miserable by today's standard, dragging along on $6 a day in present-day prices. Then liberalism and its encouragements to innovism—the permission to, as the British say, "have a go"—brought a Great Enrichment, to $100 a day by now, a factor of about 17. If the higher quality of goods (food, housing, education) is taken

---

45 Friedrich Hayek, *The Road to Serfdom* (Oxford: Routledge Press and Chicago: University of Chicago Press, 1944).
46 Thomas Paine, *Common Sense* (1776), 3, www.gutenberg.org/files/147/147-h/147-h.htm.
47 Henry David Thoreau, *On the Duty of Civil Disobedience* (or *Resistance to Civil Government*) (1849), 1, first sentence, www.gutenberg.org/files/71/71-h/71-h.htm.
48 Personal communication, November 2014.
49 H. H. Williams, "Ethics," in *Encyclopædia Britannica*, 11th ed. (Cambridge and New York: Cambridge University Press, 1910).

into account, the Great Enrichment is more like a factor of 30 or 40. That is, it was in total not the 100% or 200% since the year 1800 that people will reply if you ask them. It was a startling 3,000 or 4,000 percentage enrichment of the poor, coming from the commercially tested betterments of kerosene and electricity, cardboard and container ships, subways and autos, movies and universities, airplanes and the internet. Startling though such thousands of percentages are, no competent student of economics, economic history, or public health would disagree.[50] The poor are not always with us, not since political liberalism and economic innovism out of liberalism took hold.

§

Yet, the intellectuals had in Reverend Williams' time, as George Bernard Shaw noted in 1912, long since turned against economic innovism arising from political liberalism. The priests and artists and journalists and professors looked back in conservative-socialist fashion to the lovely Christian commonwealth of the Middle Ages: "The first half [of the nineteenth century] despised and pitied the Middle Ages," wrote Shaw.

> The second half saw no hope for mankind except in the recovery of the faith, the art, the humanity of the Middle Ages.... For that was how men felt, and how some of them spoke, in the early days of the Great Conversion, which produced, first, such books as the *Latter Day Pamphlets* of Carlyle, Dickens' *Hard Times*, . . . and later on the Socialist movement.[51]

By 1919, Tillich and Wegener were claiming, recall, that innovism is a matter of non-cooperation. They were mistaken. An economy is a massive device for cooperation. The competition so offensive to them is merely the permission to enter a trade badly served by the present powers, an entry that then radically improves the lot of the poor. Yet, as the professional economist and amateur theologian Robert Nelson in 2001 commented on such sentiments,

> If the private pursuit of self-interest was long seen in Christianity as a sign of the continuing presence of sin in the world—a reminder of the fallen condition of humanity since the transgression of Adam and Eve in the garden—a blessing for a market economy has appeared to many people as the religious equivalent of approving of sin.[52]

---

50 Hans Rosling, Anna Rosling Roennlund, and Ola Rosling, *Factfulness: Ten Reasons We're Wrong About the World—and Why Things Are Better Than You Think* (New York: Flatiron Books, 2018); Deirdre Nansen McCloskey, *Bourgeois Dignity: Why Economics Can't Explain the Modern World* (Chicago: University of Chicago Press, 2010). See McCloskey, *Bourgeois Equality* for details and evidence.

51 George Bernard Shaw, introduction to *Hard Times* (London: Waverly, 1910; repr., New York: Norton, 1990), 333–40.

52 Robert H. Nelson, *Economics as Religion: From Samuelson to Chicago and Beyond* (University Park: Pennsylvania State University Press, 2001), 331.

The economy in this view is a zero-sum game, a species of football. One might claim correctly, acknowledging a sad and sober fact, that before 1800 or so the economy *was* zero sum, one person's advantage conditioned by the sinful ruin of the other.[53] The fact justifies the claim implicit in some passages in the Hebrew Bible (though contradicted in others) and explicit in the New Testament that a rich man cannot with ease, or enjoying his ease, enter the Kingdom of Heaven. Such a view, though commonplace in the twentieth century among Christian people, is factually mistaken. Since 1800 or so, the zero-sum claim has been spectacularly belied. Income per head of the poorest has increased in Brazil and Japan and Finland and now China and soon India by that 3,000%, dwarfing any gain to the poor to be had by redistribution in a zero-sum economy. It is as though the old football game yielding typical scores of 28 to 7 in favor of the rich came after a while to yield in the new game scores of 840 to 210. The rich still "won," if sports-talk or a socialism of envy is how one wishes to think. But the formerly poor now enjoyed fully human lives, denied in the days of their old score of 7.

And, conceptually speaking, innovism is the opposite of the sinful "deliberate egoism" that the young pastors of Germany claimed. It achieves the solidarity of all people through voluntary exchanges among the 6 or 300 or for that matter 7,800 million souls rather than through the coerced allocation as though in *folkhemmet*. The people's home is run by lordly parents, or by lordly economists, or by lordly commissars with, it may be, their own motives distinct from those of the citizen-children inside. Liberalism by contrast is the adult system of thoroughgoing cooperation with strangers. The Good Samaritan's one-on-one gift was glorious. Yet, all the more is the one-on-many, or many-on-one, of modern innovism evoked by profit and craft and property. After all, no profit is achieved, and any craft is pointless, and any property fruitless, unless the seller's product made out of them is advantageous to the others, in the opinion of the others—who then willingly give over some of the profit from their own selling of labor or craft or property. It is liberal innovism, mutual gain, a positive sum.

The Christian clerisy since the Great Conversion has not much listened to such liberal reflections. Yet, physical coercion by one human over another is an evil in Christian theology, too, being an offense against the liberated will granted by a loving God. Socialism (technicalities and intentionalities aside) is the making of economic decisions by the general will, Rousseau's *volunté générale*, enforced (note the word) by physical coercion. Rousseau believed that the phrase *volunté générale* resolved the obvious tension between individual action and state coercion.[54] If you voluntarily join in the general will, he asked, what's the problem? And, happily, you will so join, as the nature of man under socialism evolves away from a wickedly bourgeois nature, "an economy," said the pastors, "in which each

---

53 See Walker Wright, "'Ye Cannot Serve God and Mammon: An Institutional Interpretation of the Gospels," *Faith and Economics* 74 (Fall 2019): 5–18.
54 Jean-Jacques Rousseau, *Du Contrat social*, book IV (1762; Paris: Groupe Flammarion, 2001), paragraph 4.

is the enemy of the other." Rousseau's oxymoronic notion of a voluntary coercion survives in political theory as the notion of a social contract.

The only alternatives to such socialized decision-making are the decisions made by the God-given individual wills interacting with other humans without physical coercion, as in the evolution of language or music or science. The result need not be a harsh and unchristian social Darwinism, a country-club disdain for the poor. Liberalism gives to others in an ethical manner the dignity of respect, autonomy, self-rule, liberty of the will, but within serious ethics. Most human arrangements are of this character, and especially so outside of tyrannies: language, is for example; and art; science, love, sports, and manners, too.

Admittedly, Rousseau's notion is paralleled in theology to voluntarily acceding to God's inevitable law. And admittedly, the economy, the language, love, football, and art, science, and manners make use of customary agreements to arrive at this or that action—what the liberal economist James Buchanan called "constitutional political economy," and what linguists and linguistic philosophers call "conversational implicatures."[55] Yet, since Rousseau the implicit agreement with the general will has of course been used routinely to justify evil coercions. In the USSR, for example, someone who did not agree with the general will as discerned by the state was judged to be quite mad, and would be put under the coercing care of psychiatrists.

The state, as Max Weber put it in 1919, can with justice claim "the monopoly of the legitimate use of physical constraint/ force/ violence/ coercion" ("*das Monopol legitimen physischen Zwanges*").[56] Good. Such a monopoly is greatly to be preferred to oligopolies of multiple gangs prowling around to physically coerce people. The liberal recommendation is to have a single guardian, and then watch over him. *Quis custodiet ipsos custodies?* Who guards the very guardians? Who watches the Chicago police? We better.

But we must keep in mind, as the riot police gather, that the justified monopoly does necessarily involve physical coercion. After all, they have the guns. Markets by contrast do not involve physical coercion, and Apple and Facebook do not have guns to coerce you into buying their wares. At any rate, they do not coerce unless the word "coercion" is so extended in meaning so that any influence, voluntary or physical, words or actions, advertising or billy clubs, is deemed "coercive." The dean of the College of the University of Chicago during the student disorders against the Vietnam War, the great rhetorician Wayne Booth, was trying to persuade a student to leave the Administration Building, which had been seized by the students. The student, irritated, said, "Now don't try to *reason* with me!"[57] Without reason, disagreement, rhetoric, free speech, all is [defined to be]

---

55 James M. Buchanan, "The Constitution of Economic Policy," *Nobel Lecture*, December 8 (reprinted in *American Economic Review* 77 (June 1987)): 243–50, http://nobelprize.org/nobel_prizes/economics/laureates/1986/buchanan-lecture.html; H. P. Grice, *Studies in the Way of Words* (Cambridge: Harvard University Press, 1989).
56 Max Weber, "The Profession and Vocation of Politics," in *Weber: Political Writings*, eds. and trans. P. Lassman and R. Speirs (Cambridge: Cambridge University Press, 1994), 310.
57 Booth used it as the title of a collection in 1970 of his essays on the turbulent era.

coercive, nothing is non-coercive, and we are doomed to an absence of will, by definition. Liberty of the will becomes a laughable fairy tale, not God's grace.

§

The ancient stoics, with many Christian quietists, went to the other extreme, claiming that external slavery allows nonetheless an internal freedom. As the philosophical stoic emperor of Rome and stoic slave from Asia Minor both noted, even a slave has choices, within a more or less constrained position. An old *New Yorker* cartoon shows two prisoners chained hand and foot, hanging from a prison wall. One says to the other, "Here's my plan."

Such extensions of meaning are rife in the philosophical discussion of liberty of the will.[58] I raise my arm voluntarily rather than not, or accept a poorly paid job in Vietnam making running shoes rather than starving. But, the determinist argues, in a world of causation, the will to raise the arm or the will to accept the job has itself causes, back to the big bang and (the theist adds) God's Beyond. One hears such an opinion expressed often on the left nowadays. It implies that being offered a job that is not heavenly, or being presented with an argument that is not pleasant, is an aggression, no better than state coercion in employment or in opinion, as in Stalin's and now Putin's Russia or Mao's and now Xi's China.

Erasmus, in his debate during the 1520s with Luther over liberty of the will, turned the discussion towards the social and ethical consequences of a supposed lack of liberty of the will. Such a liberal trope of argument was characteristic of the Prince of the Humanists. By contrast, the arguments about liberty of the will have mostly taken place at the top level, so to speak, of God's grant of liberty. Erasmus in the debate moves down to the level of human psychology, arguing for a middle position between the dual dangers of "indifference"/"hopelessness" in predestination or an "arrogance" in supposing that one can by works alone achieve salvation.[59] Staying at such a level has the merit that we have actual information and experience about it, and can reflect with some chance of conclusion about ethics and law. Rising to the level of metaphysics yields only paradoxes, irresolvable it would seem short of the Second Coming.

The theology about liberty of the will hangs on the word "intentional." Progressive Christians such as Pope Francis' economist, Stefano Zamagni, declare, contrary to the historical evidence and the economic logic, that conscious, planned, intentional action at the group level, the *volunté générale*, is what is needed in order to improve the world.[60] Francis himself, a child in Argentina of the Theology of the People, said to reporters on a flight from Poland to Rome, "as long as the world economy has at its center the god of money and not the

---

58 Robert Hilary Kane, ed., *The Oxford Handbook of Free Will* (Oxford: Oxford University Press, 2002).
59 Desiderius Erasmus, "The Free Will," in *Discourse on Free Will: Desiderius Erasmus and Martin Luther*, trans. and ed. (London: Bloomsbury Academic, 2013). 85. It is like Anglicanism.
60 Stefano Zamagni, "Catholic Social Thought, Civil Economy, and the Spirit of Capitalism," in *The True Wealth of Nations: Catholic Social Thought and Economic Life*, ed. Daniel K. Finn (Oxford: Oxford University Press, 2010), 63–93.

person . . . [it] is fundamental terrorism, against all humanity."[61] But no businessperson makes money without pleasing the person, saving her from starvation, educating her children, giving her a fuller life in which she can praise God. Contrary to such an obvious link between "money" and the person, say Zamagni, and Francis, the society cannot rely on any of those "neo-liberal" invisible hands or spontaneous orders of the sort that determine, say, the evolution of the Italian language or of Milanese fashion. Thus, my own Episcopal priest in the United States declared in her July 4 sermon that "independence is not a Christian value," and that what is Christian is a dependence on God and community (God's Will, but then also the General Will in central panning of innovation, say).

A Christian liberal disagrees on the matter with Zamagni and with Pope Francis and with my beloved pastor, as with many other good-hearted folk. The initial independence of the person in a liberal economy results in the great and good interdependence of modern life. You don't grow your own wheat or make your own accordion. You trade for then with people many thousands of miles away. Liberalism celebrates a non-coercive and ethical *inter*dependence.

Catholic social teaching of the sort Zamagni advocates doesn't face up to the point. One-to-one cooperation is splendid, and certainly subject to "intentionality." You can choose in a liberal society the life of a desert hermit if you feel so inclined, and then eschew the profit of social relations in an economy. But most people are not so inclined. If so, they should reject "national self-sufficiency" as vigorously as they would reject a law preventing them from buying a baguette at Bouton's boulangerie rather than Bateau's. The primitive calls for national self-sufficiency in response to the COVID-19 pandemic deny the massive gain from one-on-many trade. If applied consistently, the protectionists would call for cutting off trade with your neighbor down the street. Grow your own wheat; make your own accordion. To the contrary, listen again to Smith: "The woolen-coat, for example . . . is the produce of the joint labor of a great multitude of workmen [and workwomen, please, dear Adam]. The shepherd, the sorter of the wool, the wool-comber or carder, the dyer, the scribbler, the spinner, the weaver, the fuller, the dresser, with many others, must all join their different arts in order to complete even this homely production."[62]

The American theologian and writer Frederick Buechner set down as an axiom that

> We have freedom to the degree that the master whom we obey grants it to us in return for our obedience. We do well to choose a master in terms of how much freedom we get for how much obedience.[63]

---

61 Francis X. Rocca, "Pope Francis Says Ills of Global Economy, Not Islam, Inspire Terrorism," *The Wall Street Journal*, August 1, 2016, World | Europe, www.wsj.com/articles/pope-francis-urges-poles-to-embrace-migrants-on-final-day-of-visit-1469963264.
62 Smith, *Wealth of Nations*, 22–23.
63 Frederick Buechner, *Beyond Words: Daily Readings in the ABC's of Faith* (San Francisco: Harper Collins, 2009), 119. I am grateful to Amity Carrubba for the reference.

His economistic talk of a tradeoff is commendable, and the theological point is, too—that one can for instance be enslaved to corrupting desires, and that a loving Lord is a better choice of master than Satan. But the concession to non-liberty has illiberal dangers. St. Paul drove the axiom of universal lordship, typical of the slave society in which he lived, to its secular conclusion: "Let every one be subordinate to higher authorities. For there is no authority except under God" (Rom 13:1). "Render unto Caesar" was perhaps a necessary rhetorical tactic at the time for a Judean with suspect politics. But the British King James I or the French King Louis XIV could not have put better the case for a merger of religious and secular tyranny.

In short, a secular, human lordship, an absence of liberty, is not inevitable, we moderns have believed since 1776. And human lordship is not at all—*pace* St. Paul—an entailment of God's Lordship. Even theology shows, that is, how very illiberal St. Paul's, St. Augustine's, Calvin's, and James I's metaphysics is, how much against the discovery in the eighteenth century of the merits of human wills constrained by ethics but liberated from human coercion.

§

We are God's creatures. God therefore owns us, by an analogy with Lockean mixing of labor with unappropriated land, or by an analogy with the ownership of children by parents. But God chooses to liberate us, not leave us as slaves. A parent, and God, wants us to be liberated adults, not perpetual children. We Jews and Christians say at Passover/Easter that God brought us out of slavery in Egypt, and then (we Christians add) by Christ's sacrifice out of death. We Jews or Moslems say that a child undergoes a bar/bat mitzvah or instruction in the Holy Koran to become an adult, a *mukallaf*—in modern English a "responsible" person.[64]

As the theologian and biblical scholar Shawna Atteberry puts it, the people-as-pets theory of our relation to God and His universe inspires

> one of the greatest modern heresies of the church: the Prosperity Gospel . . . [which] says that if we are truly in God's will we'll get everything we want: wealth, health, and all the toys that money can buy.[65]

To the contrary, she observes, God and the universe sometimes say No. It is a position natural to the world of the economist, though God's grace be free. If we lived in Eden, it would not be so. But, as liberated adults in a real world governed by natural and social laws, we choose, as Eve chose—and as in the tale as Adam too chose, exercising the sadly persuadable will of a liberated man.

---

64 See Thomas L. Haskell, "Responsibility, Convention, and the Role of Ideas in History," in *Ideas, Ideologies, and Social Movements: The United States Experience since 1800*, eds. P. A. Coclanis and S. Bruchey (Columbia: University of South Carolina Press, 1999), 1–27, on the extraordinarily recent history of "responsibility."

65 Shawna Atteberry, "When God Says No," sermon at Grace Church, May 26, 2019, Chicago, IL, www.shawnaatteberry.com/sermon-when-god-says-no/.

132  Deirdre Nansen McCloskey

The über-liberal "Austrian" economics speaks of liberty of the will as "human action." Orthodox, non-liberal public theology, by contrast, wants the state and God to treat us like obedient pets or children or slaves, not liberated wills. And orthodox, non-Austrian economics nowadays views people as reactive, maximizing utility under a constraint, like grass seeking the light and the water optimally. No, replies the liberal Christian. God made us in the *imago Dei/Deae*. Liberated.

The point is that there *is* a third way between a coercive state and an atomistic individual: namely, the cooperation yielded by entry and exit in markets. When Jesus' fishermen sold their catch—the abundant one arranged for them that day by Jesus—they intended only to help their own families. But by the miracle of interdependence in the market for fish, thousands ate. The unintended consequence of specialization and trade is a social miracle analogous to the divine miracle of loaves and fishes.

The great economist Frank Knight (1885–1972), in an anti-clerical fury, mistook the Christian morality of charity as a call to common ownership in a big society and not merely in a literal home. He attacked it as unworkable. (It is said that the only time the University of Chicago has actually refunded tuition money to a student was to a Jesuit who took Knight's course on "the history of economic thought" and discovered that it was in fact a sustained and not especially well-informed assault on the Catholic Church.) Knight wrote a book in 1945 with T. W. Merriam called *The Economic Order and Religion*, which mysteriously asserts that Christian love destroys "the material and social basis of life," and is "fantastically impossible," and is "incompatible with the requirements of everyday life," and entails an "ideal . . . [that is] not merely opposed to civilization and progress but is an impossible one." Under Christian love, "continuing social life is patently impossible" and "a high civilization could hardly be maintained long,. . to say nothing of progress."[66]

It develops that Knight and Merriam are arguing that social life in a large group *with thoroughgoing ownership in common* is impossible. *That* is what they believe Christian love entails.[67] Compare Tillich and Wegener. The source for Knight and Merriam is always the Gospels, never the elaborate compromises with economic reality of the Church of Power, or of other Christian writings, such as the 38th article of the Anglicans: "The riches and goods of Christians are not common, as touching the right, title, and possession of the same, as certain Anabaptists do falsely boast."

But, yes: social life without private property *is* impossible, at any rate in large groups. So said Pope Leo XIII in 1891 in *Rerum Novarum*, re-echoed by Pius XI in 1931, John XXIII in 1961 and 1963, by Paul VI in 1967 and 1971, and by John Paul II in 1981 and 1991.[68] These men were not nineteenth-century liberals—

---

66  Frank Knight and T. W. Merriam, *The Economic Order and Religion* (New York: Harper and Bros., 1945), 29–31, 46.
67  See for example ibid., 48.
68  These are Pope Pius, "Quadragesimo Anno: Encyclical of Pope Pius XI on Reconstruction of the Social Order to our Venerable Brethren, the Patriarchs, Primates, Archbishops, Bishops, and Other Ordinaries in Peace and Communion with the Apostolic See, and Likewise to

especially, as the Catholic but liberal public intellectual Michael Novak explained, not "liberals" in the harshest Continental sense.[69] The popes admitted private property—when used with regard to soul and community. They were nothing like the Sermon on the Mount socialists that Knight and Merriam attacked.

Thus Leo: "private possessions are clearly in accord with nature" (15), following his hero, Aquinas.[70] "The law of nature, . . . by the practice of all ages, has consecrated private possession as something best adapted to man's nature and to peaceful and tranquil living together" (17). "The fundamental principle of Socialism which would make all possessions public property is to be utterly rejected because it injures the very ones whom it seeks to help" (23). "The right of private property must be regarded as sacred" (65).

> If incentives to ingenuity and skill in individual persons were to be abolished, the very fountains of wealth would necessarily dry up; and the equality conjured up by the Socialist imagination would, in reality, be nothing but uniform wretchedness and meanness for one and all, without distinction.
>
> (22)

---

all the Faithful of the Catholic World," May 15, 1931, St. Peter's, Rome, www.vatican.va/content/pius-xi/en/encyclicals/documents/hf_p-xi_enc_19310515_quadragesimo-anno.html; Pope John XXIII, "Mater et Magistra: Encyclical of Pope John XXIII on Christianity and Social Progress," May 15, 1961, St. Peter's, Rome, www.vatican.va/content/john-xxiii/en/encyclicals/documents/hf_j-xxiii_enc_15051961_mater.html; Pope John XXIII, "Pacem in Terris: Encyclical of Pope John XXIII on Establishing Universal Peace in Truth, Justice, Charity, and Liberty," April 11, 1963, St. Peter's, Rome, www.vatican.va/content/john-xxiii/en/encyclicals/documents/hf_j-xxiii_enc_11041963_pacem.html; Pope Paul VI, "Populorum Progressio: Encyclical of Pope Paul VI on the Development of Peoples," March 26, 1967, St. Peter's, Rome, www.vatican.va/content/paul-vi/en/encyclicals/documents/hf_p-vi_enc_26031967_populorum.html; Pope Paul VI, "Octogesima Adveniens: Apostolic Letter of Pope Paul VI," May 14, 1971, Vatican, www.vatican.va/content/paul-vi/en/apost_letters/documents/hf_p-vi_apl_19710514_octogesima-adveniens.html; Pope John Paul II, "Laborem Exercens: To His Venerable Brothers in the Episcopate to the Priests of the Religious Families to the Sons and the Daugters of the Church and to All Men and Women of Good Will on Human Work on the Ninetieth Anniversary of Rerum Novarum," May 15, 1981, Castel Gandolfo, www.vatican.va/content/john-paul-ii/en/encyclicals/documents/hf_jp-ii_enc_14091981_laborem-exercens.html; Pope John Paul II, "Centesimus Annus: Encyclical Letter to His Venerable Brotehr Bishops in the Episcopate the Priests and Deacons Families of Men and Women Religious all the Christian Faithful and to All Men and Women of Good Will on the Hudnredth Anniversary of Rerum Novarum, Blessing," May 1, 1991, St. Peter's, Rome, www.vatican.va/content/john-paul-ii/en/encyclicals/documents/hf_jp-ii_enc_01051991_centesimus-annus.html; Michael Novak Is My Guide Here: Michael Novak, *Catholic Social Thought and Liberal Institutions: Freedom with Justice*, 2nd ed. (New Brunswick: Transaction, 1989), chapters 6–8.

69 Novak, *Catholic Social Thought*, chapters 6–8.

70 Leo XIII, "Rerum: Novarum: Encyclical of Pope Leo XIII on Capital and Labor," May 15, 1891, St. Peter's, Rome, www.vatican.va/content/leo-xiii/en/encyclicals/documents/hf_l-xiii_enc_15051891_rerum-novarum.html. See Thomas Aquinas, *Summa Theologica*, trans. Fathers of the English Dominican Province (1270), IIa, IIae, Q 66; quoted and discussed in Fleischacker, 35 note 40.

"The love-gospel," write Knight and Merriam, "condemning all self-assertion as sin . . . would destroy all values."[71] Knight and Merriam are correct if they mean, as they appear to, that love *without other and balancing virtues* is a sin. Knight's understanding of Christianity appears to have derived from his childhood experience in a primitive Protestant sect, the Campbellites (evolved now into the less primitive Church of Christ and Disciples of Christ), and theirs is what he took to be the core teaching of Christianity: "No creed but the Bible. No ethic but love."

But love without prudence, justice, temperance, and their combinations is not Christian orthodoxy—for example the orthodoxy of Aquinas or of Leo XIII. And, yes, such a single-virtue ethic would *not* be ethical in a fallen world. Economists would call the actual orthodoxy a "second-best" argument, as against the first best of "to him who washes to bring judgment against you, so he may take away your tunic, give him your cloak as well" (Matt 5:40). Given that people are imperfect, the Christian, or indeed any economist, would say: we need to make allowances, and hire lawyers, and call the police. Otherwise, everyone will live by stealing each other's tunics and cloaks, with a resulting failure to produce tunics and cloaks in the first place, and the life of humans will be solitary, poor, nasty, brutish, and short.

St. Paul himself said so, admittedly in a letter that not all scholars regard as authentic:

> And we [that is, Paul, recalling his visit to the Thessalonian Christians] ate bread not as a gift from anyone, but rather by labor and struggle, working night and day so as not to place a burden on any of you. . . . If anyone should not wish to work, neither let him eat. For we hear of some who walk in idleness.
>
> (2 Thess 3:8, 10–11)

Startlingly, Lenin adopted it as a motto. To put it more positively, as Michael Novak did, "one must think clearly about what actually does work—in a sinful world—to achieve the liberation of peoples and persons."[72] "In the right of property," wrote even John XXIII in 1961, "the exercise of liberty finds both a safeguard and a stimulus."[73] Frank Knight couldn't have put it better.

Charity is not socialism. Generosity is not a system at all. It is of a person, then two, then a few. God arranges such encounters, a Christian might say. But humans value them, too, the gift-economy of grace above material concerns.[74]

---

71 Knight and Merriam, *The Economic Order*, p. 50.
72 Novak, *Catholic Social Thought*, xvi.
73 John XXIII, "Mater et Magistra: Encyclical of Pope John XXIII on Christianity and Social Progress," May 15, 1961, St. Peter's, Rome, www.vatican.va/content/john-xxiii/en/encyclicals/documents/hf_j-xxiii_enc_15051961_mater.html; quoted in Ibid., xxii.
74 Given an exceptionally eloquent expression in David Klemm, "Material Grace: The Paradox of Property and Possession," in *Having: Property and Possession in Religious and Social*

Yet, to make them into a coerced-contributory social system is to undermine their virtue. We are mostly not friends, but strangers, and even in the Society of Friends the property was not held in common. Knight and Merriam were not really facing Christian orthodoxy and Christian ethics. They were misunderstanding them. One owes love to a family first. Property, with the virtue of justice, protects the beloved family, on the analogy with God's love for us. If any would not work, neither should he eat. Work, depending on temperance and prudence, is desirable to create and to acquire the property. So is prudent stewardship in managing it, though the lilies of the field toil not. For big groups of humans, being neither lilies nor little families, the right prescription is admiring the bourgeois virtues. A Bourgeois Revaluation giving permission to people to have a go has since 1800 occurred in Holland England, Scotland, France, Germany, the US, Sweden, Japan, Hong Kong, Ireland, China, India, and ended, or is ending, famine and other miseries.

§

So much, then, for a sketch of the political economy of liberty possible in Christian theology. It suggests a new and truly liberal public theology. For it is liberalism, a fulfillment of the Abrahamic equality of souls, that brings human flourishing and human virtue, as God wishes.

---

*Life*, eds. William Schweiker and Charles Matthews (Grand Rapids, MI: Eerdmans, 2004), 224–45.

# 7 Neutral Principles and Legal Pluralism

*Víctor M. Muñiz-Fraticelli*

> What is at stake here is the power to exercise religious authority. That is the essence of this controversy.[1]

Katy Perry wanted to buy a convent. In 2014, the pop singer—who began her career in Christian rock but found fame in decidedly more secular musical performance—expressed interest in purchasing a property in the Los Feliz neighborhood of Los Angeles to use as a private residence for her and her mother. The building, until recently, had been a convent for the California Institute of the Sisters of the Most Holy and Immaculate Heart of the Blessed Virgin Mary. Known at different times as Villa San Giuseppe or the Waverly property, it was purchased by the Institute at the time of its founding in the 1970s. By 2012, after a long period of conflict and decline, the handful of nuns who remained in the Institute had been relocated, and the property remained vacant or was rented out for film productions and events.[2]

The Sisters had a turbulent history with the Archdiocese of Los Angeles. In the late 1960s, the order had split over the nuns' embrace of—and then-Archbishop James Francis McIntyre's resistance to—the reforms in religious discipline encouraged by the Second Vatican Council.[3] Many nuns left the Institute to establish a separate lay community, independent of the Archdiocese. But those that remained would still have occasional squabbles with the archdiocesan authorities over control of the Institute and its property.

The crux of the matter was that the legal status of the Institute was always bifurcated. On one hand, it was a religious corporation organized under the law of the state of California;[4] on the other, it was an institute of consecrated life

---

1 F. Frankfurter, concurring in *Kedroff* v. *Saint Nicholas Cathedral of the Russian Orthodox Church in North America*, 344 U.S. 94 (1952), 121.
2 There is a threadbare account of the events leading up to the sale in *Callanan v. Roman Catholic Archbishop of Los Angeles*, B275366 (Cal. Ct. App. July 25, 2017).
3 The schism is recounted by the leader of the departing faction, Anita M. Caspary, *Witness to Integrity* (Collegeville, MN: Liturgical Press, 2003).
4 California Corporations Code, sections 9110–9690.

DOI: 10.4324/9781003309291-8

organized under the Code of Canon Law of the Roman Catholic Church.[5] Over a little more than a decade, a series of agreements between the Sisters and the Archdiocese had the latter assume greater oversight over the Institute. Especially important were two agreements between the Sisters and the Archdiocese: the first, in 1992, amended the Articles of Incorporation to provide that the Institute "shall not sell, lease, encumber, convey, exchange, transfer or otherwise dispose of . . . the buildings and real property located at [Waverly Drive] without the prior written approval of The Roman catholic Archbishop of Los Angeles"; the second, in the following year, recognized that, as an institute of consecrated life, the Institute was subject to the provisions of the Code of Canon Law but, as a religious corporation, it was also subject to the Corporations Code of California.[6] In addition, the canon law of the Church requires that the alienation of goods owned by ecclesiastical juridic persons (including institutes of consecrated life) receive the permission of the Holy See if they are above a certain value.[7] The Waverly property was well above this value. The title of the Waverly property was in the name of the Institute under the law of California, but the authority to administer and alienate the property was restricted by both state and canon law.

It is in this context that Ms. Perry, supported by the Archbishop of Los Angeles, made an offer to purchase the Waverly property. But some of the Sisters objected to the financial structuring of the deal, the use to which the property would be put, and, frankly, the notoriety of the buyer. Believing that, as directors of the religious corporation, they had the right to dispose of the property, they concluded a separate sale agreement with Dana Hollister, a hotelier and restaurateur. The Archdiocese filed suit against Hollister to invalidate the sale agreement and grounded much of their claim on canon law and on the internal ecclesiastical agreements of the previous decades. In response, the dissenting Sisters brought an action in canon law to the Supreme Tribunal of the Apostolic Signatura, the highest court in the Church, to assert their right to control the Institute's affairs. Both the Apostolic Signatura and the California court would eventually rule in favor of the Archbishop.

The ruling of the California court is especially interesting in this case because it is compelled to resolve a problem that is common in many religious organizations: the convergence of civil and ecclesiastical regulation of not only physical assets but also labor and services and various other relations that are part of ordinary market exchange.[8] This convergence presents problems for secular liberal democracies.

---

5 At the time of the property dispute, this would have been Book II, Part III, section I of the 1983 Code of Canon Law (CIC), and in particular the norms governing the administration of temporal goods of such institutes (CIC arts. 634–640). When the Institute was created, the 1917 Code was in force.

6 "Order Granting Plaintiff's Motion for Summary Adjudication" in *Roman Catholic Archbishop, et al. v. Hollister*, Case No. BC585604 (April 4, 2017), pp. 11–13.

7 CIC arts. 1290–1298. At the time of the dispute, permission was required for property above $7.5 million.

8 I use "civil law" in contraposition to ecclesiastical or canon law, that is, as the law enacted by the state and not the church, and not by reference civil (as opposed to criminal) law, or to the civil (as opposed to common) tradition, unless otherwise noted.

While all religious bodies generate norms that may be at odds with prevailing political and social principles, the convergence of civil and ecclesiastical law is felt most patently in traditions that are historically strongly communal and hierarchical. Secular liberal democracies are generally solicitous of religious expression, but they are also driven by their internal logic to favor legal solutions that do not embroil them in religious controversies, do not perpetuate hierarchical governance, and do not give force to exceptional legal systems that are outside of popular control.[9]

The temptation of secular liberal democracy is, then, to resolve religious disputes by reference to a neutral standard that can be adjudicated by state courts. But the precise meaning of neutrality varies between and within jurisdictions. Express reliance on theological reasons—prophecy, mystical experience, revelation—is ruled out by general principles of secularism, but what of more intelligibly legal reasons offered by churches as complex organizations? These may be recognizably legal (and sometimes legalistic to a fault). Yet, attempts to liquidate religious law into civil law inevitably result in distortion of the tenets of religious communities and may even provoke a retrenchment of these communities into even more formally centralized structures.

For present purposes, I will focus on property disputes in churches and other religious communities, rather than disputes over employment, ministry, membership, and management of these institutions. All these disputes involve things of value coming into the church from the market or the holdings of economic actors, whether as gift, labor, or acquisition or, in the case of employment and membership, by promise, agreement, or contract. While under the control of the church they may be withdrawn from commerce or put to use in the economy, according to the norms and instructions of religious authorities. As such, it is reasonable that they should be guided by a common framework that recognizes the problems of governance involved, the assessment of economic value of not only real assets but also labor and of the worth of membership in an organization, and the rulemaking authority of churches.

I recognize that property presents a special case. Property disputes are often discussed separately from other disputes because of the centrality of clear title to property in a modern market economy, the guarantee of which is one of the core functions of the state. Such disputes may also involve third parties who are not themselves members of a religious congregation and thus not subject to religious law directly. And, in conflicts so fraught with animosity that they lead religious congregations to schism, property is a tangible asset, the ownership of which must be enforced by the state. Two dissenting factions may decide to worship separately without requiring adjudication, but not so if they contest control over the place of worship or the funds dedicated to its maintenance and mission.

---

9 For a criticism of the liberal "logic of congruence" see Nancy L. Rosenblum, *Membership and Morals: The Personal Uses of Pluralism in America* (Princeton: Princeton University Press, 2018), especially pp. 73–111 on religious associations. For a defense of liberal paramountcy over religious legal authorities, see Cécile Laborde, *Liberalism's Religion* (Cambridge: Harvard University Press, 2017) especially pp. 160–96.

Civil courts have developed a succession of doctrines to resolve disputes within religious organizations in a way that protects a religious organization's self-understanding but, at the same time, ensures stability and predictability in relations of property and contract. The doctrine that has garnered near universal approval is the "neutral principles approach" first articulated by American courts but reproduced, whether by importation or spontaneous development, in other jurisdictions.[10] The application of neutral principles has varied widely between American states, mainly because of different assumptions about the nature of the church and its relation to the state. Against the strictest interpretation of the neutral principles approach (which would have courts rely only on civil legal documents to the exclusion of ecclesiastical law), I will raise some objections derived from the tradition of political and legal pluralism. A pluralist understanding of neutral principles does not resolve all the problems that arise from the participation of churches in the market, but it reduces the violence done to religious bodies by civil intervention into their structures of governance.

## The Judicial Adjudication of Property Disputes

Quarrels often arise within religious institutions that pit individuals against ecclesiastical superiors, or local congregations against more general bodies. In cases of internal disputes within a church, the parties may resort to the state courts to settle their disagreements, since these often entail questions about determination of ownership of property, appointment or dismissal of ministers or employees, or enjoyment of the benefits of membership.[11] The question of how state courts should respond to these quarrels, what legal principle or standard they should use to settle them, has vexed temporal authorities over the centuries and is especially challenging for secular liberal democracies. The liberal commitment to normative individualism in the formulation and pursuit of both religious and secular objects conflicts with the prevalence of custom and hierarchy in some religious traditions. The democratic insistence on popular sovereignty bristles at the insistence of many churches on their legal and political autonomy. That the church is a space in which the general norms that structure political and commercial relations may not operate is, for some, the normative ideal and, for others, an inefficiency or injustice to be overcome.

The recent disputes within the Anglican Communion—in both the Episcopal Church in the United States and the Anglican Church of Canada—the Presbyterian Church, and the United Methodist Church again bring to the fore the peculiar position of ecclesiastical polities in the broader legal and economic sphere.

---

10 I will mainly compare the United States doctrine with the most recent application of neutrality by Canadian courts.
11 I use the term "church" as a stand-in for religious institutions more broadly, which follows from the historical prevalence of Christian denominations as parties in the legal controversies I consider. But growing religious pluralism has resulted in similar cases arising in other religious traditions.

The context of the present division is the debate over LGBT rights, where the hierarchies of national churches have taken a more liberal position on the ordination of gay and lesbian priests and bishops and on the recognition of same-sex marriage. A minority of local congregations have decided to disaffiliate from either the general church or one of its regional divisions because of perceived doctrinal incompatibilities with the hierarchy's position. But previous disagreements have precipitated similar disputes. In the early nineteenth century, the American Revolution caused a rift in Roman Catholicism that nearly led to heresy and schism and profoundly transformed the organization of the Catholic Church in North America.[12] Profound divisions racked Presbyterianism after the United States Civil War, and similar disagreements divided Russian Orthodoxy during the Cold War. Every great crisis and controversy that divides the secular polity seems to have a similar effect on the ecclesiastical polities within it, and these rifts are most salient in religious bodies of hierarchical churches with long traditions of governance and substantial real and pecuniary holdings.

Across common law jurisdictions, judicial review of ecclesiastical disputes takes one of three or four paradigmatic forms: direct adjudication of the underlying theological controversy, complete deference to religious authority, or adjudication on the basis of more or less strict neutral principles of law. The forms here referred to emerge from United States constitutional law, but they can be generalized to other legal systems, as they are regularly referenced in Canadian doctrine—despite a very different history and ostensibly divergent constitutional language[13]—and have even entered into doctrinal literature in the United Kingdom.[14] But, more broadly, the three approaches can be classified according to the kinds of reasons (religious or legal) taken into account when conducting review, and according to the body (church or civil court) that has final authority to create and interpret the legal norms that apply to the ecclesiastical polity. The model could, in principle, be applied to other legal traditions.

## *Doctrinal Fidelity (or the "English Rule")*

The traditional common law standard of review for disputes over ecclesiastical property was an examination of the fidelity of each disputing party to the original doctrinal tenets of the church. The reasons English courts adopted the standard had to do with the ways in which ecclesiastical polities were ordinarily constituted

---

12 Patrick W. Carey, *People, Priests, and Prelates* (Notre Dame: University of Notre Dame Press, 1987).
13 M. H. Ogilvie, *Religious Institutions and the Law in Canada*, 4th ed. (Toronto: Irwin Law, 2017). I discuss the Canadian doctrine under "Church Law in a Comparative Context," later in this chapter.
14 Rex Ahdar and Ian Leigh, *Religious Freedom in the Liberal State*, 2nd ed. (Oxford: Oxford University Press, 2013); Jane Calderwood Norton, *Freedom of Religious Organizations* (Oxford: Oxford University Press, 2016); Julian Rivers, *The Law of Organized Religions* (Oxford: Oxford University Press, 2010).

and in which they received and held property. Some churches, especially established churches, received a corporate charter from the state that stated their purpose in terms of continued adherence to certain doctrines. Deviation from those doctrines would have been an *ultra vires* act and thus invalid *ab initio*. Most often, however, the institution of ecclesiastical polity was a matter of internal concern for the church, and the state courts only cared about the disposition of assets. Churches themselves were sometimes constituted as trusts, because that institution was easier to set up and avoided some of the formalities and complications of the corporate form, including Parliamentary and judicial oversight over corporate charters.[15] These assets were usually acquired as charitable trusts, and a dispute over control of the property was made to turn on which of the contesting parties most faithfully promoted the intent of the settlor.[16] Since the terms of the trust seldom made express and detailed reference to specific purposes, save the support of a giver church or parish, in cases of disputes over property given to a church in trust, courts had to determine to whom the settlor intended to leave it. Usually, they determined that

> in the absence of evidence of an express trust provision the court assumed that property was held in 'implied trust' by and for the benefit of individuals or groups that adhered to the same religious standards and beliefs as the donors did.[17]

As a result, the court was called upon to make extensive theological determinations about the content of church doctrine and the merits of various interpretations of it.

The implied church doctrine faced criticism even from theologians such as John Neville Figgis, an ardent defender of the right of religious institutions to autonomous development, because of two related but independent reasons. In the first place, the implied trust doctrine inhibited religious organizations from changing and adapting and effectively bound them to the wishes of their original founders or of powerful donors against the structures of governance of the institution. This was more than an abstract worry for Figgis. A disastrous dispute over the control

---

15 As Maitland explains, the functional difference between trusts and corporate charters from the perspective of the church itself was largely irrelevant. F. W. Maitland, "Trust and Corporation," in *Maitland: State Trust and Corporation*, eds. David Runciman and Magnus Ryan (Cambridge: Cambridge University Press, 2003), 75–130.
16 A charitable trust is a legal instrument through which a *trustee* administers a certain property at the request of a *settlor* (who donates the property) for the benefit of a stated *cause* or *purpose* (say, the sustainment of a parish). This differs from an ordinary trust in that it is the cause or purpose, and not the welfare of a specific person, that is the beneficiary of the trust. The trust itself may have a religious object, but it is a civil (secular) instrument, and disputes arising from it are subject to resolution by state court.
17 H. Reese Hansen, "Religious Organizations and the Law of Trusts," in *Religious Organizations in the United States*, eds. James A. Serritella, et al. (Durham: Carolina Academic Press, 2006), 279–314, 286 discussing *Craigdallie v. Aikman* 4 Eng Rep 435 (1820).

of the assets of the Free Church of Scotland at the turn of the twentieth century had exposed the fragility of church autonomy if the state were allowed to determine religious doctrine. The Free Church had sought to merge with another congregation that held uncompromising views on disestablishment and demanded that all ties of sponsorship or patronage with both the state and private donors be severed. The overwhelming majority of the Free Church accepted the position, but a very small yet powerful minority, supported by wealthy Scottish patrons with powerful allies in Parliament who had grown accustomed to control parsonages in the Scottish church, objected to the merger. These so-called *Wee Frees* claimed that the endorsement of the strict disestablishmentarian position was a departure from the longstanding religious doctrine of the church, and by adopting it the majority had abdicated their duty to the original donors and founders of the congregation. The House of Lords confirmed the *Wee Frees* and granted them ownership of the vast educational and charitable assets of the Free Church, which led to a protracted crisis that would take decades to sort out, as the number of *Wee Frees* was too small to manage the spoils effectively. Eventually, however, compromises were reached that allowed the assets and missions to be managed effectively by both sides of the conflict.[18]

More important was Figgis' second objection: that the implied trust doctrine placed authority over the life of the church in a power wholly outside of it, depriving it of institutional autonomy. The latter objection would have greater resonance across the Atlantic. In the United States, the implied trust doctrine was quickly seen to be inapplicable because it embroiled the state courts in theological disputes that would force them to grant their imprimatur to some religious congregants over others *on religious grounds*. The usual solution was for the courts to strip gifts granted in trust to the church of any reference to purpose, unless one was expressly stated in the trust instrument itself, and consider it an unencumbered gift to the congregation which was controlled by its officials "without the limitation of trust obligations and without regard to religious doctrines, affiliations, or practices."[19]

It is important to consider that the implied trust approach, with its attendant examination of religious doctrine by a secular court, was not obviously wrong, and only seems so given the constitutional arrangement in the United States and the general but recent reluctance of courts in Canada and the United Kingdom to consider religious disagreements as matters of fact to be decided by the courts.[20]

---

18 *Bannatyne v. Overtoun* (Free Church case), [1904] A.C. 515 (H.L.). Ultimately, the decision was overturned by legislation of Parliament in favor of an equitable division of property between the two religious factions. For a broader discussion in relation to Figgis' political thought, see Víctor M. Muñiz-Fraticelli, *The Structure of Pluralism* (Oxford: Oxford University Press, 2014), 183–91.
19 Oaks, *Trust Doctrines in Church Controversies*, 36–37, cited in Hansen (note 15, above), 287.
20 The leading Canadian scholar on religious organizations has argued that Canadian courts should reject the American reluctance to examine doctrinal issues as they arise, but lately recognizes that current Canadian practice is to defer to the ecclesiastical authorities of religious

Secular courts are unclear about the grounds for their reluctance to interpret religious doctrine, usually settling on an admission of their own incompetence to do so. But it is not clear that the incompetence refers to a lack of expertise (which could be resolved through expert testimony), a lack of jurisdiction, or an inability to enter the right (i.e., devotional) frame of mind necessary to properly address a religious dispute.

## *Polity Approach*

The doctrinal fidelity approach had the twin effects of involving state courts in theological disputes and disregarding instances of actual practice of religion. State courts in the United States rejected it early on. Finally, in *Watson v. Jones*,[21] the US Supreme Court officially rejected doctrinal fidelity in favor of a hierarchical deference or polity approach. The Court faced a Presbyterian congregation divided over opposition to slavery during the Civil War that had just ended. Both sides claimed fidelity to church teachings and procedures and quarreled over the continued union of the presbytery of Louisville, Kentucky, with the national General Assembly.

Rather than examine which party held most steadfastly to doctrine, the Court established a hierarchy of sources on which to decide the question: it would first defer to explicit deeds of trust, if they exist; then to hierarchical authority, if there is one; and if there is none, to a majority of the membership.

> In this class of cases we think the rule of action which should govern the civil courts, founded in a broad and sound view of the relations of church and state under our system of laws, and supported by a preponderating weight of judicial authority is, that, whenever the questions of discipline, or of faith, or ecclesiastical rule, custom, or law have been decided by the highest of these church judicatories to which the matter has been carried, the legal tribunals must accept such decisions as final, and as binding on them, in their application to the case before them.

The *Watson* decision went unchallenged for nearly a century, but it had significant problems, not least the fact that religious bodies come in more varieties than hierarchical and congregational; Presbyterian churches, which ironically were the cause of the suit, don't fit neatly into either category. Moreover, the polity

---

organizations. Contrast M. H. Ogilvie, "Church Property Disputes: Some Organizing Principles," *University of Toronto Law Journal* 42 (1992): 377, criticizing the reluctance of Canadian courts to consider departures from religious doctrine in adjudicating disputes, to M. H. Ogilvie, "Three Recent Cases Confirm Canadian Approach to Church Property Disputes," *Canadian Bar Review* 93 (2015): 537, discussing the recent adoption by Canadian courts of a version of the American "neutral principles" approach (despite some judges' repeated disavowals that they are doing so).

21  80 US 679 (1872).

approach is not universally deferential to church polity. Under it, courts generally deferred to the ecclesiastical tribunals of hierarchical churches (understood as churches in which the national church held authority over local churches) but not to the decision-making bodies of congregational ones, whose disputes were to be settled according to ordinary law.

The polity approach at least attempted to take religious institutions seriously and accord them a place in the protection of religious liberty. But there are important and troubling similarities between the doctrinal fidelity and polity approaches. In both cases, the court is led to make a religious judgment, in the former case about the content of doctrine, in the latter about the locus of authority. Especially in cases when the locus of authority is articulated in religious rather than legal terms, there can be as much controversy about doctrine as there is about its proper interpreter. In some cases, the interpretive authority has textual support in internal church law. In other cases, the judgment will be irreducibly religious, despite the express attempt of the court to disallow such exercise of judicial discretion.

### Neutral Principles of Law Approach

Nearly a century after *Watson*, the Court turned in a decidedly different direction. In a series of cases on ecclesiastical property disputes, the Court reaffirmed the principle that state courts could not decide church disputes by interpreting religious doctrine,[22] but permitted lower courts to apply a so-called neutral principles approach. The advantage to the courts was avoidance of considerations of religious doctrine.

> The primary advantages of the neutral-principles approach are that it is completely secular in operation, and yet flexible enough to accommodate all forms of religious organization and polity. The method relies exclusively on objective, well-established concepts of trust and property law familiar to lawyers and judges. It thereby promises to free civil courts completely from entanglement in questions of religious doctrine, polity, and practice.

The advantage to churches was the ability to organize their polities as they saw fit, though amendment and revision of legal documents.

> Furthermore, the neutral-principles analysis shares the peculiar genius of private-law systems in general—flexibility in ordering private rights and obligations to reflect the intentions of the parties. Through appropriate reversionary clauses and trust provisions, religious societies can specify what is to happen to church property in the event of a particular contingency, or what

---

22 *Presbyterian Church v. Hull Church*, 393 US 440 (1969), *Maryland v. VA churches* 396 US 368, and *Jones v. Wolf*, 443 US 595.

religious body will determine the ownership in the event of a schism or doctrinal controversy. In this manner, a religious organization can ensure that a dispute over the ownership of church property will be resolved in accord with the desires of the members.[23]

These two passages together suggest that religious organizations may use the institutions of the common law—trusts and property arrangements, for instance—to give secular legal force to their ecclesiastical polities, and it expresses confidence in the flexibility of the common law to accommodate nearly any such polity, from the congregational structure of Baptists and Quakers to the elective eldership of Presbyterian and Reformed Churches, through to the centralized episcopal government of Anglicans and Roman Catholics (the last of which extends to the transnational authority of the Holy See).

But the *Jones* court went further than recommending to churches that they employ the instruments of secular law. It also recognized them as legal authorities in their own right and allowed state courts to consider their internal legal instruments as dispositive when secular legal instruments were unclear or incomplete.

At any time before the dispute erupts, the parties can ensure, if they so desire, that the faction loyal to the hierarchical church will retain the church property. They can modify the deeds or the corporate charter to include a right of reversion or trust in favor of the general church. Alternatively, the constitution of the general church can be made to recite an express trust in favor of the denominational church. The burden involved in taking such steps will be minimal. And the civil courts will be bound to give effect to the result indicated by the parties, provided it is embodied in some legally cognizable form.[24]

The neutral principles approach, which states could adopt as an alternative to the polity approach, "requires a civil court to examine certain religious documents, such as a church constitution, for language of trust in favor of the general church" but instructs it to "take special care to scrutinize the document in purely secular terms, and not to rely on religious precepts in determining whether the document indicates that the parties have intended to create a trust." The interpretation of the meaning of religious concepts in these documents, however, required the court to "defer to the resolution of the doctrinal issue by the authoritative ecclesiastical body."[25]

Following the *Jones* decision, the neutral principles approach was adopted by an overwhelming majority of US states. But the apparent unanimity is deceptive. In truth, the *Jones* decision offered two guiding principles in tension with each

---

23 *Jones v. Wolf*, 443 US 595, 603–04 (1979).
24 *Jones v. Wolf*, 443 U.S. 595, 606 (1979).
25 *Jones v. Wolf*, 443 U.S. 595, 604 (1979).

other—the permission for state courts to apply neutral principles of law and the invitation for churches to enact their own law and state courts, while claiming fidelity to *Jones*, have steered their opinions along different interpretive currents commonly referred to as a "strict" and a "hybrid" neutral principles.[26] The more restrictive "strict" current would look only to ordinary civil legal documents—deeds of trust, contracts, corporate charters—to determine who had title to property and exclude any formal or informal church rules, such as norms of canon law or long traditions of practice. The more capacious "hybrid" approach would also consider these internal church documents as sources of law—constitutions, regulations, and the like—as well as past behavior by the church or congregation, as long as those documents could be interpreted without reliance on theological reasons.

## A Pluralist Understanding of Neutral Principles

In a recent article, Michael McConnell and Luke Goodrich make the strongest case yet for the strict neutral principles approach against the hybrid alternative.[27] Their argument is compelling not least because the authors defend strict neutral principles on the grounds of preserving the autonomy of religious bodies. McConnell and Goodrich's three grounds of defense of the strict neutral principles approach roughly correspond to the vertices that animate the chapters in the present volume: democracy, religion, and the market. Democracy, insofar as disputes over property often pit local versus regional or national interests and call into question the effective voice of parishioners versus bishops, presbyters, or councils in determining the direction of the religious community. Religion, insofar as the discussion of internal church documents would seem inevitably to require the passing of judgment by secular courts on religious questions. And the market, insofar as the protection of stable property rights ensures the orderly management of valuable economic assets by the church, their transfer to and from ecclesiastical authority, and their use in (or withdrawal from) commerce.

McConnell and Goodrich identify two constitutional principles that structure judicial interpretation of ecclesiastical disputes: the Establishment Clause demands that courts abstain from deciding ecclesiastical questions, and particularly questions of doctrine, while the Free Exercise Clause allows churches "to be free from state interference in their internal affairs."[28] A corollary of the latter point is that the intention of denominations, congregations, and charitable donors

---

26 Jeffrey Hassler, "A Multitude of Sins? Constitutional Standards for Legal Resolution of Church Property Disputes in a Time of Escalating Intradenominational Strife," *Pepperdine Law Review* 35 (2008): 399; Cameron Ellis, "Church Factionalism and Judicial Resolution: A Reconsideration of the Neutral-Principles Approach," *Alabama Law Review* 60 (2009): 1001.
27 Michael W. McConnell and Luke Goodrich, "On Resolving Church Property Disputes," *Arizona Law Review* 58 (2016): 307.
28 Ibid., 316.

in structuring their governance and property relations should be respected, as they are motivated by constitutionally protected religious reasons. All the historical approaches to the church property question, as well as the contemporary interpretations of the neutral principles approach—including those adopted in Canada and the United Kingdom—agree on these points. But McConnell and Goodrich contend that the English doctrinal-continuity rule, the *Watson* deference approach, and the "hybrid" interpretation of the post-*Jones* neutral principles approach make unwarranted assumptions about the nature of churches that, in different ways, undermine the constitutional principles of non-establishment and free exercise. The English rule assumes that churches are defined by doctrinal continuity, the *Watson* deference approach assumes that churches are defined by submission to hierarchy (or else are defined by no principles at all), and the hybrid approach assumes that churches are defined by internal church rules.

This last assumption, that a church is defined by its internal rules, they argue, undermines the two constitutional principles that undergird judicial treatment of ecclesiastical disputes and, in effect, creates a ratchetting effect that entrenches hierarchy even in less centralized churches.

> By giving special weight to internal church rules, the hybrid approach creates a dilemma: if the rules are interpreted by civil courts, those courts become entangled in religious questions; but if the court defers to an interpretation by the highest church authority, the church is converted into a hierarchical structure whether or not that is what the founders, donors, or members wanted. Even worse, they write, the hybrid approach gives courts discretion to decide how much weight to give to internal church rules, and how much to defer to denominations on the interpretation of those rules. This gives judges tremendous flexibility to reach almost any result—making the outcome unpredictable and "largely depende[nt] upon the predilections of the judges."[29]

By contrast, the strict approach makes no assumptions about the essence of an ecclesiastical association.

> The strict approach is preferable to the hybrid approach in three main respects. First, it protects free exercise rights by giving churches flexibility to adopt any form of governance they wish. Second, it prevents civil courts from becoming entangled in religious questions. And third, it promotes clear, stable property rights.[30]

McConnell and Goodrich attempt in good faith to give weight to the internal principles of religious institutions through the common law, but they are either

---

29 Ibid., 339.
30 Ibid., 327.

too optimistic about the capacity of secular institutions to accommodate ecclesiastical norms, or they share with American religious culture a preference for local governance. That secular institutions have been ambivalent in their treatment of churches over time and across denominations only exacerbates the lack of fit between civil and ecclesiastical governance.

There are at least three concerns that a legal and political pluralist might have about a strict application of the neutral principles approach. First, that it treats churches as ordinary voluntary associations *constituted* by the civil law, rather than as law-making institutions in their own right, whose adoption of secular forms is always imperfect and contingent. Second, the strict neutral principles approach expresses a preference of the *local* over the denominational that is not theologically neutral and becomes especially relevant when the civil courts change their doctrine for dealing with religious disputes. And, third, that the strict approach underestimates the *stability and predictability* that a rule of deference to ecclesiastical law might offer in securing property rights in cases of dissention or schism.

## Constitutive and Declarative Functions of Civil Law

It would be good to begin by explaining what is meant by a pluralist approach to the problem of church governance. Pluralism, in law and politics, is a descriptive claim about normative phenomena. Political pluralists claim that, in any society, there exist multiple claims to ultimate authority, each grounded on an independent basis of legitimacy and not reducible or rankable against the other. Legal pluralists make similar claims about legal systems, that there exist a multiplicity of legal systems that overlap over a given population.[31] While there are many historical sources to political and legal pluralism, some of the most influential—and most relevant to our case—are religious. The Anglican theologian and historian John Neville Figgis described the church, from a political perspective, as "the body of all the faithful with rights and powers inherent and unconnected with the state."[32] And historian and legal theorist Harold Berman insisted that the claims of the medieval church to legal autonomy "is reproduced in contemporary resistance to legal control over belief and morality."[33]

It is true that a church is many things, not only an institution constituted by a system of rules. Even those churches most commonly identified with hierarchy and legal form, like the Roman Catholic Church, can be conceived in different ways. In a celebrated treatise, Avery Cardinal Dulles, enumerates conceptions of the church as "mystical communion," "sacrament," "herald," "servant." But the

---

31 Víctor M. Muñiz-Fraticelli, *The Structure of Pluralism* (Oxford: Oxford University Press, 2014), 17–30; Víctor M. Muñiz-Fraticelli, "Theorizing Justice under Conditions of Global Legal Pluralism," in *The Oxford Handbook to Global Legal Pluralism*, ed. P. S. Berman (Oxford: Oxford University Press, 2020), 295–313, 297–98.
32 John Neville Figgis, *Churches in the Modern State* (London, New York [etc.]: Longmans, Green and Co., 1913), 217.
33 Harold Berman, *Law and Revolution* (Cambridge: Harvard University Press, 1983), 269.

first definition that he gives is that of the church as a *societas perfecta*, "a 'perfect society' in the sense that it is subordinate to no other and lacks nothing required for its own institutional completeness."[34] Put in less expressly theological language, the church as an institution is a compete legal system that contains both primary and secondary rules, including rules of recognition that do not depend on those of civil law.[35]

A salient example of this is the assertion of authority over temporal goods in the Roman Catholic Code of Canon Law, which asserts that "to pursue its proper purposes, the Catholic Church by innate right is able to acquire, retain, administer, and alienate temporal goods independently from civil power," though commentators clarify that it is "the right and duty of the civil authority to regulate the exercise of religious freedom in the interest of public order."[36] It is true that not all religious denominations make their assertions of autonomy in a tone as categorical or juridical as the Roman Catholic Church, but all are norm-making and law-making bodies or, in Robert Cover's terms, *jurisgenerative*.[37] In an exhaustive study of Christian law-making, Norman Doe declares that

> Christians are prolific legislators. The laws they make are a meeting-place of faith and action. Of the twenty-two world church families, the churches of the ten studied here all have laws and other regulatory instruments. Alongside the Bible and service books for worship, these law books are central to the institutional lives of these churches.[38]

Now, McConnell and Goodrich readily concede that internal church rules "are understood as a species of church law, enforceable through the internal mechanisms of church authority, such as excommunication, refusal to ordain ministers unless the canon is obeyed, or other means."[39] They are not, however, ordinarily enforceable in civil court. In their view, it is not the internal rules of churches that should be used to discern the intention of parishes and denominations with regard to property, but rather the civil instruments that congregants have used to give civil form to their intentions. This analogizes churches to voluntary associations of various kinds and to entities like the charitable trust and the not-for-profit corporation.

In the case of ordinary business or nonprofit corporations, however, it is generally accepted that the entity does not come into existence until the legal

---

34 Avery Cardinal Dulles, *Models of the Church* (New York: Image Books Doubleday, 2002), 26.
35 Even if a church admits to being governed by the civil law of the state—as some national churches might—this concession operates ordinarily by virtue of internal church rules themselves.
36 Canon 1254, John P. Beal, James A. Coriden, and Thomas J. Green. *New Commentary on the Code of Canon Law* (New York: Paulist Press, 2000), 1453–54.
37 Robert Cover, "Nomos and Narrative," *Harvard Law Review* 97 (1983): 4.
38 Norman Doe, *Christian Law* (Cambridge: Cambridge University Press, 2013), 384.
39 McConnell and Goodrich, "On Resolving Church Property Disputes," 322.

formalities have been met. A corporate charter or a deed of trust are constitutive of the business corporation and the trust. In the case of most religious institutions, this is not the case. From a purely historical perspective, the existence of many churches—and especially those churches most often embroiled in property disputes—the existence of the institution is prior to the secular legal forms through which it is recognized. Even for churches of more recent vintage, the religious community preexists the formal constitution of the church.

Perry Dane suggests that the "rhetoric [of the neutral principles approach] does not as clearly recognize the independent juridical and normative dignity of religious institutions"[40] One way to recognize this normative dignity is by emphasizing the distinction between merely secular associations and churches. In the case of churches, civil forms are merely *declarative*, not constitutive, of the churches' corporate existence, and only imperfectly so. State legal form would need to be complemented by looking at the organization's principles of the church and not adhered to blindly as if the secular form constituted the entire reality of the organization.

The distinction between *declarative* and *constitutive* legal form is consistent with the tradition of British political pluralism and the more obviously pluralist members of the New Religious Institutionalism.[41] Among the British pluralists, Frederick W. Maitland argues that the positive law should offer associations the broadest catalogue of instruments to order their affairs as they see fit.[42] John N. Figgis agrees and adds that the changes and amendments of the political constitution of a church should be in the hands of the corporate body, and that the state should have no part in shaping it, although he admits that the state may require marks of registration to ensure that the existence of the association is public, that it can answer to third parties, and that the state is to be "guardian of property and interpreter of contract."[43]

## *Legal Change and Ecclesiastical Law*

The limitation of the strict neutral principles approach is magnified if we take a historical view of the regulation of ecclesiastical polities. Civil legal norms should not encourage certain ecclesiastical forms over others, by either directly favoring hierarchy or creating incentives towards it. But because the fit between

---

40 Perry Dane, "The Varieties of Religious Autonomy," in *Church Autonomy: A Comparative Survey*, ed. Gerhard Robbers (Frankfurt am Main: Peter Lang, 2001), 11.
41 See, for instance, Richard W. Garnett, "Do Churches Matter? Towards an Institutional Under-standing of the Religion Clauses," *Villanova Law Review* 53 (2008): 273; Richard W. Garnett, "The Freedom of the Church," *Journal of Catholic Social Thought* 4 (2007): 59; Paul Horwitz, *First Amendment Institutions* (Cambridge: Harvard University Press, 2012).
42 F. W. Maitland, "Trust and Corporation," above note 16.
43 John Figgis, "The Church and the Secular Theory of the State," in *The Pluralist State: The Political Ideas of JN Figgis and His Contemporaries*, ed. David Nicholls, 2nd ed. (Oxford: St. Martin's Press, 1994), 158.

ecclesiastical and civil law is never perfect, the decisions of civil courts tend to create incentives (or disincentives) for churches to make the effort to craft the secular legal instruments that would most closely approximate their self-understanding.

Sometimes, the hostility of civil courts can provoke a defensive response by the church that can distort and deform an ecclesiastical tradition. Other times, even a sympathetic attitude can have a negative effect, as a change in the standard interpretation used by civil courts may change the assumptions under which a church was operating and require that the ecclesiastical authorities make explicit in civil law what had only been articulated in ecclesiastical law. In nearly all these cases, adherence to a strict neutral principles standard has historically favored the local over the denominational interest, either deliberately or by omission.

McConnell and Goodrich worry that the "hybrid" approach's reliance on internal church documents creates a bias in favor of national churches, who ultimately control the drafting of internal rules. This leads to a centralizing ratchet of authority over church property and governance. Ultimately, the worry about centralization of authority is directed at the *Watson* deference approach. The *Watson* court classified churches as hierarchical or congregational and gave complete deference to the internal rules of hierarchical churches. The "hybrid" approach reaches the same conclusion in the opposite direction. By making internal church rules dispositive of internal church disputes, the "hybrid" approach effectively defers to the body within the church that has the power to make, alter, and interpret those rules.

But it is not clear that either a strict or a hybrid approach leads to a ratcheting effect. The clearest example of increased hierarchization in American legal history involved Roman Catholic ecclesiastical retrenchment in the face of a strict application of principles of law that ignored (willfully, in that case) the history, traditions, structure, and internal norms of the religious body. The other instance in which hierarchical structures were formally instituted occurred at the (admittedly equivocal) invitation of the Supreme Court itself, and only because an unexpected change in the approach taken by civil courts. These situations are best illustrated by example.

### *The Trusteeism Controversy in the Roman Catholic Church*

In the early nineteenth century, the Roman Catholic Church in the United States (and, to a lesser extent, in the Atlantic provinces of Canada) was fraught with struggles over the control of ecclesiastical institutions. Catholics in European countries where the Roman church was established or recognized through a concordat were used to having the authority of bishops recognized through the direct application of canon law over parish, priests, and laity, or through special legislation governing the organization of Roman Catholic institutions. The parish retained legal personality and the laity were often involved in its administration, but if there was a dispute, Episcopal authority was recognized as paramount, regardless of who ostensibly held title in a secular legal document. The structure of the church was laid out in canon law and considered binding on Catholics regardless of state forms of property ownership or administration.

In colonial America (both the future United States and Canada), American Catholics had set up their institutions without a thought for the legal and political condition of the new country. After the revolution, tensions arose between laypersons and the episcopate over control. The issue was the discrepancy between canon law, which dictates that while parishes have independent legal personality (thus allowing them to contract for services and purchase or lease property on their own), they ultimately answer to the bishop of the diocese, as do all Catholics. But in the early nineteenth century, many parishes were administered by boards of lay trustees and organized through secular state trust instruments. Because of a mix of ethnic tensions in the immigrant Catholic population and the infusion of republican enthusiasm, some lay trustees (and a few sympathetic priests) decided that if they held title to property under common law, they would use their legal position to assert their preferences over church policy and personnel, even over the bishop's objections.

State courts—encouraged as much by principled republican advocates as by nativist know-nothings—often upheld the legal title of rebellious lay trustees over the assertions of ecclesiastical discipline by local Catholic bishops.[44] After two decades of dispute, the Vatican became involved and threatened the insurgent lay trustees with heresy (the heresy of "trusteeism"). In the United States, the Third Plenary Council of Baltimore laid down regulations that effectively ended the controversy. They recommended that all diocesan property in common law countries be vested in a trust whose only trustee was a corporation sole in the person of the bishop. This effectively eliminated formal lay participation in the management of church property and made the American Church far more hierarchical than it had been even in countries with a formal concordat or established Roman Catholic worship. The effects of the turn towards episcopal control, and especially the ownership of diocesan property by a corporation sole in the person of the bishop (buttressed by the supervisory authority granted by the Code of Canon Law, e.g., canon 1276) have been a continual problem for the Roman Catholic Church, especially in periods of greater lay involvement.[45] But the concern that civil courts will see any relaxation in ownership rules as an opportunity to force the church to democratize is a deterrent to more decentralized administration.

## *Legal Change, the Dennis Canon, and the Episcopal Church*

The history of the Episcopal Church in the United States shows that ecclesiastical authority was contested in the early days of the republic but settled into a stable form in which bishops, in council, eventually constituted a national body justified theologically on the ground that episcopal authority exists by mutual recognition

---

44 Patrick W. Carey, *People, Priests, and Prelates* (Notre Dame: University of Notre Dame Press, 1987), 50–56, 93–106.
45 Ibid., 290–92.

of the conclave. There was no doubt, however, that the church was hierarchical, all the way though to its name. What distinguished Episcopalians from Congregationalists or Baptists, for instance, was the local congregation's subjection to a bishop. This was rarely articulated in explicit trust language, in part because the *Watson* standard of deference made this unnecessary.

> The *Watson* deference rule, while ostensibly favorable to the national churches, laid a trap for those denominations such as the Protestant Episcopal Church and United Presbyterian Church that relied on it. Because deference to ecclesiastical tribunals does not require the national church to create explicit trust documents with its parishes in order for a court to find for the denomination when the parish breaks away, denominations largely avoided creating such explicit trusts with individual parishes. This was a reasonable decision at the time; the legal system produced the result that individual parish trusts would have created anyway, but without the added cost and awkwardness.[46]

When the Supreme Court decided *Jones v. Wolf*, the national churches were unprepared for the new standard of deference. But the underlying juridical reality of the churches had not changed. Three months after the *Jones* decision, the Episcopal Church held its General Convention. Guided by the paragraphs in the decision that invited churches to modify ecclesiastical instruments to ensure that parish property would be retained by the national church in cases of schism, and worried about growing dissent about the church, modified the Canons of the Episcopal Church to state that "All real and personal property held by or for the benefit of any Parish, Mission, or Congregation is held in trust for this Church."[47] The worry was that many parishes that dissented from the national church's stance towards the consecration of women and LGBT persons as bishops would leave the church, or at least the more liberal dioceses, and take the parish property with them.

The worries proved correct, and many decades of lawsuits followed, but the decisions of state courts were inconsistent. Almost invariably, courts that adopted a hybrid approach and took into consideration the constitution and canons of the denominational churches sided with the national bodies, while those that took a strict approach and only looked to the civil law of trusts sided with the dissenting congregations. In the view of the "strict" courts, the national church could only impose a trust on the local congregation with the latter's consent, and not unilaterally. But, in the view of the Episcopal Church, the amendment to the church's canons had only clarified what had been the longstanding relationship between the national church and its local congregations.

---

46 Brian Schmalzbach, "Confusion and Coercion in Church Property Litigation," *Virginia Law Review* 96 (2010): 443, 446.
47 The Presbyterian Church adopted similar language in its constitution. Schmalzbach, "Confusion and Coercion in Church Property Litigation," 454.

In relation to the Episcopal Church cases, Kent Greenawalt observes that,

> Ignoring provisions regarding property because they happen to be in a church constitution that covers matters of faith is, for example, quite unjustified. Demanding explicit trust language for transactions that occurred at a time when general churches reasonably expected to succeed without such language is also unjustified.[48]

In practice, the stricter interpretation of the neutral principles approach inverted the Episcopal form of government and effectively transformed the Episcopal Church into a congregational body by demanding that the hierarchy obtain the consent of individual parishes. Adherence to a strict neutral principles approach, in this case, forced a clearly hierarchical church to ratchet *down* its form of polity towards a more democratic model, even when this is contrary to its theology or traditions.

It would be good to contrast the case of the American Roman Catholic Church with that of the American Baptist Churches. But the power of the central body is itself determined by church rules, and rules can be drafted to facilitate or inhibit ratcheting. In a strongly congregational denomination, authority can be explicitly reserved to the local body. Examples include the *Covenant of Relationship* and the *By-Laws of the American Baptist Convention*, which repeatedly declare that each congregation is autonomous, has sole rights over its property, and has the right to withdraw from the covenant with a simple unilateral declaration, but also makes clear that none of the instruments that establish the coordinating bodies of the denomination can alter or affect this autonomy.[49]

The assumption McConnell and Goodrich make is that the central governing body of a denomination has nearly unfettered control over rulemaking inside the church, and thus that relying on internal church rules would create a ratchet towards ever-increasing centralization and away from local or democratic control. But the example of the American Roman Catholic Church shows that a centralizing ratchet may be encouraged by overzealous application of civil law against a clear theological structure, and the example of the Episcopal Church demonstrates that the strict neutral principles approach can ratchet down a church's hierarchical structure contrary to its history and traditions. Churches whose

---

48 Kent Greenawalt, *Religion and the Constitution*, vol. 1 (Princeton: Princeton University Press, 2006), 286.
49 "The Covenant of Relationships is not a legally binding instrument; it creates no legal rights or legal obligations between and among the organizations which enter in or for non-parties to it. The parties to the Covenant of Relationships disclaim any intent to form a legal joint venture or association. No party to the Covenant of Relationships has any power or authority over, or any legal responsibility for, the beliefs, persons or property of any American Baptist or any other organization or its governing board or property; nor does the Covenant of Relationships create or establish any organization which has such power, authority, or responsibility." *Autonomy and Interdependence within the American Baptist Denomination: A Declaration* [December 1983; GB1279].

ecclesiological principles mandate a congregational polity are able to prevent a ratchet towards increasing hierarchy by carefully structuring their own constitutions, but it is not a neutral stance for the civil law to create a presumption or inventive towards more democratic forms of polity.

The problem of correspondence between civil and ecclesiastical norms is a problem of change over time. Churches draft internal norms and civil instruments to reflect their ecclesiological self-conception, but they do so against certain assumptions about existing social and legal norms. When those norms change, the assumptions may no longer hold. What was implicit or taken for granted at the time a trust was created may require more explicit language if courts no longer adopt a deferential attitude towards church law. It is not clear, then, if an amendment to church rules changes relations between the congregation and the denomination or if it clarifies the existing norm. We should always ask, as Perry Dane wonders, "whether the state's secular legal categories have put the religious community in a straitjacket, or have, to the contrary, given it the means by which to successfully express its own constitutive norms."[50]

### Church Law in a Comparative Context

The final concern McConnell and Goodrich have about the hybrid approach is that it makes property rights uncertain. "If ownership no longer turns on publicly recorded deeds and trust instruments," they argue, "but on the meaning of internal church rules and relationships, no one can know for certain who owns church property—at least not without the benefit of a thorough trial."[51] Concern over the stability of property rights is arguably what encourages state courts to become involved in these disputes. Property appears to courts as an irreducibly temporal matter, inherently within their jurisdiction. As seen in the Waverly property case, disputes about property also affect more than the mere conscience of congregants. The interests of third parties may be intertwined with who owns a particular piece of real estate, which may serve as collateral for a loan or as an asset to be liquidated to compensate for damages in litigation. And, finally, there is an economic and equitable interest in having property be put to use, whether directly in the market or indirectly in service of the purposes—temporal or spiritual—of those whose interests are most closely aligned with it, because they either have materially contributed to the property or are most affected by its use.

The concerns over the stability of property rights are the most concrete objection to a pluralist approach, if no more because churches, congregants, and third parties rely on the rules of property and contract to make long-term plans and carry out their mission.[52] In order to function effectively, these rules have to be susceptible to a final authoritative interpretation—rules of property are no

---

50 Dane, "The Varieties of Religious Autonomy," 12.
51 McConnell and Goodrich, "On Resolving Church Property Disputes," 340.
52 I discuss this in more detail in *The Structure of Pluralism*, ch. 11, "Property, Personality, and Public Justification," 227–39.

rules at all if they are not settled (or capable of being settled, in cases of uncertainty). Does a strict neutral principles approach that relies exclusively on secular, civil documents in the adjudication of church property disputes provide greater certainty than one that allows the consultation of internal rules, canons, and constitutions? Almost certainly so. The question is whether, in simplifying the resolution of property disputes in the church, or any other organization, the structure of the religious tradition is distorted.

Some of these concerns have been addressed already but bear repeating. It is quite reasonable to argue that most of the work of building a parish is borne by the parishioners. Nearly all Christian traditions, whatever their ecclesiology, uphold the local church as the immediate site of spiritual and social life towards which the efforts of congregants are primarily directed. They differ, however, on whether the parish or local congregation is the ultimate locus of authority. It is the very definition of a hierarchical church that the locus of authority is beyond the local congregation, that local efforts are nonetheless ultimately guided by superior authority and may be directed away from the local congregation by the hierarchy. This is a tension that the hierarchy must bear in mind when making decisions that might alienate or frustrate local parishioners. Almost by definition, most disputes over church property arise when a majority of the local parish wants to sever relations with a superior denominational body. If the denomination prevails in court, they are often left with a much emptier building. This is a practical problem that the denomination must take into account—an externality of successful litigation, as it were, that it must internalize. This may lead to further negotiations with the unsuccessful litigants, who still hold a valuable asset in sheer number of parishioners. But it may just be that some churches are disinclined to sacrifice the principle of hierarchical governance for a larger congregation. The practical difficulties that such a result might have for parish and denominational life, however, is not a legitimate concern of the civil court. The alignment of the economic and equitable interests of local parishioners with authority and control over local property is an ecclesiological position that a civil court may not legitimately assume. Only a congregationalist preference towards localism would dictate that church governance follows local interest.

Other concerns about the predictability of property rights remain, especially regarding the stability of property rights in the long run. The question is not which standard would secure such stability simpliciter, but rather which would secure it while doing the least violence to the structures of governance of religious communities. The difficulties that have been visited on hierarchical churches over the decades after *Jones v. Wolf* have had as much to do with the change in doctrine and the lack of a clear standard as with the specific approach that has been adopted by the courts. It is helpful, then, to look to other jurisdictions that have faced similar controversies to see if an alternative is sufficiently stable. I will focus on the Canadian example because it is the one most closely influenced by American doctrine and concerns the same ecclesiastical bodies (mainly the Anglican Church in Canada, equivalent to the Episcopal Church in the United States).

Canadian courts have taken a different approach towards the resolution of ecclesiastical disputes, at once more doctrinally conservative yet more deferential towards church autonomy. The result is that Canadian law has generally recognized in churches the authority to generate, interpret, and revise both internal norms and theological doctrine while maintaining continuity in the ecclesiastical community.

Some clarification of the Canadian constitution and of the judiciary would be useful. The Canadian judiciary is differently structured than the American, as Canada has a unified judiciary with general jurisdiction. There are provincial trial courts and courts of appeal, but all disputes may be appealed to the Supreme Court. This differs sharply from the American case in which federal courts are courts of limited subject-matter jurisdiction and state courts have the final say on the interpretation of state law, including most property disputes. Nonetheless, few ecclesiastical disputes have reached the Supreme Court of Canada, and the most recent ones have remained at the level appellate level.[53] Canada, as its courts are quick to note, has no formal separation of church and state. Where the Constitution of the United States makes no reference to God and expressly enjoins Congress and the states from establishing religion or prohibiting its exercise, the Canadian Constitution opens with a declaration that "Canada is founded upon principles that recognize the supremacy of God and the rule of law."[54]

For many years, Canadian courts ostensibly followed the English "implied trust" rule that reserves the right of civil courts to examine the fidelity of a religious organization to its traditional doctrine when settling disputes over property, ministry, and membership and, with few exceptions, favored whichever faction in a dispute kept most truly to the substantive religious doctrine of the church at the time of creation of the trust.[55] Courts in Canada, as opposed to their American counterparts, were not constitutionally barred from resolving ecclesiastical disputes on a doctrinal basis. Nonetheless, despite these constitutional differences, Canadian courts have adopted a similar analytic framework as American courts regarding their involvement in religious disputes. The Canadian *Charter of Rights and Freedoms*, part of the constitutional reforms of 1982, rather than having a prohibition on legislative action respecting religion, affirmatively guarantees to "everyone . . . freedom of conscience and religion."[56] And while there is no "explicit textual limitation on government establishment of religion" in the Canadian Charter,[57] a textual basis for state neutrality can be found in a

---

53 The exception is a long line of cases involving Hutterite communities, which were as much disputes over membership as over property. For a thorough treatment of these, see Alvin Esau, *The Courts and the Colonies* (Vancouver: University of British Columbia Press, 2004).
54 Preamble to *Constitution Act*, 1982, being Schedule B to the Canada Act 1982 (UK), 1982, c 11.
55 M. H. Ogilvie, "Church Property Disputes," 387, in note 20 above.
56 *Canadian Charter of Rights and Freedoms*, s 2(a), Part 1 of the *Constitution Act*, 1982.
57 Jeremy Patrick, "Church, State and Charter: Canada's Hidden Establishment Clause," *Tulsa Journal of Comparative & International Law* 14 (2006): 25, 27.

combination of *Charter* clauses,[58] which has led scholars to conclude that, with some exceptions, there is substantial convergence in the constitutional regime on religious neutrality in Canada and the United States.[59]

Recent church property cases are no exception to the tendency towards convergence. Since the early 1990s, Canadian churches have been riven by the same divisions as their southern neighbors. In one of the first such disputes to come before the courts, the Superior Court of Ontario, in *United Church of Canada v. Anderson*, considered the case of three UCC congregations that voted to break with the national church because they could not accept the position of the General Council of the United Church on the issue of homosexuality, namely, the ordination of openly gay and lesbian ministers.[60] The court sided with the national church, on the basis of the express trusts created by the original incorporating documents of the United Church of Canada. It did not consider, however, the religious doctrine contained in the *Basis of Union*, the main creed of the United Church—"to preserve the inviolability of marriage and the sanctity of the family"—as it would have been held by congregants at the time of founding of the church, and which was incorporated into the founding documents of the United Church.

In a response to the *Anderson* decision, M. H. Ogilvie criticized the reluctance of the Canadian court to consider doctrinal continuity as a question of fact, a reluctance she attributed to American influence.[61] However, she suggested that courts move towards a stronger emphasis on internal ecclesiastical procedures, ensuring that religious groups follow their own norms for the adjudication of disputes and enforcing the decision of the appropriate church officials as a form of judicial review, which was the approach Canadian courts had taken in other internal disputes concerning church membership and discipline. This is the direction in which the courts moved in later years.

In a lengthy comparative study of American and Canadian approaches to church property disputes, Alvin Esau argued that in theory, Canadian courts are

---

58 The specific clauses are the guarantee of freedom of religion in section 2(a) and equality rights in section 15.
59 Christopher L. Eisgruber and Mariah Zeisberg, "Religious Freedom in Canada and the United States," *International Journal of Constitutional Law* 4 (2006): 244; Donald L. Beschle, "Does the Establishment Clause Matter? Non-Establishment Principles in the United States and Canada," *Journal of Constitutional Law* 4 (2002): 451. Some of the differences, such as the financing of religious schools, have converged even further in recent years, after the US Supreme Court decision in *Trinity Lutheran Church of Columbia, Inc. v. Comer*, 582 U.S. ___ (2017), while in other areas, such as the acceptance of public prayer at municipal events, the courts have reached different decisions but not diverged much in terms of doctrine. Cf. the US Supreme Court decision in *Town of Greece v. Galloway*, 572 U.S. 565 (2014) with the Supreme Court of Canada's decision in *Mouvement laïque québécois v. Saguenay (City)*, 2015 SCC 16. I discuss these cases in more detail in "*Mouvement laïque québécois v. Saguenay*: Neutrality and Narrative," *SCLR* (2d) 76 (2016): 219.
60 *United Church of Canada v. Anderson* (1991), 2 OR (3d) 304 (Sup Ct).
61 Ogilvie, "Church Property Disputes," 393.

empowered to "untangle the mysteries of doctrinal religious trusts and declare that one group was heretical."[62] There are, in fact, several doctrines of "implied trusts" in Canadian law, and the courts have moved from a doctrinal to a more political or institutional trust doctrine. The original English doctrine, Esau explains, was of an *implied original doctrinal trust*, by which courts presume that church property is held in trust by the group that is most faithful to the original doctrine of the church at the time the property was acquired. The presumption is that churches cannot depart from fundamental doctrine unless the trust makes provision for such change. But such a rule arbitrarily assumes that church property grantors intended that religious doctrine be frozen in time.[63] Esau considers other possibilities. There is no reason to outright reject the possibility that the grantors intended an *organic trust*, by which a religious organization can change its doctrine by majority action (or by other specified provision).[64] Esau argues that switching to implied *organic* trust could open the door to courts abandoning the all-or-nothing approach to determining property entitlements in the case of schisms within the church. Implied organic trusts allow courts to change the underlying presumptions, including those of resolving property disputes. But implied *organic* trusts leave the disposition of property in more uncertain terms and are vulnerable to the very valid criticism that it will lead judges to enact their preferences for fairness or equity into ecclesiastical orders.

Esau suggests instead that Canadian courts have gravitated towards express or implied *original affiliation* trusts, which only require the courts to decide whether affiliation with the mother church was part of the original trust.[65] In more recent articles discussing later developments in church property disputes, M. H. Ogilvie confirms that Canadian courts have moved in an institutional direction.[66] The current Canadian doctrine ostensibly rejects the American neutral principles approach because of its First Amendment pedigree, but in effect adopts the "hybrid" model. The Ontario court acknowledges that "disputes about religious doctrine are not appropriate for judicial determination" and expresses concern about "the real risk of misunderstanding the relevant religious tradition and culture, and that a mistaken decision could saddle the organization with difficult if not unworkable consequences."[67] The latter concern does not lead the court to

---

62 Alvin Esau, "The Judicial Resolution of Church Property Disputes: Canadian and American Models," *Alberta Law Review* 40 (2003): 767, 773–74.
63 Ibid., 775–76.
64 Ibid., 777.
65 Ibid., 783. M.H. Ogilvie has notes, correctly in my view, that Esau's considered position is analogous to Kent Greenawalt's, cited above in note 48.
66 M. H. Ogilvie, "Three Recent Cases" and "Judicial Restraint and Neutral Principles in Anglican Church Property Disputes: *Bentley v. Diocese of New Westminster*," *Eccl Law Journal* 13, no. 2 (2011): 198, discussing *Bentley v. Anglican Synod of the Diocese of New Westminster*, 2010 BCCA 506; *Incorporated Synod of the Diocese of Huron v. Delicata*, 2013 ONCA 540; and *Pankerichan v. Djokis*, 2014 ONCA 709.
67 *Pankerichan v. Djokic*, par. 54–55.

ignore internal constitutions and canons of the church, however, but rather to consider them as it would the governance instruments of any other organization.

> [The Ontario Court of Appeal case] *Pankerichan* [*v Djokic*] confirmed two propositions. First, the proper approach to internal religious institutions disputes, including property disputes, is for courts to ensure that the religious institution has followed its own constitution by applying the normal rules of construction to constitutional documents such as incorporating legislation, by-laws and internal canons or codes of law and practice. Secondly, the normal principles of the common law relating to contract, trust and property apply, including any applicable legislation, whether public or private. Religious institutions operate within the secular realm and it should not surprise when secular law is applied.[68]

This position adopts the same standard in church property disputes as the one Canadian courts have adopted in disputes about membership and discipline within churches: that the role of the courts is circumscribed to ascertaining whether internal rules were complied with and, even then, substantial deference is given to the determination of the authorities within the religious institution.[69] In this way, the Canadian approach is a close approximation to the pluralist position. It takes religious organizations seriously as autonomous bodies, whose self-understanding, expressed through their internal norms, bears on the interpretation of the civil instruments that govern their temporal assets. That is not to say that these civil instruments are of no importance in discerning the relationship between past and present parishioners, local congregations, and national bodies, but rather that they are created, used, and interpreted against a background that includes and takes account of the institutional structure of the church.

## Conclusion

What distinguishes the pluralist position is that it takes seriously the misfit between civil law instruments and the organizing principles of religious organizations and does not substitute the judgment of the court above that of religious authorities in making sense of the structure of religious authority. The Canadian approach is no less neutral than the corresponding American approaches, strict or hybrid,

---

68 Ogilvie, "Three Recent Cases," 542.
69 See, most recently, *Highwood Congregation of Jehovah's Witnesses (Judicial Committee) v. Wall*, 2018 SCC 26, and *Ethiopian Orthodox Tewahedo Church of Canada St. Mary Cathedral v. Aga*, 2021 SCC 22. Both cases involved the expulsion of members from their respective congregations. But see *Sandhu v. Siri Guru Nanak Sikh Gurdwara of Alberta*, 2015 ABCA 101, in which the Alberta Court of Appeal found that a minority in a religious corporation had been treated oppressively by the majority under general principles of corporate law. I doubt that the decision would stand after the two cases cited earlier, but the matter has not come before the Supreme Court.

but locates neutrality not in the instrument of civil law but in the institutional integrity of the religious institution. The result has been no less predictable or less certain than the American approaches, although the track record for national denominations has certainly been more positive. But it is incorrect to say that the fact that the Anglican Church of Canada has been able to retain its property in Canada—and in most American states adhering to the hybrid principles approach—is evidence that the approach is itself biased. The same may be said, in reverse, of the strict neutral principles approach, which almost always results in a victory for breakaway parishes.

The Anglican and Episcopal churches may succeed in asserting the authority of the hierarchy because they are in fact hierarchical. If the denominational structure is congregational, as is the Baptist church, parishioners can rest assured that labor and property contributed to the local church will remain in its hands. More complex corporate structures, like the Roman Catholic Church, may divide ownership and authority in different ways, some not clearly contemplated by civil instruments. For instance, every parish in the Roman Catholic Church possesses its own legal personality, as do dioceses and other religious bodies, but all are subject to the authority of bishops and, in some cases, the Roman Pontiff, so they may possess title to their parochial and diocesan property—which may be important in cases of insurance or liability—but lack authority to alienate this property without authorization by a superior. The details of governance may change, but there is tremendous continuity in the form of ecclesiastical polity, certainly more so than in the civil instruments adopted by religious bodies or the standard that civil courts use to evaluate them.

The pluralist position, whether in the Canadian approach or some version of the American hybrid neutral principles, is not without problems. It certainly assumes, as McConnell and Goodrich rightly observe, that whatever else a church is, as a religious *institution* it is constituted by its own internal rules. But the pluralist denies that this assumption is unwarranted. Rather, it asserts that greater violence is done to a church's self-understanding in *not* assuming that donors, parishioners, and third parties are aware of a congregation's denominational membership and take that affiliation into account when considering their dealings with the church. All disputes about church property involve uncertainty about the intention of a donor or the priorities of past and present congregants. The question is whether it serves the church best to have a civil judge discern the intent of past and present members, or to treat the church as a self-regulating institution, in effect, as a separate and autonomous jurisdiction.

# 8 Markets as Moral Contexts
## An Account Based in Catholic Theological Anthropology

*Christina McRorie*

### Introduction

American public and legal discourse often operates with an implicit view of markets as definitionally "free" spaces in which individuals exercise their preferences without being coerced, and without themselves coercing others. As a result, we tend to assume markets are largely apolitical contexts—and, in a sense, even private ones, in that they are not spaces in which we expect to make explicit claims over each other's actions, preferences, or religious and moral identities. Instead, the reigning law is generally something like "to each their own." The main exception to this is the power held by government, of course, but we often think of regulation as being justified on the grounds that it simply ensures that markets maximize freedom in practice as well as in theory, and that we are indeed leaving each other alone. This conception thus casts political and economic contexts as dramatically different.

Despite the hold that this caricature has upon the American imagination (and perhaps on our jurisprudence, as well[1]), it has obvious problems. This is evident in current disagreements over whether putatively private expressions of moral preferences in business can "spill over" and become coercive to others (perhaps by unduly shaping the opportunity horizons of one's customers or employees, for example), and what to do about if they can. In considering this possibility, we are grappling with the fact that private economic choices sometimes *do* seem to impact others in quantifiable and observable ways. In our struggle to clarify what is at stake in those cases, we often turn to rights language, although this pushes beyond the American expectation that the only rights relevant in markets are negative ones and therefore leads us into conceptually murky waters. While the ideal typical depiction of markets as realms of pure freedom in which agents do not influence each other is not necessarily the sole cause of this confusion, it certainly compounds it.

The point of this chapter is to outline an additional, and distinctively theological, account of why this implicit picture of markets serves us so poorly, and of

---

1 See e.g., Paul Horwitz, "The Hobby Lobby Moment," *Harvard Law Review* (2014): 154–89, https://harvardlawreview.org/wp-content/uploads/2014/11/vol128_horwitz_comment.pd.

DOI: 10.4324/9781003309291-9

what is at stake with regard to decisions about how to shape markets and how to act within them. Specifically, it explains that the presuppositions structuring the Catholic account of human nature led to the conclusion that markets enable us to impact each other in often invisible and perhaps even unquantifiable ways, because they allow us to influence each other's moral character. In this view, markets are thus significantly *moral* contexts (although, to be clear, their specific moral quality varies from setting to setting). Their moral character is not the result of any unique or especially formative powers residing in markets themselves, however, but the result of the fundamental plasticity of human nature and our susceptibility to moral formation by all our social contexts. The analysis modeled here thus suggests that economic life is much more akin to political and cultural life than the assumption that markets are uniquely "free" would lead us to expect. In the economy as much as in politics and culture, we are all potentially influencing each other as moral agents, whether we know it or not (and, of course, with varying levels of power). And, even more to the purposes of this volume, because moral formation inevitably has political implications, this indicates that apparently private economic decisions may still bear importantly on the character of our shared democratic life, and therefore that markets are to a certain extent always political and public spaces.

Given its specific focus on habituation, the Catholic theological perspective deployed here provides a lens of analysis that renders this fact of our mutual influence in markets particularly visible. Moreover, it offers a rich language with which to take up the questions raised when we notice this influence. As this chapter will explain, this language situates human life in markets within the larger theological drama of salvation and the moral life, through the use of concepts like sin, grace, and sanctification. Indeed, on a Catholic reading, markets enable us to mediate God's grace to each other by encouraging virtue in one another—or to do the opposite. Because this tradition links virtue and freedom, markets also thus enable us to support each other's experience and exercise of true freedom, or to oppose it.

While this chapter develops its analysis in this confessional idiom, its goal is not necessarily to convince readers to share this specific theological reading of markets. Rather, it aims to invite the reader to examine their own presuppositions about human nature, and the implications of these for how we view markets. Above all, it argues that insofar as readers find any of the anthropological starting points used here plausible or compelling (with regard to the formative power of habituation, for example, or the inadequacy of accounts of freedom that focus exclusively on choice), that they therefore have solid grounds on which to reject caricatures of markets as straightforwardly "free" spaces in which we merely express our agency, but are not ourselves significantly acted upon or formed as agents. Indeed, in the view sketched here, the fact that we are always potentially being formed by our contexts, indicates that stakes of decisions about and within markets are quite high.

What to do about these stakes, of course, is a separate question entirely, and not one that the analysis offered here proposes to neatly resolve. Theological concerns about freedom and character do not map tidily onto existing arguments "for" or "against" free trade or regulation, and by no means supersede or replace important considerations of observable coercion, material justice, and rights. If anything, attention to moral formation only promises to further complicate public discussions about the place of law in markets, given the plurality of views on what counts as virtue in contemporary America. In addition to modeling how the resources of this specific religious tradition can be used to approach this complexity, the larger argument of this chapter is that this is a complexity we cannot avoid, if we are to speak adequately and responsibly about markets as social contexts.

In what follows, this chapter develops this argument in three sections. The first of these explains the confessional perspective from which it hails by providing a sketch of a broadly Catholic account of moral agency. This focuses on the role of habituation in moral formation and provides a brief introduction to how this is linked with the tradition's "substantive" account of liberty, noting what distinguishes this from more choice-centered or "procedural" accounts. This section explains that this theological anthropology assumes that we each have a role to play in supporting each other's moral formation and experience of freedom and describes this role as one of mediating God's grace.

The second section applies the approach to social analysis generated by this theological anthropology to markets and explains what it means to view a social context as moral. It explains how this theological analysis aligns with and differs from the attention paid to the morally formative powers of markets in other disciplines and offers a few illustrations of this perspective being brought to bear upon specific market settings.

A final section reflects on what a Catholic perspective can contribute to wider conversations about markets, law, and democracy. Above all, this chapter suggests, it urges us to consider how high the stakes are of all decisions about how to structure the economic contexts in which we live, whether those decisions are made by public or private actors. Moreover, this view invites us to engage in granular, specific analysis of specific markets, with attention to their moral complexity. Such analysis does not promise to yield tidy conclusions about what to do about hard cases at the intersection of religion, democracy, and economics. To avoid it, however, would be to ignore an important aspect of the exercise of moral agency in markets, and perhaps to miss part of why we feel so vexed by hard cases in the first place, as well.

## Catholic Theological Anthropology

I begin by sketching the broad contours of the Christian view of the human person as a moral agent, focusing on two themes particularly present in Catholic thought: habituation and a substantive account of human freedom as something we receive at least as much as we exercise. As we will see, both of these direct our attention to the complicated way that an individual's social context interacts with his or her moral agency.

## Habituation

The first of these is summed up easily enough: it is the presupposition that character is formed through repeated action. This is an insight at the foundation of virtue ethics, which locates the goal of the moral life not in isolated instances of performing good actions but in an overall process of becoming the kind of person who acts well, because they are good. In this approach, one builds virtues and thus becomes this good person by acting well over time. In the *Nichomachean Ethics*, Aristotle likened this to the process of learning to play the harp through repeated practice; so, in turn, do "we become just by doing just acts, temperate by doing temperate acts, [and] brave by doing brave acts."[2] Through repetition, a course of action that may have initially been awkward, extrinsically motivated, or even accidental eventually becomes natural and reflexive to an agent, who thus acquires the related virtue as a kind of skill, or habit.

This habit not only makes its specific activity increasingly effortless for the agent but also shapes the agent's perception of the subject overall; just as a skilled carver and a novice may see a particularly knotty piece of wood in a different light, so might a brave and a cowardly person view a dangerous situation with different eyes. As the scholastic Thomas Aquinas (who integrated Aristotelian thought into the Christian tradition, and whose articulation of virtue ethics remains foundational in Catholic moral theology today) put it, the virtues are "operative habits," or dispositions, that perfect and order "the powers of the soul . . . to that which is outside."[3] Virtues (and vices) thus shape persons as entire agents, not merely strengthening certain powers of action, but also orienting them to the world around them in new ways.

Being attentive to the power of habituation directs us to consider the moral stakes, in a sense, of any force or factor influencing an agent's choices. In this view, the moral import of an individual action exceeds its specific and one-time moral valence, since actions add up to character. Therefore, anything that attempts to influence my actions—however subtly—may also be making a bid to influence me as a moral agent, and to affect my very personhood—at least, if the nudge in question relates to anything more than trivial, non-moral matters. And this influence can go either way, since virtues and vices alike are habits and dispositions formed through repeated action.

With regard to this influence, the reader will have noticed that the use of qualifying language such as "attempts" and "making a bid" places a certain amount of distance between external forces and the agent's ultimate character; this distance is critical. Neither Aquinas nor Aristotle before him assumed that individuals were merely the product of their environment. And neither ever suggested that an agent

---

2 Aristotle, *Nichomachean Ethics*, ed. H. Rackham, Loeb Classical Library (Cambridge, MA: Harvard University Press, 1926), 73, https://www-loebclassics-com.proxy.wm.edu/view/aristotle-nicomachean_ethics/1926/pb_LCL073.73.xml.
3 Thomas Aquinas, *Summa Theologiae*, trans. Fathers of the English Dominican Province (New York: Benziger Brothers, 1948), I–II q. 55, a. 2.

could be morally formed against or without reference to their own will (à la behaviorism). Indeed, as a tradition based in the profession of belief, Christianity is known for an emphasis on the centrality of the individual's free will to their moral progress, and even to their identity as Christian and salvation status—we must freely choose to profess faith, and then exert the moral effort required to live our lives accordingly. A theological analysis of the importance of an agent's context, then, will never go so far as to suggest that external influences determine or remove our agency.

However, even this brief mention of the individual's salvation status points us toward the complexity and even elusive nature of the Christian concept of free will—because, of course, the basic Christian narrative begins from the assumption that a defect in our will is part of why humanity needs saving in the first place. As a result of an initial Fall due to sin,[4] we have been left with damaged moral agency, in a sense, and no longer have truly free will. Specifically, we are not capable of wholeheartedly desiring or effectively pursuing our highest good, which is God. For this we need divine assistance, or grace. One of the effects of this grace operating in and on our lives is that it slowly reshapes our agency itself, by reorienting our desires in a positive direction, and "freeing" our will.

## *Freedom*

This brings us to our second central theme within Catholic anthropology: its conception of freedom. While the fact that we are reformed with divine assistance might sound as if grace thus tampers with our agency, the theological claim is that actually this lends us the integrity and freedom we previously lacked. This conclusion relies on the presupposition that true freedom is found in the experience of desiring and being able to act for the good, rather than in the mere ability to express one's preferences through choice, without regard for the content of those preferences. If we need to be helped along and even reformed so as to enjoy this kind of freedom, then so be it. Indeed, we might go so far as to claim that only when our wills are "tampered" with so as to be oriented toward our true flourishing, do our choices become truly free. Or, put differently, we might say that true freedom is something we receive and cooperate with, rather than something we can claim or exercise unaided.[5]

This account of freedom is clearly at odds with the classic and ideal-typical conception of freedom operative in most of Western and modern thought, in which agents are free if others refrain from acting upon them, and if they are not themselves constrained when acting.[6] Modern thought thus tends to rely on a

---

4 An "event" which, it may be worth noting, is more usually understood in Catholic thought as etiological than historical, and as explanatory or sense-making than as juridical. E.g., see Joseph Cardinal Ratzinger, *'In the Beginning . . .': A Catholic Understanding of the Story of Creation and the Fall* (Grand Rapids: Eerdmans, 1995).
5 On this, see *The Catechism of the Catholic Church*, 1730–42.
6 Aside from the minimal limits required to protect the same freedoms for others, naturally—but in this view, those are so legitimate as to arguably not count as true "constraints."

negative, or procedural, account of liberty, which makes determining whether an agent is free a fairly straightforward and technical matter.[7] Such a determination does not require normatively evaluating the ends toward which an agent acts; these are taken as given, and irrelevant. In contrast, in this theological narration freedom is a markedly value-laden and substantive concept, the application of which leads into the murky waters of normative judgments about which desires are truly good, and about what flourishing truly entails.

This conception of freedom adds another layer to the theological analysis of context being developed here. The above section explained that a social setting that encourages us to act in morally significant ways is potentially influencing our character through a process of habituation. Now, the link between moral formation and freedom indicates that this influence may further be supporting or inhibiting our ability to experience true freedom, as well. One implication of this is that observable coercion is not the only threat to our liberty: forces that encourage us to form vicious habits and to desire ends inimical to our flourishing also make a bid to chip away at our ability to be free, however subtle these forces may be. Another is that when we put in place forces that support right action, we are empowering (or, at the very least, encouraging) each other to be more free.

This all suggests that we each wield a significant amount of power over each other. This is especially true given the connections between moral formation, freedom, and God's grace. While the term grace carries a number of related meanings in theology, here it has the sense of sanctifying grace, or the unmerited assistance humans receive from God that helps them grow in virtue.[8] While talk of such sanctifying grace can sound rather ethereal and otherworldly, since Vatican II the tradition has emphasized that this process intersects with and is mediated through the ordinary activities of our everyday lives. Our wills are reoriented not in a spiritual vacuum but through the mundane and yet also mysterious process of moral progress over time, as we exert effort in an attempt to cooperate with grace.[9] Neither do we undergo this process alone: often, the morally strengthening aid that we so need comes to us through the actions of others, who mediate this grace to us by supporting or encouraging our positive habituation, sometimes by being winsome and accessible moral exemplars. Indeed, because we need grace in order to experience the freedom to which we are called, we need the help of others—and we are charged with mediating grace to them, in

---

7 For further reflections on the distinction between this and the theological view of freedom mentioned here, see David Burrell, *Faith and Freedom: An Interfaith Perspective* (Malden, MA: Blackwell, 2004), especially 143–55.
8 This represents a significant difference between Aristotelian and Thomistic/Christian virtue ethics; in the latter, all growth in virtue is ultimately underwritten by God, even if its proximate cause in this life is human effort.
9 Our capacity and therefore duty to cooperate with grace is a characteristic emphasis of Catholic theology and anthropology in particular, where it is called "synergism," in contrast with some "monergistic" Protestant theologies, which focus exclusively on God's agency in salvation and/or sanctification.

turn, as well. While not reducible to each other, the moral life and the social life are inextricably intertwined, and our experience of God's help often arrives to us through the neighbor.

## Markets in This View

The application of this theological worldview to markets is simply stated: in this view, when market settings facilitate or encourage us to make good choices, they are also facilitating or encouraging us to become good persons, and thus supporting our ability to receive grace and experience freedom. Where markets do the opposite, they are in turn inhibiting our (correct) moral formation and militating against our ability to receive grace and be truly free. And, because markets are not self-instituting, this further implies that those who design, limit, or in any morally significant way shape the markets in which we act are thus possibly influencing our character, and possibly either mediating grace to us or working against its mediation.

A number of points of clarification are in order. The first is that the same claim could be made about any of the other spaces, structures, or institutions that host our everyday lives, and those who shape them. Nothing in this view suggests that markets are special, at least when it comes to the fact that they may interact with our moral agency. Familial, ecclesial, political, cultural, and other settings can also predispose us to virtuous or vicious action, and thus contribute to our moral formation or malformation (and indeed, often do both at once, in complicated admixtures). Markets are merely some of the spaces in which we are exposed to influences that can free or constrain us, and thus to which we ought to be alert.

The next point to keep in mind is that neither is there anything in this theological anthropology that tells us the precise nature of these moral influences *ex ante*, and apart from a consideration of particulars. There is certainly nothing that leads to the conclusion that markets are necessarily all the same, or even that any individual market is necessarily either all good or all bad as a moral context. It is true that the Christian tradition has long encouraged a moral suspicion of wealth, and especially of wealth in the face of poverty, as illustrated in its consistent depiction in the New Testament as both a "peril and obligation."[10] However, the intuition that wealth presents its own morally dangerous setting of sorts has never developed into a condemnation of either buying or selling, or what could be considered a specifically anti-market ethic.[11] Rather, Christian ethics has long enjoined buyers and sellers alike to treat each other fairly, based on the recognition that markets regularly host both coercion and justice.

---

10 Sondra Wheeler, *Wealth as Peril and Obligation: The New Testament on Possessions* (New York: Eerdmans, 1995). Before the modern era ushered in the recognition that wealth could be created (or, that not all financial transactions were zero sum), this suspicion extended to finance and seemingly effortless profit as well.
11 For one accessible introduction to the history of economic thought in Christianity, see Daniel Finn, *Christian Economic Ethics* (Minneapolis: Fortress Press, 2013).

Given this, assessing any moral suasion presented by an economic setting will require inquiry into a host of details: what sort of options and information does this market make available and salient to various parties, such as consumers, vendors, employees, managers, and so forth? Toward which choices does it steer them? How do these ways of acting reinforce, interrupt, or reshape these agents' existing dispositions, sensibilities, desires, and habits of attention? Do the ways that this setting encourages them to act conduce to their growth in virtue, and therefore their receipt of God's grace and experience of freedom—or does it work against this?[12]

It bears repeating that the answers to such questions will never indicate that a market will wholly determine an agent's character—it cannot. Neither can any other moral context: a childhood in a vicious family does not always lead to an adulthood of vice, for example, nor does citizenship in a virtuous polity necessarily lead to individuals becoming as tolerant, responsible, and solicitous of the common good as their neighbors and legal institutions have encouraged them to be. For both better and worse, we humans often push back quite successfully against that which and those who would form us. Out of recognition of our very formability and plasticity, however, most of us would argue that children who have been raised with morally problematic habits start the moral life at a kind of disadvantage, just as members of a generally morally upright community have been given a moral head start. In both situations, certain patterns of activity and relating to self and others will lead individuals to acquire certain dispositions almost automatically, which can only be changed later through effortful and reflexive work. Recognition of the immense power of this formation funds the Catholic tradition's longstanding emphases on parenting as a grave moral responsibility, and on the need for laws that inculcate virtue.[13] Even if they are never determinative, our social contexts *do* matter, quite a bit.

A current illustration of a theologically rooted attention to the ways in which specifically economic contexts matter can be found in Pope Francis' observations regarding the affective and spiritual dangers of inequality. In his 2013 exhortation *Evangelii Gaudium*, Francis laments the corrupting influences that economic segregation and inequality together can have upon those whose lives are comfortably insulated from vulnerability: our distance from suffering too often reorients our attention, distorts our sense of what counts as "news," and slowly

---

12 And alas, this already dense and granular line of questioning is *further* complicated by the fact that different individuals may experience a given economic contexts differently, due to variations in culture as well as individual character.

13 On law, e.g., see Aquinas, ST I-II q. 90–92; on the responsibility of parents to form their children, e.g., see John Chrysostom, *On Raising Children* and *On Marriage and Family*. For contemporary introductions to these topics that include surveys of the history of thinking in these areas, see Cathleen Kaveny, *Law's Virtues: Fostering Solidarity and Autonomy* (Washington: Georgetown University Press, 2012); Julie Hanlon Rubio, *Family Ethics: Practices for Christians* (Washington: Georgetown University Press, 2010), respectively.

renders us "incapable of feeling compassion at the outcry of the poor."[14] While Francis' primary concern is for the deprivation and exclusion that an unjust system metes out to the world's poorest, he does not overlook the moral influence that this same system can have on those who are well off. Given the nature of papal documents, Francis speaks to this subject largely in generalities; moral theologians have for some time addressed this phenomenon as it occurs in more local contexts, as well. Those addressing business ethics have taken up topics such as what constitutes and sustains virtuous leadership, how organizational structure "affects the moral formation" of employees, and how good businesses can "contribute greatly to the ... spiritual well-being of society."[15] Most recently, theologians have employed tools from critical realist social theory to analyze how specific economic structures enable, restrict, and incentivize various actions, and to illuminate the ways that our embeddedness within various social positions leads us to make decisions that are thus "free-but-constrained."[16]

### *Relation of This to Other Fields, and Illustrations*

Of course, theologians are not the only ones to have noticed that markets seem to have an effect on our character; since at least the Enlightenment there exists a well-developed legacy of reflection addressing precisely this. One strand of this celebrates markets' civilizing effects, and the way that engaging in commercial activity promotes virtues such as prudence, frugality, industry, honesty, and tolerance. In particular, early proponents of what came to be known as the *doux commerce* thesis observed that the expansion of trade seemed to reduce violence and warfare—that, in the words of Montesquieu, commerce "polishes and softens barbarian ways."[17] More recently, this has been extended to the claim that life in markets also inculcates democratic attitudes and the virtues required for

---

14 Pope Francis, "Evangelii Gaudium: Apostolic Ehortation of the Holy Father Francis to the Bishops, Clergy, Consecrated Persons and the Lay Faithful on the Proclamation of the Gospel in Today's World," November 24, 2013, St. Peter's, Rome, §53, www.vatican.va/content/francesco/en/apost_exhortations/documents/papa-francesco_esortazione-ap_20131124_evangelii-gaudium.html.

15 Michael Naughton, "Participation in the Organization: An Ethical Analysis from the Papal Social Tradition," *Journal of Business Ethics* 14, no. 11 (1995): 923–35, here 923; and Pontifical Council for Justice and Peace, *Vocation of the Business Leader: A Reflection* (2012), 2, respectively.

16 David Cloutier, "Introduction," in *Moral Agency Within Social Structures and Culture: A Primer on Critical Realism for Christian Ethics*, ed. Daniel Finn (Washington, DC: Georgetown University Press, 2020) 14. On this, see also Daniel Daly, *The Structures of Virtue and Vice* (Washington: Georgetown University Press, 2021).

17 Montesquieu, *Spirit of the Laws*, XX, 1, cited in Albert O. Hirschman, *The Passions and the Interests: Political Arguments for Capitalism Before Its Triumph* (Princeton: Princeton University Press, 1977), 60. See this for an introduction to this thesis and key critiques of it, as well as Albert O. Hirschman, *Rival Views of Market Societies and Other Recent Essays* (New York: Viking, 1986).

self-governance.[18] An equally robust strand of reflection argues precisely the opposite: that modern markets inevitably corrupt our character, enervate our political agency, and distract us from what truly matters in life. With roots in Romantic and Marxist critiques of modernity, and perhaps most fully developed in Frankfurt School-inspired analyses of consumerism, this line of thought continues to inform public conversations through scholarship on whether and where markets "crowd out" morals.[19]

While the concerns animating these literatures clearly overlap and resonate with the theological approach to markets outlined here, none perfectly map onto its ambivalent attitude or undertake the kind of granular inquiry it requires. This may be because a Catholic perspective on markets isn't ultimately *about* markets, per se; it begins in a theological reflection on the experience of being a moral agent and works out from there to how this ought to lead Christians to engage their various social contexts, which happen to include markets. In contrast, these non-theological fields tend to take as their sole subject "the market," and address its (singular) relation to our moral agency in the broadest of strokes. In terms of the attitudinal approach proposed here, perhaps closer to the mark are practical disciplines such as marketing or behavioral economics. Instead of addressing a single market writ large, these probe how economic behavior often responds to subtle and even minute shifts in our immediate contexts.[20] These fields may have even less in common with the fundamental values animating Catholic thought; the aim of advertising, in particular, is not to examine the plasticity of our agency for its own sake, but to ever more effectively steer (or, as some worry, manipulate[21]) behavior for the purpose of generating revenue. Nonetheless, the attention to detail in this scholarship provides useful insight into the constantly

---

18 See, e.g., Benjamin Friedman, *The Moral Consequences of Economic Growth* (New York: Knopf, 2005). For other recent work in this vein, see Deirdre Nansen McCloskey, *The Bourgeois Virtues: Ethics for an Age of Commerce* (Chicago: University of Chicago, 2006); Nathan B. Oman, *The Dignity of Commerce: Markets and the Moral Foundations of Contract Law* (Chicago: University of Chicago, 2016); for a Catholic defense of this thesis, see Michael Novak, *The Spirit of Democratic Capitalism*, 2nd ed. (Lanham, MD: Madison Books, 1991), 180–81.

19 The language of "crowding out" is Michael Sandel's; see, e.g., his *What Money Can't Buy: The Moral Limits of Markets* (New York: Farrar, Straus and Giroux, 2012), especially 44–93. For an introduction to Romantic and Marxist critiques of markets as they relate to theological critiques, in particular, see Eugene McCarraher, *The Enchantments of Mammon: How Capitalism Became the Religion of Modernity* (Cambridge, MA: Harvard University Press, 2019).

20 For an overview of a number of interesting studies that suggest rather small changes in context can have a measurable effect on economic behavior, see Kathleen Vohs, Nicole L. Mead, and Miranda R. Goode, "The Psychological Consequences of Money," *Science*, New Series 314, no. 5 (2006): 1154–56. For a broadly accessible introduction to the field of behavioral economics more generally, see Daniel Kahneman, *Thinking, Fast and Slow* (New York: Farrar, Straus and Giroux, 2011).

21 E.g. Shoshanna Zuboff, *Age of Surveillance Capitalism: The Fight for a Human Future at the New Frontier of Power* (New York: PublicAffairs, 2019).

changing ways that many of us are being shaped by the environments in which we make financial choices.

As an illustration of contexts that mediate influences to which we may wish to attend, consider three examples: the quasi-hidden market of slotting fees; the use of fuel economy labeling on new cars for sale; and marketing and product labeling used by mission-driven businesses. These vary widely, from the specific moral influences they exert and the populations they engage to the agents and parties responsible for the institution of these influences. Moreover, an initial glance at each invariably leads to further questions, many of which do not admit a single answer but nonetheless ought to have a place in a theologically informed consideration of various markets.

Through the use of slotting fees, producers and manufacturers pay supermarkets to carry and display their items, with higher prices for areas that yield more sales, such as aisle ends and at eye level. The fact that this practice has ballooned to become a multibillion-dollar industry speaks to its effectiveness: tweaks in product placement and presentation have million-dollar ramifications and yield measurable variance in consumer behavior.[22] The sorts of food products that generate the kinds of profit margins necessary to make such fees feasible are, of course, processed; one does not often see fresh vegetables or bulk whole grains displayed near cash registers, and for good reason. With this in mind, a theological analysis might ask whether many modern supermarkets are exposing us all to a kind of unfortunate moral luck, by paving the way for us to develop poor dietary habits. If so, in this regard they present a morally unhelpful context that subtly works against our integral flourishing. This line of inquiry only gains in urgency when considered alongside inequities in access to healthy foods, such as food deserts in impoverished and minority communities.

The opposite sort of influence may be operative in the case of the gas mileage disclosures required on new cars for sale in the United States after 2011. This was one of a number of attempts by the Obama administration to employ insights from behavioral economics to encourage what Cass Sunstein has termed "choice architectures," or decision-making contexts, that "influence people's behavior in order to make their lives longer, healthier, and better."[23] The idea was to take into account the cognitive biases and heuristics that structure and sometimes distort our decision-making processes to present choices in such a way as to "nudge"

---

22 While it is difficult to estimate the size of this industry, one study estimated it already at 16 billion in 2001: Ramarao Desiraju, "New Product Introductions, Slotting Allowances, and Retailed Discretion," *Journal of Retailing* 77, no. 3 (Fall 2004): 335–58, cited in Adam Rennhoff, "Paying for Shelf Space: An Investigation of Merchandising Allowances in the Grocery Industry," *Food Marketing Policy Center Research Report* 84 (2004). It may be worth mentioning arguments on behalf of the utility of slotting fees, most compellingly that they enable grocers and producers to share risk. However, such considerations do not address concerns about the promotion of products that do not support consumer health.

23 Richard Thaler and Cass Sunstein, *Nudge: Improving Decisions About Health, Wealth, and Happiness* (New Haven: Yale University Press, 2008), 5.

individuals without actually limiting their freedom of choice (through, for example, the use of default options, or labeling that frames options differently). In the updated fuel economy disclosures, the nudge in question was to encourage consumers to select more energy efficient cars through the use of labels that prominently feature an estimate of annual fuel costs for each vehicle, alongside how much this would "save" or "cost" a consumer in comparison to the average car in each vehicle class.[24] If these new labels have had the impact intended, an argument could be made that these have improved the auto sales market as a moral context, by making it easier for individuals to make choices that prudently steward not only the planet's resources but also their own.[25] However, we might also ask whether fuel economy labeling (on new cars, no less!) is rather "too little" and "too late" to amend our casual attitude toward fossil fuels, and whether a truly morally wholesome market would not be one that encourages individuals to structure their lives so as to rely less on scarce resources—through public transportation and walkable communities, perhaps.

Finally, consider the impact upon markets of benefit (or "B") corporations, social enterprises, and other forms of business organization that explicitly marry business' traditional pursuit of profit with a social or environmental mission. Such organizations have proliferated in recent years following the passage of legislation allowing directors of mission-driven corporations to consider non-financial interests in corporate governance. Most scholarly treatment of these organizations assesses the effectiveness of their "bottom up" attempts to promote social change by converting customers "a cup at a time," as in the case of the fair-trade coffee market.[26] Arguably, however, this attempt at conversion may also provide a related but distinct moral service to the consumers themselves. In their marketing and advertising, these companies regularly educate their audiences about the particular need or problem they address. Insofar as the issue or need addressed by such firms is morally urgent, where such marketing does in fact reorient consumers' sensibilities, habits of attention, and preferences, it could be said to support their moral formation, and perhaps even mediate them a kind of grace.

Here, too, however, a range of further questions presents itself. In light of the fact that ethical consumption is often costly, we might ask whether part of its appeal is that it offers to distract affluent individuals from the true depths of their social, environmental, and political responsibilities, and whether it subtly suggests that the Christian responsibility to care for the neighbor can be replaced with

---

24 This thought was that this corrects for a bias that leads most of us to underestimate the cost differences between vehicles with low and moderate fuel economy, and to overestimate the differences between those with moderate and high fuel economy. See Cass Sunstein, *Simpler: The Future of Government* (New York: Simon & Schuster, 2013), 81–89.
25 It is always an open question whether attempts to nudge behavior work as intended; they have at times been ineffective, and at other times produced unintended outcomes. Behavioral manipulation is, it turns out, more an art than a science!
26 This language drawn from Margaret Levi and April Linton, "Fair Trade: A Cup at a Time?" *Politics and Society* 31, no. 3 (2003): 407–32.

high-end consumerism. Do mission-driven markets strengthen or dissipate our commitment to the common good, and encourage vice more than they do virtue? To be useful, of course, such a question ought to be directed not to these markets in the abstract, but to a specific setting—the context of a particular brand or product, say. Even here, however, answers may be ambiguous, and certainly will vary with the cultures and even individuals involved.

It may seem unsatisfying that such analyses end with questions rather than answers. However, an iterative process of questioning is central to a Catholic analysis of economic life (and all social phenomena, for that matter). On the opening page of their 1986 pastoral letter *Economic Justice for All*, the United States Catholic Bishops frame their reflections as a meditation on three fundamental questions: "What does the economy do *for* people? What does it do *to* people? And how do people *participate* in it?"[27] These are not questions that lead to obvious, tidy, or permanent answers. Nonetheless, they are ones we must keep asking, not only at the level of the "the economy" as a whole, but also on more local levels—of individual employers and lenders, retail brands and stores, advertising platforms and campaigns, software and algorithms mediating consumer activity and interactions between employers and employees, and goods and services themselves. Of and in each of these we ought to ask: what is *this* corner of the economy doing for people, and doing to people? How does this particular market allow and invite us to participate in our shared economic life—and who does it encourage us to become?

## Markets, Law, and Democracy

How does this all of this relate to this volume's conversation on the relation of markets, law, democracy? The first thing to be said is that this way of seeing markets does *not* immediately translate into a single or clear legislative agenda. The purpose of this chapter certainly has not been to build a religious argument for legally requiring markets to maximally encourage virtue and discourage vice, if such a thing were even possible. As noted, the Catholic jurisprudential tradition rooted in Aquinas does assume that one of the purposes of human law is to "lead men to virtue, not suddenly, but gradually."[28] However, this tradition also holds that law cannot and ought not aim to repress all acts of vice or to compel all acts of virtue, but only to address those acts most directly related to the common good and necessary for the maintenance of social order.[29] How to balance these two ends of law was an open question even in Aquinas' time[30] and is only even more so now, given that modern democracies are characterized by significant value pluralism.

---

27 United States Conference of Catholic Bishops, *Economic Justice for All* (Washington, DC: United States Conference of Catholic Bishops, 1986), 1, Emphasis in original.
28 Aquinas, ST I-II q. 96, a. 2. For more on this subject, see Kaveny, *Law's Virtues*.
29 Ibid., a. 2 and 3.
30 He assumed that laws would and should vary according to the different customs of different places; see e.g., ST I-II q. 95, a. 3, and q. 97.

At the very least, this pluralism means that any attempt to use law to limit or reshape markets based on concerns about moral formation will likely be contentious. On the whole, this is a good thing; in the past, economic laws justified mainly in terms of a paternalistic concern for morals were frequently oppressive and, from the perspective of today, unnecessarily inhibited entrepreneurship. Such laws also backfired on a regular basis, leading to unintended consequences arguably worse than the putative moral evils they aimed to suppress.[31] With the failures of this paternalistic legacy in mind, some have objected to the use of behavioral economics by government, arguing that even if it is successful it will subject us to the unaccountable and unseen manipulations of unelected technocrats.[32] In such a view, it would be better to restrict the role of law in markets to protecting negative rights and to leave markets as they were and ought to be: realms of free expression, not of coercive moral formation by some outside, meddling party.

Such critics are right to highlight the importance of transparent and democratic deliberation over when and how the state uses its power to encourage citizens' moral behavior. In the perspective sketched here, however, this reaction misses much about the nature of markets as contexts, perhaps because it first misunderstands humans as economic and moral agents. An analysis of why brings us to the heart of what Catholic anthropology can bring to our public conversations about markets.

In the view outlined here, markets are *never* merely realms of free expression, in which individuals express preferences without themselves being influenced, as if in a social vacuum. This is not because of anything special or particular to markets, however—it is simply how human nature works. We are the sort of beings whose preferences and choices are influenced by the way others present options to us, and whose character is formed through the practice of choosing, pursuing, and then having the ends we desire. We are, in short, plastic, and our wills are always in flux. We are perennially in a process of becoming, in which our selves, our activity in the world, and our social contexts (and, Christians hope, God's grace) are in constant and dynamic interaction.

Thus, the removal of government from markets cannot solve the "problem" of how markets shape us as persons, if the problem is the mere fact of that shaping. Markets will shape us no matter who is in charge of them or how they are designed. Even in an imaginary world where markets emerge spontaneously and without the need for law, we would be no less susceptible to the moral influences they would mediate. The authors of those influences in that case, however, would be simply proportionately more "private" actors: corporations, managers, advertising and content creators, those who design the algorithms that use our

---

31 One notorious example of this is that of Prohibition in the US, and its connection with the rise of organized crime; another is the problem of STIs and crime against sex workers in places where sex work is criminalized.
32 See Sherzod Abdukadirov, ed., *Nudge Theory in Action: Behavioral Design in Policy and Markets* (Cham: Palgrave, 2016), for a number of arguments along these lines.

personal data to predict how to more effectively capture revenue, and so forth. Our character is always in *someone's* hands, we might say.

And this is the real takeaway of the theological argument here: to indicate how high the stakes are of all decisions made about markets, whether made by public or private actors. Whether public or private, anyone who has a hand in shaping the moral contexts in which we live is also making a bid to shape us, as persons, whether they realize it or not. These influences—and thus, the agents who set them in place—can help us be better persons and enjoy true freedom, or they can work against it, by enabling and incentivizing morally unhelpful choices. In the theological idiom modeled here, we might go so far as to say that through the way we each contribute to and shape markets, we can either mediate grace to each other, or we can fail to do so. Politically, we can certainly say that markets are as important for democracy as any other realm of life in which individuals influence each other and are morally formed.

For those who find this narration of life in markets plausible or compelling, this can explain part of why we feel such anxiety about them, and about what others are allowed to do in them—almost as much as we do, say, about politics. In this analysis, to dichotomize markets and politics as different kinds of moral contexts—and above all, to characterize the former as pure realms of expressive freedom, in which we morally leave each other alone as we act out our private (and even religious) preferences—is misleading, and perhaps also naïve. Instead, markets are at least as complex, ambiguous, and variable as any other moral setting. Moreover, in them our decisions influence each other quite a bit, potentially in morally significant ways—even mundane decisions about whom to hire and on what terms, how to organize stores and design webpages, or how to present various options to employees, subcontractors, and supply chain vendors. As private and nonpolitical as these all seem to be, they can impact the habits of those involved and shape their sense of what ways of being and acting in the world are normal, possible, and expected.

In short, this view suggests that markets and in politics alike, we can and do exercise power over each other—different sorts of power, to be sure, but power nonetheless. What to do once we notice this fact is a separate question entirely, and not at all easy to answer. To try to avoid taking up such questions by ignoring the complexity of markets as moral contexts (and, underneath that, our susceptibility to moral suasion and need for assistance in developing virtue) is to miss part of what happens in markets already, and is part of why they matter so much for our shared public life.

# 9 Regulating Religious Performance on the Commercial Stage

*Nathan B. Oman*

It is not uncommon for market actors to imbue their commercial activities with religious significance. This can take a bewildering variety of forms. Kosher food is big business, a religiously infused segment of industrial food production.[1] Sharia-compliant financial instruments constitute a multibillion-dollar international market.[2] Other believers have created investment funds that seek to earn a profit while advancing religious goals and avoiding entanglement with sin.[3] Religious business owners have found themselves on the front lines of the culture wars as they have clashed with state anti-discrimination laws in the wake of the legal recognition of same-sex marriage.[4] More prosaically, religious institutions are often commercial actors, purchasing the services of ministers, issuing bonds, and buying and selling assets.[5] Some for-profit businesses exist primarily to advance a religious message, such as publishers that are closely allied to a particular denomination or theological position.[6] Thus, ArtScroll exists to publish Jewish works from an Orthodox perspective,[7] while Zondervan is basically an Evangelical press.[8] In more subtle ways, religion often guides the decisions of market actors even when the decisions

---

1 See Michael A. Helfand and Barak Richman, "The Challenge of Co-Religionist Commerce," *Duke Law Journal* 64, no. 5 (February 2015): 771 (discussing the Kosher food industry).
2 See generally Mahmoud A. El-Gamal, *Islamic Finance: Law, Economics, and Practice* (New York: Cambridge University Press, 2006); M. Kabir Hassan and Mervyn K. Lewis, eds., *Handbook of Islamic Banking* (Northampton, MA: Edward Elgar Publishing, 2007).
3 See Ronald J. Colombo, "The Naked Private Square," *Houston Law Review* 51, no. 1 (Fall 2013): 22–23 (discussing such investment funds).
4 See Masterpiece Cakeshop v. Colorado Civil Rights Commission, 138 S. Ct. 1719 (2018) (holding for religious bakers in a conflict with state anti-discrimination laws).
5 See generally Bruce P. Powers, ed., *Church Administration Handbook*, rev. ed. (Nashville, TN: B&H Academic, 2008); Michael Anthony and James R. Estep, eds., *Management Essentials for Christian Ministries* (Nashville, TN: B&H Academic, 2005).
6 See, e.g., "Tyndale | Our Purpose," accessed July 13, 2020, www.tyndale.com/purpose (noting that the company serves to "spread the Good News of Christ around the world").
7 See generally Jeremy Stolow, *Orthodox by Design: Judaism, Print Politics, and the ArtScroll Revolution* (Berkeley: University of California Press, 2010).
8 See generally David D. Kirkpatrick, "Evangelical Sales Are Converting Publishers," *The New York Times*, June 8, 2002, Books, www.nytimes.com/2002/06/08/books/evangelical-sales-are-converting-publishers.html.

DOI: 10.4324/9781003309291-10

might lack any overt religious content to an uninformed non-believer.[9] And so on. What is the law to make of all of this religious commerce?

In this chapter, I borrow ideas from feminist theory to understand the role of religion in the commercial space. Just as gender can be understood as in part a matter of performing one's personal identity so as to constitute it, religion is also an aspect of identity that is constituted through performance. The law has long recognized that unlawful discrimination can take the form of restrictions on the performance of gender, a theory that has been extended to include protections for gays, lesbians, and transgender people.[10] I argue that a similar set of concerns might orient our thinking on religion in the marketplace, at least in part.[11] This has, I argue, concrete implications for legal rules. I use the example of bankruptcy law, showing how understanding religion as a performance both justifies and critiques the way that law accommodates religious activity around the payment of debts. I choose this relatively prosaic example deliberately. Because the intersection of law, religion, and the marketplace often involves some of the most hotly contested cultural issues in our politics, everyone's political priors on those cultural questions frequently overwhelm more abstract reflection. Few readers, however, are likely to have strong opinions about bankruptcy law. Accordingly, the discussion ought to make it easier for readers to consider my approach "on the merits."

## The Law of Church and Market

Many legal actors have expressed skepticism about, if not hostility toward, the idea of religiously infused commerce. Justice Ginsburg, for example, drew a sharp distinction between those that "use labor to make a profit" and those that seek "to perpetuate the religious values shared by a community of believers."[12] This suggests some kind of clear demarcation between the commercial and the religious spheres. In recent years, this intuition has often been couched in terms of whether for-profit corporations should be able to claim legal protections for religious practices.[13] Although I have argued elsewhere that the legal mechanism used for asset partitioning (the corporate form, partnership, sole proprietorship,

---

9 See Mark L. Rienzi, "God and the Profits: Is There Religious Liberty for Moneymakers," *George Mason Law Review* 21, no. 51 (2013): 74 (giving examples of for-profit businesses guided by religious beliefs).
10 See Bostock v. Clayton County, 140 S.Ct. 1731 (2020) (holding that Title VII applies to LGBT employees).
11 To be clear, I am not claiming that the arguments put forward in this chapter exhaust the legitimate concerns one might have with the place of religion in the market or provide the sole way in which to approach such questions. Rather, I put it forward as one possibly useful way of approaching this question.
12 See Burwell v. Hobby Lobby Stores, Inc., 134 Sup. Ct. 2751, 2797 (2014) (Ginsburg, J., dissenting) (quoting *Gilardi v. United States Department of Health and Human Services*, 733 F.3d 1208, 1242 (D.C. Cir. 2001) (Edwards, J., concurring in part and dissenting in part)).
13 See generally Burwell v. Hobby Lobby Stores, Inc., 134 Sup. Ct. 2751(2014) (holding that for-profit corporations could be "persons" for purposes of the Religious Freedom Restoration Act).

etc.) is largely irrelevant to questions of how the law should regulate religious commerce, debates over the religious exercise of corporations are beyond the scope of this chapter.[14] Those debates, however, are often simply a confused proxy for a deeper set of issues about the relationship between commercial and religious practices. The sharp line drawn by Justice Ginsburg and others must be understood as normative rather than empirical. The examples with which this chapter began demonstrate that as an empirical matter, in many situations there simply isn't a clear distinction between commercial and religious activities. Of course, this doesn't mean that these normative lines are mistaken. We might think that religious believers commit some error when they inject their faith into commerce. Even if one rejects a sharp separation between church and market of the kind suggested by Justice Ginsburg, one might still believe that there is something suspect or dangerous when the faithful seek to charge commerce into a pious activity.

The liberal state that gradually emerged after the end of the wars of religion in the 17th century is dedicated to the ideal of religious pluralism.[15] One of the chief ways in which that pluralism has been negotiated is by consigning religion to a "private" space that is sealed off from the "public" arena of government.[16] In this schema, spaces such as homes, churches, mosques, or synagogues are clearly thought of private spheres where religious exercise is most legitimate and most deserving of legal solicitude.[17] On the other hand, government spaces such as courts or legislatures are seen as inherently "public."[18] In these public spaces religion, even if it is not entirely excluded, must tread carefully if it is not to upset the liberal order. How these basic intuitions are cashed out in practice is, of course, hugely controversial. The scope of religious freedom even in the private spaces can be debated, as can the vigor with which religion should be excluded from public spaces. This is the stuff of our traditional debates over "church and state." The basic approaches—seperationism v. accomodationism, etc.—are well defined. Those skeptical of claims for religious protections understand that within the liberal framework their opponents will have the strongest claims in private spaces, while those seeking greater freedom of action for religious exercise realize that their claims are weakest when applied to government actors and public spaces. Once fitted into this framework, disputes over particular cases can proceed using the well-rehearsed rhetorical moves of each approach, and debates can take on the comforting predictability of a frequently danced minuet.[19]

---

14  See Alan Meese and Nathan B. Oman, "Hobby Lobby, Corporate Law, and the Theory of the Firm: Why For-Profit Corporations Are RFRA Persons," *Harvard Law Review Forum* 127 (2014): 273–301.
15  See, e.g., Martha Craven Nussbaum, *Liberty of Conscience: In Defense of America's Tradition of Religious Equality* (Princeton: Basic Books, 2008).
16  See Colombo, "The Naked Private Square," 12–13.
17  Ibid., 33.
18  Ibid., 1.
19  For a good summary of these traditional debates, see Michael W. McConnell, John H. Garvey, and Thomas C. Berg, *Religion and the Constitution*, 4th ed. (New York: Wolters Kluwer, 2016).

Markets, however, problematize the public–private religious divide that structures traditional church–state debates. On one hand, commerce is the quintessential example of a "private" activity. Markets are structured by the rules of private property and private contracts. Contract and property, in turn, are among the primary categories through which liberal political orders have understood the idea of private spaces. Indeed, on one view, what it means for a particular social space to be private is for it to be owned by an individual rather than the state. Similarly, market orders emerge from the decentralized activity of millions of private decisions, in contrast to centrally planned economies where government fiat dictates economic life. When we talk about commercial activity, we speak of the "private sector." And so on. At the same time, in modern liberal societies, no area of social life is as subject to legal regulation as the marketplace. Trucking and bartering are no longer—if they ever were—purely a matter of private property and private contract. Rather for better or for worse, employment, trade, and manufacturing are all subject to pervasive state oversight. Likewise, our political discourse, while often focused on questions of culture and identity, assumes that "the economy" is one of our primary objects of political concern.[20] We task our leaders with delivering material prosperity; we expect them to be adept at the pulling the levers of regulatory, fiscal, and monetary policy to produce it; and, we hold them accountable at election time for economic performance.[21] The single best predictor of whether presidents will be re-elected is whether they are running for re-election during a recession.[22] All of these factors point toward the idea that the market is one of our central "public" spaces.

The ambiguous status of commerce in the public–private framework creates a problem for how we think about religion in the market. Because in this space the traditional categories of public and private break down, it is difficult to insert religiously infused commerce into the traditional minuet of church–state debates. Rather, we must re-examine why it is that we might value religious exercise and what it might have to do with the market.

Markets are not natural. Rather, they are human achievements that require a host of formal and informal practices and institutions in order to function. They are not wholly creatures of the law, but law has a profound impact on the nature and extent of markets.[23] Thus, the law will inevitably shape and regulate religious commerce. This fact raises the normative question of how the law *ought* to shape

---

20 See Stuart Chinn, "Political Parties and Constitutional Fidelity," *Marquette Law Review* 102, no. 2 (Winter 2018): 416 (discussing the role of economic management in modern politics).
21 See generally Adi Brender and Allan Drazen, "How Do Budget Deficits and Economic Growth Affect Reelection Prospects? Evidence from a Large Panel of Countries," *American Economic Review* 98, no. 5 (2008): 2203–20.
22 See generally Joshua Green, "Presidents Lose When There's an Election-Year Recession," *Bloomberg.com*, June 9, 2020, www.bloomberg.com/news/articles/2020-06-09/presidents-lose-when-there-s-an-election-year-recession.
23 For a discussion of the complex interplay of law and the maintenance of markets see Nathan B. Oman, *The Dignity of Commerce: Markets and the Moral Foundations of Contract Law* (Chicago, IL: University of Chicago Press, 2016). For a discussion of how religion itself

the relationship between religion and commerce. That question, in turn, requires that we have a sense of the virtues of commercial activity and the way in which religion might reinforce or threaten those goods.[24] It likewise requires that we consider the limits and potential pathologies of markets and consider how they might threaten religion or be mitigated by faith-based commerce.

The most common way of understanding the market is as a social mechanism for the allocation of goods and services. This is the familiar vision of the market from economics. In contrast to systems of centralized control, markets represent an emergent order—albeit one that is decisively shaped by political choices about the structure of legal institutions—in which decentralized, private, formally voluntary interactions dictate the flow of assets. Given a system of well-specified property and contract rights, markets hold out the promise of efficiently allocating resources and producing material prosperity. Adopting this view, one could examine the effect of religious commerce on market efficiency. Hence, for example, some commenters have suggested that religious activities by for-profit corporations threaten their efficiency.[25] Others have argued that by solving problems of information and interpersonal trust, religious commerce can increase the efficiency of markets.[26] Both responses take it as given that the primary normative question to be asked when thinking about the relationship between religion and commerce is the efficiency of the market.

The efficiency of the market is the most common question for contemporary legal theory, particularly the law and economics scholarship that has come to dominate thinking in virtually all areas of commercial and business law. Nevertheless, there are alternative ways of understanding the normative stakes in commerce. In the 18th century, thinkers such as Montesquieu, Voltaire, Adam Smith, and Thomas Paine propounded the so-called *doux commerce* thesis, arguing that markets are an unusually effective mechanism for promoting cooperation in the face of ethnic, national, and religious divisions.[27] In addition, commerce promotes peace and toleration by both creating pro-social incentives and inculcating habits of mutual forbearance and respect.[28] Pieces of this tradition have been invoked by contemporary legal

---

can provide a similar structuring force for commerce, see Nathan B. Oman, "Commerce, Religion, and the Rule of Law," *Journal of Law, Religion and State* 6 (2018): 213–35.

24 See Nathan B. Oman, "Doux Commerce, Religion, and the Limits of Antidiscrimination Law," *Indiana Law Journal* 91 (2017): 693–733.

25 See Leo E. Jr. Strine, "A Job Is Not a Hobby: The Judicial Revival of Corporate Paternalism and Its Problematic Implications," *Journal of Corporation Law* 41, no. 1 (Fall 2015): 71–116.

26 See Barak D. Richman, *Stateless Commerce: The Diamond Network and the Persistence of Relational Exchange* (Cambridge, MA: Harvard University Press, 2017); Nathan B. Oman, "Commerce, Religion, and the Rule of Law," *Journal of Law, Religion and State* 6 (2018): 213–35; Barak D. Richman, "How Community Institutions Create Economic Advantage: Jewish Diamond Merchants in New York," *Law and Social Inquiry* 31, no. 2 (2006): 383–420.

27 See Albert O. Hirschman, *The Passions and the Interests: Political Arguments for Capitalism Before Its Triumph* (Princeton: Princeton University Press, 1977).

28 See Nathan B. Oman, *The Dignity of Commerce: Markets and the Moral Foundations of Contract Law* (Chicago, IL: University of Chicago Press, 2016), 40–58 (discussing how

theorists to understand certain legal institutions,[29] and elsewhere I have argued that structuring a market that is capable of delivering the goods of *doux commerce* can provide a normative approach to questions of religious commerce.[30] On this view, we should consider the function of markets in sustaining liberal democracy and think about how religious commerce both advances and potentially threatens that function. Any such analysis, however, requires that we think through the logic of religious commerce. Why do believers inject religion into the market and how should that inform how the law regards religion in this context?

## What Is Religion Doing in the Market?

In the beginning, American law conceptualized religion in terms of either assent to theological claims or a circumscribed set of somehow inherently religious activities such as prayer. Hence, in thinking about "freedom of religion," American courts spoke in terms of "freedom of belief" or "freedom of worship."[31] During the course of the 20th century, however, American law became much more ambitious, claiming the authority to regulate and organize larger and larger swaths of life. Increasingly, the regulatory state runs up against religiously motivated conduct that doesn't fall neatly into the concepts of belief or worship narrowly construed that it has often used to define religion.[32] How are we to understand what is going on, for example, when Jewish merchants insist on arbitration before a beth din in the face of a bankruptcy court's automatic stay or when a Christian debtor insists that a Chapter 13 plan must budget funds for the payment of a tithe to her church? Let me suggest that in part these religious believers are using commercial activity to affirm, define, and even create their religious identities.

There are many ways of thinking about the nature of identity. One might think of identity as a matter of autonomous choice as in the philosophy of Joseph Raz.[33] Alternatively, one might follow Aristotle and insist that identity only makes sense within the context of a community that generates the social resources such as language that make identity possible.[34] Another way of approaching the question

---

markets inculcate liberal virtues and provide a mechanism for peacefully managing moral pluralism).

29 See Jules Coleman, *Risks and Wrongs* (New York: Oxford University Press, 2002).
30 See Nathan B. Oman, "Doux Commerce, Religion, and the Limits of Antidiscrimination Law," 693–733; see generally Oman, *The Dignity of Commerce.*
31 See, e.g., Reynolds v. United States, 98 U.S. 145 (1879) (holding the free exercise clause of the first amendment protected only the freedom to believe and not the freedom to act on beliefs); Jones v. City of Opelika, 319 U.S. 105, 119 (1943) ("The constitutional right of freedom of worship does not guarantee anybody the right to sell anything" (internal quotations omitted)).
32 See, e.g., William A. Glaser, "Worshiping Separation: Worship in Limited Public Forums and the Establishment Clause," *Pepperdine Law Review* 38, no. 4 (2011 2010): 1106 (discussing the difficulty of providing a legal definition of religious "worship").
33 See Joseph Raz, *The Morality of Freedom* (New York: Oxford University Press, 1988).
34 See Aristotle, *Aristotle's Politics*, trans. Carnes Lord, 2nd ed. (Chicago: University of Chicago Press, 2013).

is to note the identity that arises out of actions; it is something that we perform. For example, feminist theorists such as Judith Butler have argued that gender is always a performance.[35] Butler is ultimately building on the thought G. W. F. Hegel, who argued that identity arises dialogically through the process by which a self is recognized as such by another.[36] Hegel's ideas were first used to understand gender by Simone de Beauvoir and has since been expanded on by other feminist theorists.[37] Hence, for Butler gender identity is simply the process by which one performs "being a man" or "being a woman" and is recognized as such by others.

The idea of identity through performance and recognition reaches far beyond feminist theory. Charles Taylor has made a similar point more generally, pointing toward what he calls the "politics of recognition."[38] Hannah Arendt wrote of how for ancient Greeks and Romans identity was only possible in the public space of the agora and the forum because it was only in political life that one had sufficient freedom to act as an individual and thus become an individual.[39] Today, however, we recognize that there are multiple stages on which one can enact one's identity, from the intimate sphere of the family to the public stage of politics. The market is one of these theaters. This can take a relatively trivial form, as in the fashion choices that people make when they purchase their clothes. Certainly, advertisers have long recognized that identity is often tied to the decisions to buy and sell, furiously trying to convince consumers that buying a favored product is part of being the kind of person that the consumer is or wishes to become.[40] At a deeper level, in modern societies we inevitably spend much of our lives in commercial settings. We are employers and employees, buyers and sellers. These activities occupy most of our waking hours. Along with the public square of politics and the intimate space of the home, we play out our identities amid our trucking and bartering; our getting and spending. All the world's a stage, including the market.

---

35 See Judith Butler, *Gender Trouble: Feminism and the Subversion of Identity* (New York: Routledge, 2006).
36 Hegel makes this argument in his famously obscure master–slave parable. See G. W. F. Hegel, *The Phenomenology of Spirit*, trans. A. V. Miller (New York: Oxford University Press, 1977), chap. 4 (good luck).
37 See Simone De Beauvoir, *The Second Sex*, trans. Constance Borde and Sheila Malovany-Chevallier (New York: Vintage, 2011).
38 See Charles Taylor, "The Politics of Recognition," in *Multiculturalism: Examining the Politics of Recognition*, ed. Amy Gutman (Princeton, NJ: Princeton University Press, 1995), 25–74.
39 See Hannah Arendt, *The Human Condition*, 2nd ed. (Chicago: University of Chicago Press, 1998).
40 See Guy Champniss, Hugh N. Wilson, and Emma K. Macdonald, "Why Your Customers' Social Identities Matter," *Harvard Business Review*, January 1, 2015, https://hbr.org/2015/01/why-your-customers-social-identities-matter ("Social identities are important for marketers because they guide people's behavior at any given moment. Some behavior will bolster and support the group, and, equally important, some behavior will betray the group.").

## Performing Identity and the Law

Consider *Price Waterhouse v. Hopkins*,[41] a case construing the scope of federal anti-discrimination law decided by the US Supreme Court in 1989. Ann Hopkins was denied promotion to partnership at her accounting firm. While the firm had promoted (a few) female partners previously and indicated a willingness to promote female partnerships in the future, Hopkins' upward climb was halted because she was too "macho."[42] One of the partners considering her candidacy suggested that she "take a course at charm school,"[43] and another suggested that his colleagues "objected to her swearing only because it's a lady using foul language."[44] The US Supreme Court wrote:

> But it was the man who ... bore responsibility for explaining to Hopkins the reasons for the Policy Board's decision to place her candidacy on hold who delivered the *coup de grace*: in order to improve her chances for partnership ... Hopkins should walk more femininely, talk more femininely, dress more femininely, wear make-up, have her hair styled, and wear jewelry.[45]

According to the Court, the firm's reliance on gender stereotypes was sufficient to make out a prima facie claim for employment discrimination under Title VII.

There are at least two ways that we can understand the relationship between gender stereotypes and the legally actionable discrimination in *Hopkins*. We might think that the stereotypes were simply a proxy for gender-based hostility more generally. In other words, we might think that the reason that Price Waterhouse denied Hopkins her promotion was that she was a woman. Even though a few women had been promoted in the past and the firm claimed that they were willing to promote women in the future, the reality is that they were simply hostile to the promotion of any female partners. On this reading of the situation, the discussion of femininity and acting in a properly lady-like fashion was a smoke screen. Even if Hopkins didn't cuss and wore more jewelry, she wouldn't have received the promotion because Price Waterhouse simply wasn't going to promote a woman, no matter how lady-like she might be. If this is the situation, we have a conceptually simple case of gender discrimination, even if getting at the fact of the matter requires that we see through the pretextual reasons offered by Price Waterhouse.

On an alternative reading of the case, Price Waterhouse was not offering pretextual reasons for denying promotion to Hopkins. The firm really was ready and willing—even eager—to promote women, but only so long as they conformed to

---

41 490 U.S. 228 (1989) *superseded by statute on other grounds* 42 U.S.C. § 2000e-5(g)(2)(B) (1991) *as stated in* Landgraf v. USI Film Prods., 511 U.S. 244, 251 (1994).
42 490 U.S. at 235.
43 Ibid. (internal quotation marks omitted).
44 Ibid.
45 Ibid.

certain gender stereotypes. It might be that the problem in this situation is that standards of lady-like behavior aren't also applied to male applicants. Hence, if Hopkins' sin consisted of swearing and having an abrasive personality, but Price Waterhouse was happy to promote foul-mouthed and unpleasant male partners, then we simply have a standard that is applied inconsistently on the basis of gender. Notice that for there to be this kind of discrimination there is no necessary connection between gender stereotypes and the inconsistently applied standard. If Price Waterhouse required that female partners have a graduate degree but did not impose the same burden on male partners, there would be comparable discrimination, even if graduate education isn't related to crude gender stereotypes.

However, there is another, far more interesting way of understanding the case. It might be that Price Waterhouse was genuinely committed to gender stereotypes. What it wanted was a certain kind of feminine behavior from Hopkins. It is difficult to imagine that such a standard could be applied in way that didn't place unique burdens on employees based on their sex, and that would be enough to make out a prima facie case of discrimination. However, there is an additional concern at work in the outcome in *Hopkins*. We could say that Price Waterhouse ought not to impose on Hopkins a particular script for what it means to be a woman. Taking our cues from Butler, we could acknowledge that identity is constituted through public performance. Accordingly, respect for identity requires that we create a protected space in which people are free to perform their identities. On this view, the problem was not simply that Price Waterhouse denied Hopkins promotion based on her gender (although it did so), but that it sought to undermine her female identity as such. Of course, no one can be afforded infinite freedom to perform their identity. In the context of employment discrimination, employers must be able to impose neutral, bona fide occupational requirements on employees, even if doing so might limit their ability to constitute some protected aspect their identity.[46] However, absent such a neutral, bona fide reason, it was not for Price Waterhouse to tell Hopkins how she was to construct her identity through the performance of her gender. On this reading, what was at issue in the decision was not simply equal access to commercial life. It was also about recognizing commercial life as an important sphere where people need room in which to engage in the process of performance from which gender emerges.

Religion is similar to gender in its performativity.[47] There is a sense in which one is a Jew or a Christian or a Muslim by virtue of "performing" one's religion

---

46 See, e.g., 42 U.S.C. § 2000e-2(k)(1)(A)(i) (2012) (an employer may use employment practices that cause a disparate impact on protected employees, provided "the challenged practice is job related for the position in question and consistent with business necessity").

47 Butler makes particularly strong claims about the nature of gender, insisting that it consists only or necessarily of performance. I am drawing on her argument, however, to make a more modest claim, namely that performance plays an important part in constituting identity. My argument here is neutral with regard to any deeper claim about the essence of gender or religion. Nothing in the argument hinges on how one resolves such questions. For a collection

and having that performance recognized as such by others, if only by God. Writing more than 25 years ago, Stephen Carter argued that within the United States a "culture of disbelief" has a tendency to relegate to religion to the status of a hobby or personal preference to be pursued mainly within the private sphere.[48] This, however, isn't an adequate way of conceptualizing how religious identity works. Consider the case of two Jewish business men who agree to submit their commercial dispute to a rabbinic court.[49] In part they are simply trying to resolve an ordinary business conflict, such as collecting on a debt or getting a final interpretation of a contract. In some cases, the rabbinic court may apply ordinary secular law to the dispute by honoring a choice of law clause in their contract. One might tell a story about how the rabbinic court provides a better quality of dispute resolution than an ordinary commercial arbiter, and in some cases, this is no doubt true. The beth din may be faster or less expensive than a secular court. It may also be used opportunistically or strategically by Jewish business owners to engage in religious and secular form shopping. However, none of this gets at why many Jewish business owners wish to resolve their disputes before a beth din. Doing so is a way in which one becomes Jewish, albeit not in the formal sense of being born Jewish or converting to the faith. Rather, the use of the beth din performs Judaism in a certain way. It is similar to how wearing a skirt or cussing at subordinates performs a certain way of being a woman.

We can understand the nature of identity in this argument by looking at its roots in Hegel. Since at least the 17th century, philosophers have used the idea of a state of nature to elucidate various philosophical puzzles.[50] Hegel has his own state-of-nature story, although one told in almost completely impenetrable prose.[51] Very roughly speaking, it goes like this: two individuals meet. Each sees the other as an independent person, and in the other's recognition of the self as a rational agent and vice versa, each comes to self-awareness. At the same time, the presence of another person is threatening, and the two grapple in a death struggle. The battle ends only when one yields, becoming a slave and thus giving up the freedom that was so threatening to the other. The victory of the master over the slave, however, is hollow. Only in the free recognition of himself by another can the master be assured of his own identity. Indeed, it was the very

---

of essays discussing the relationship between Butler's theory and the study of religion, see Ellen Armour and Susan St Ville, eds., *Bodily Citations: Religion and Judith Butler* (New York: Columbia University Press, 2006).

48 See Stephen L. Carter, *The Culture of Disbelief: How American Law and Politics Trivialize Religious Devotion* (New York: Anchor Books, 1994).

49 See Michael A. Helfand, "Fighting for the Debtor's Soul: Regulating Religious Commercial Conduct," *George Mason Law Review* 19, no. 1 (2011): 157–96.

50 See generally Thomas Hobbes, *The Leviathan* (New York: Barnes & Noble Books, 2004); John Locke, *Two Treatises of Government* (New York: Cambridge University Press, 1988); Ann Cudd and Seena Eftekhari, "Contractarianism," in *The Stanford Encyclopedia of Philosophy*, ed. Edward N. Zalta, Summer 2018 (Metaphysics Research Lab, Stanford University, 2018), https://plato.stanford.edu/archives/sum2018/entries/contractarianism/.

51 See Hegel, *The Phenomenology of Spirit*, chap. 4.

confrontation with the other that led to the master's initial self-consciousness. Yet, precisely because the slave is a slave, his recognition can never be the kind of free recognition that vouchsafes the identity of the master.

Hegel's is a strange story, but it gets at an important point. We often understand the self in individualistic terms. Think, for example, of Ralph Waldo Emerson's paen to the personal authenticity of independence.[52] Hegel, in contrast, emphasizes that the self arises dialogically. We enact freely enact our identity, but it is in the recognition of that freedom by another that identity arises. If we take the Hegelian insight about performance and identity seriously, religious conduct is not epiphenomenal. Submitting their commercial dispute to a beth din isn't an odd thing that two Jewish business people do because they are Jewish. It is not mere accidental activity that one can subtract from an Orthodox business person while leaving his or her identity untouched. Rather, the performance is in some sense existential. Being Jewish—like being a woman—is at least in part about performing Jewishness and having that performance recognized. Public performance isn't something that one does because of one's identity. In some sense, the performance is one's identity. Identity isn't possible outside of performance and recognition.

## Applying the Theory to Bankruptcy Law

Contemporary liberal societies pride themselves on their solicitude for the identities of their citizens. The reasons for this are complex, and this solicitude is far from self-evident as a matter of political philosophy. Indeed, much of the civic republican tradition is devoted to the idea that the state should play a primary role in shaping the identity of its citizens and that full membership in the political community requires that one adopt a particular identity, that of a virtuous citizen.[53] To a certain extent such ideas persist in liberal societies, which remain concerned with the need to produce citizens suited to life in a liberal polity.[54] Nevertheless, both the practical conditions and the normative commitments of liberal democratic regimes dispose them toward a relatively hands-off stance toward identity. First, modern societies are characterized by high levels of pluralism. Indeed, liberalism itself was born from the need to find a modus vivendi in the post-Reformation world of competing religious identities. It did this by constricting the moral ambitions of politics and with it the moral ambitions of the law. Peace in pluralistic societies requires that the state not position itself as

---

52 See Ralph Waldo Emerson, *Essays and Poems*, ed. Tony Tanner (London, UK: Everyman, 1997), 21–46 (Emerson's famous essay "Self Reliance").
53 For an introduction to civic republicanism in modern political philosophy see Philip Pettit, *Republicanism: A Theory of Freedom and Government*, 1st ed. (Oxford: Oxford University Press, 1997).
54 See Peter Berkowitz, *Virtue and the Making of Modern Liberalism* (Princeton, NJ: Princeton University Press, 1999); Stephen Macedo, *Liberal Virtues: Citizenship, Virtue, and Community in Liberal Constitutionalism* (New York: Oxford University Press, 1990).

the final arbiter of identity, nor may the liberal state declare its enmity toward the enacted identity of particular groups without risking the modus vivendi that is one of its chief virtues. These practical concerns yield a second, deeper reason for commitment to a certain deference toward the pluralism of identity. Liberalism, perhaps more than other philosophical traditions, has been acutely aware of the role of violence in constituting the state.[55] This carries over into attitudes toward the law. As Robert Cover put it, "legal interpretation takes place on a field of pain and death."[56] Accordingly, liberal states are rightly reticent about using the law to shape identity because they recognize the risk of violence and suffering in such projects. Finally, for at least some strands of liberal thought, identity must be freely constructed by individuals. This commitment can come from a belief in the truth of incommensurable moral positions, which renders freedom the only acceptable response to moral pluralism, or from a belief that in the scale of human values autonomy ought to trump other concerns.[57]

Once the state's solicitude for identity is accepted, it follows that we must provide individuals with the spaces in which to engage in the performances that constitute those identities. This can be seen most clearly in recent trends in antidiscrimination law, which does more than simply ensure access to the marketplace but also ensures that, subject to bona fide business concerns, individuals are free within the commercial space to perform their identities.

In *Bostock v. Clayton County*,[58] the Supreme Court held that the federal law outlawing discrimination on the basis of sex also prohibited employment discrimination against gays, lesbians, and transgendered people. In his majority opinion for the Court, Justice Gorsuch offered a narrowly textualist analysis, insisting that discrimination against LGBT employees involved negative action against them on the basis of some aspect of their sexual identity that would be treated as unobjectionable in the opposite sex. Thus, a gay man who was fired for being sexually attracted to men was fired for behavior that would not have called forth any ire had he been a woman. Because of its textualist focus, Justice Gorsuch's opinion makes no effort to explain why discrimination against LGBT employees should be subject to legal sanction, and as the dissenters correctly point out, the outcome in the case is almost certainly beyond what the drafters of the law imagined.[59] What made an unimaginable interpretation of the statute into today's

---

55 See Judith N. Shklar, "The Liberalism of Fear," in *Liberalism and the Moral Life*, ed. Nancy L. Rosenblum (Cambridge, MA: Harvard University Press, 1989).
56 Robert M. Cover, "Violence and the Word," *The Yale Law Journal* 95, no. 8 (July 1986): 1601.
57 Compare Isaiah Berlin, *Liberty: Incorporating Four Essays on Liberty*, ed. Henry Hardy (New York: Oxford University Press, 2002); with Raz, *The Morality of Freedom*; see also George Crowder, *Isaiah Berlin: Liberty and Pluralism* (Malden, MA: Polity, 2004).
58 140 S. Ct. 1731 (2020).
59 See ibid. at 1755 (Alito, J. dissenting) ("If every single living American had been surveyed in 1964, it would have been hard to find any who thought that discrimination because of sex meant discrimination because of sexual orientation—not to mention gender identity, a concept that was essentially unknown at the time.").

controlling precedent was surely more than the bare text of the statute. Rather, LGBT rights became imaginable in part because large and influential segments of society came to recognize the particular social evils of the closet and the pernicious effect of social practices such as employment discrimination that threatened the livelihood of LGBT workers who dared to openly enact their sexual identities. Indeed, the closet is a particularly potent example of the relationship between identity, performance, and recognition. The social shift that made Bostock possible insisted that tolerance of LBGT individuals could not be made conditional on their willingness to keep their sexual identities concealed in the most narrowly defined of private spaces.

In *Equal Employment Opportunity Commission v. Abercrombie & Fitch Stores*,[60] the Supreme Court applied this logic to religion, holding that it was not sufficient that a company was willing to employ the Muslim plaintiff. It also had to allow her to wear a hijab. As a formal doctrinal matter, these cases involve the interpretation of Title VII of the 1964 Civil Rights Act. However, underlying the cases is a broader normative commitment to using the law to construct the market as a stage on which individuals can perform their identity. This normative principle can be applied more broadly to the question of how the law should regulate religious activity that emerges in the commercial sphere. We can think about the possible legal implications of this approach by considering two issues that arise in bankruptcy when a religious believer tithes to his or her church. The choice is deliberate. My goal is to take hot button cultural issues off the table for a moment, because in such cases conclusions are often over-determined by ideology and a host of other political commitments. It is the very lack of strong political saliency that makes bankruptcy law useful in this context.

For many religious believers, making regular donations to their church is a religious obligation, a way in which one consecrates one's life and property to God and his work.[61] In short, it is one of the ways in which one's religious identity is performed and thus constituted. In bankruptcy, however, complications arise. An insolvent debtor owes more money to creditors than she has assets or income. The process of personal bankruptcy represents a social choice to extend a modicum of mercy to such debtors in order to allow them to make a "fresh start." This fresh start comes, however, at the expense of creditors. In a Chapter 7 proceeding] the basic "deal" is that the debtor gives up all of his non-exempt assets to his creditors in return for a fresh start, shielding all of his future income from the claims of pre-petition creditors. In a Chapter 13, in contrast, the debtor retains her assets but gives to her creditors a limited claim on her future income, after which she will also be given a "fresh start."

---

60 See Equal Employment Opportunity Commission v. Abercrombie & Fitch Stores, 135 S. Ct. 2028 (2015).
61 See, e.g., Howard D. Swainston, "Tithing," in *The Encyclopedia of Mormonism*, ed. Daniel H. Ludlow (New York: Macmillan Publishing Company, 1992).

Tithing presents two problems. The trustee in bankruptcy, who is tasked with looking after the interests of the creditors in a Chapter 7 proceeding, is given the power to marshal all of the debtor's non-exempt assets for the benefit of creditors. This includes the right to pursue fraudulent conveyances made by the debtor in the period leading up to bankruptcy.[62] A classic fraudulent conveyance consists of a transfer of property made with "the actual intent to hinder, delay, or defraud any entity to which the debtor was . . . indebted."[63] However, one also makes a fraudulent conveyance if, while one is insolvent, one transfers property for "less than a reasonably equivalent value."[64] These so-called constructive fraudulent conveyances do not hinge on debtor's intentions, which may be wholly innocent. The basic policy idea is that a debtor cannot disperse assets at the expense of his or her creditors. As one commentator put it, debtors must comply with the commandment to "be just before you are generous."[65]

When an insolvent debtor pays a tithe to her church, she makes a constructive fraudulent conveyance.[66] The payment is a transfer of the debtor's property, for which the debtor does not receive "reasonably equivalent value." Accordingly, in bankruptcy, trustees have pursued fraudulent conveyance actions against churches that received tithing payments, requiring that churches refund the tithes to the bankruptcy estate for the benefit of the debtors' creditors.[67] The resulting actions proved troublesome for churches, some of which might lack the funds to satisfy the trustee's judgment and others that simply wished to avoid the expense of being entangled in debtor's bankruptcy proceedings. Congress responded by amending the bankruptcy code to exempt religious donations from the reach of fraudulent conveyance actions by the trustee in bankruptcy, so long as the donations do not exceed 15% of the debtor's annual income.[68]

A second issue with tithing arises in Chapter 13. In a Chapter 13 plan, the debtor retains their property but creditors get a claim on the creditor's future income for a time, after which the debtor is given a "fresh start." The creditors

62 See 11 U.S.C. § 548 (2012).
63 11 U.S.C. § 548(a)(1)(A) (2012).
64 11 U.S.C. § 548(a)(1)(B)(i) (2012).
65 Robert C. Clark, "The Duties of the Corporate Debtor to Its Creditors," *Harvard Law Review* 90 (1977): 510.
66 For a discussion of the issues around tithing and fraudulent conveyances, see Todd J. Zywicki, "Rewrite the Bankruptcy Laws, Not the Scriptures: Protecting a Bankruptcy Debtor's Right to Tithe," *Wisconsin Law Review* 1998 (1998): 1223–88; Richard Collin Mangrum, "Tithing, Bankruptcy and the Conflict Between Religious Freedom and Creditor's Interests," *Creighton Law Review* 32 (1999 1998): 815–48; Judd M. Treeman, "Blessed Be the Name of the Code: How to Protect Churches from Tithe Avoidance Under the Bankruptcy Code's Fraudulent Transfer Law," *Emory Bankruptcy Developments Journal* 25 (2008, 2009): 599–650.
67 See, e.g., In re Young, 148 B.R 886 (Bankr. D. Minn. 1992) aff'd, 152 B.R. 939 (D. Minn. 1993), rev'd, 82 F.3d 1407 (8th Cir.), reh'g denied, 89 F.3d 494 (8th Cir. 1996), vacated and remanded, 117 S. Ct. 2502 (1997), on remand, 141 F.3d 854 (8th Cir.), cert denied, 119 S. Ct. 43 (1998).
68 See 11 U.S.C. § 548(a)(2) (2012).

cannot claim the entirety of the debtor's income, as this would leave her without any means of support. Accordingly, a Chapter 13 plan will contain a budget allowing to the debtor reasonable living expenses, including a modest budget for entertainment and the like.[69] The question arose, can a Chapter 13 plan budget part of the debtor's income for the payment of tithing, or must the debtor give up religious donations until the creditors are paid under the plan. Initially, a number of courts—with the support of some commentators—ruled that Chapter 13 plans could not include a budget for religious tithes.[70] Again, however, congress intervened, amending the code so that a Chapter 13 budget could include religious donations so long as they did not exceed 15% of the debtor's income.[71]

If we think of religious spending—including spending on tithes—as a kind of performance constituting religious identity that is entitled to some breathing room from the law, how do these two statutory accommodations for tithing in bankruptcy fare? Protecting the performance of religious identity provides at best a weak support for the tithing exemption from the bankruptcy code's fraudulent conveyance statute. Fraudulent conveyance law does not prohibit the debtor from making tithing payments while insolvent. The language of fraud in these cases is somewhat misleading, as the debtor who makes a constructive fraudulent conveyance commits no legal wrong. Rather, the purpose of the law is simply to allocate the risk of the debtor's insolvency between creditors and donees. Certainly, the money that might be recovered in a fraudulent conveyance action does not benefit the debtor. Fraudulent conveyance law does not exist to allow debtors to undo regretted transfers of property. Rather, the money is recovered for the benefit of the bankruptcy estate, meaning for the benefit of the creditors.[72] Hence, the exemption exists primarily for the benefit of churches rather than for the benefit of debtors. To be sure, we might have valid reasons for favoring churches, but those reasons don't directly touch on the constitution of individual religious identity through personal performance.[73]

On the other hand, the identity-as-performance argument does provide a basis for a tithing budget in Chapter 13. The absence of such an allowance would in effect deprive a debtor of the ability to pay tithes. At the very least, it would make the payment of such tithes a legal wrong. This would constitute a prohibition on the performance of religious identity. This does not, of course, dispose of

---

69 See 11 U.S.C. § 1325(b) (2012).
70 See, e.g., In re Packham, 126 B.R. 603 (Bankr. D. Utah, 1991). See also Leonard J. Long, "Religious Exercise as Credit Risk," *Bankruptcy Developments Journal* 10 (1993): 119–70.
71 See 11 U.S.C. § 1325(b)(2)(ii) (2012).
72 See 11 U.S.C. § 551 (2012) ("Any transfer avoided [as a fraudulent conveyance] ... is preserved for the benefit of the estate").
73 See Richard W. Garnett, "The Freedom of the Church (towards) an Exposition, Translation, and Defense the Freedom of the Church in the Modern Era," *Journal of Contemporary Legal Issues* 21 (2013): 33–58; Paul Horwitz, "Freedom of the Church Without Romance the Freedom of the Church in the Modern Era," *Journal of Contemporary Legal Issues* 21 (2013): 59–132.

the issue. We do not have an unlimited ability to perform our identities. Consider again the case of *Price Waterhouse v. Hopkins*.[74] While Title VII prohibits an employer denying a woman a promotion based on the way in which she performs her gender, employers are entitled to impose bona fide occupational qualifications on employees, including qualifications that might impinge on their uninhibited ability to perform their gender as they see fit.[75] In the context of a Chapter 13 plan, the payment of tithing comes at the expense of the debtor's creditors. The problem may be particularly acute because federal law prohibits discrimination in lending on the basis of religion, meaning that lenders are unable to price ex ante the repayment risk that tithing donations may represent.[76] However, the entire point of the fresh start policy under Chapter 13 is to grant a benefit to the debtor—the fresh start—at the expense of creditors. There are numerous other places in the law where creditors' interests are balanced against concern for the debtor, including concerns for what we might think of as the debtor's identity. The most obvious example are the property exemptions created by state law that place certain assets beyond the reach of creditors. This includes—in most states—one's home but also property closely tied to the debtor's sense of self, such as family heirlooms, graves, and even pets.[77] Likewise, bankruptcy acknowledges that while a debtor is not entitled to live lavishly under a Chapter 13 plan at the expense of creditors, she need not be confined to the bare necessities of material subsistence.

## Conclusion

Recognizing that religious activity in the commercial context is part of how religious identity is constituted provides a way of thinking about how the law should structure the relationship between faith and the market, including such bedrock commercial matters as the collection of debts. A normative commitment to providing some breathing room within the market for the performance of identity does not answer all of our questions. There are other concerns that we might have such as efficiency or the liberalism-sustaining character of commerce. Likewise, concerns for identity may have to be balanced against other matters, such as the right of creditors to be paid. The advantage of such an approach, however, is that it provides a normative framework that is native to the questions of law's relationship to commerce and religion. Hence, rather than seeing religious

---

74 490 U.S. 228 (1989) *superseded by statute on other grounds* 42 U.S.C. § 2000e-5(g)(2)(B) (1991) *as stated in* Landgraf v. USI Film Prods., 511 U.S. 244, 251 (1994).
75 See, e.g., 42 U.S.C. § 2000e-2(k)(1)(A)(i) (2012) (an employer may use employment practices that cause a disparate impact on protected employees, provided "the challenged practice is job related for the position in question and consistent with business necessity").
76 See 15 U.S.C. § 1691(a)(1) (2012).
77 See, e.g., Va. Code Ann. §34–26 (2020) (the so-called poor debtor's exemption listing particular kinds of personally meaningful property exempted from the claims of creditors).

commerce as simply another site for the endless and well-choreographed debates about the relationship between church and state, recognizing the identity creating power of religious commerce focuses our attention on what might make that commerce of unique concern.[78] In so doing, it hopefully points toward a more productive framework for our debates about the law of church and market.

---

78 See generally Nathan B. Oman, "The Need for a Law of Church and Market," *Duke Law Journal Online* 64 (2015): 141–60.

# Index

abortifacients 30, 36
abortion 30
accommodationism 179
Affordable Care Act (ACA) 25, 27–38; "Women's Health Amendment" 29; "Women's Preventive Services Guidelines" 30
Afghanistan 41
agency: and grace 166; moral 164, 166, 168, 171
Aleksii II (Russian Orthodox Patriarch) 49
Alito, Samuel 4, 32
alternative dispute resolution (ADR) 69–70
American Baptist Church 154
American College of Obstetricians and Gynecologists 33, 36
American Roman Catholic Church *see* Catholic Church
Anabaptists 121, 132
anarchism 112
Anglican Church of Canada 139, 156–61
Anglican Communion 139–40
Anglicans 124, 132, 145, 148; *see also* Church of England
anti-discrimination laws 1, 184–85
Apfel, Daniel C. 24
Apostolic communion 92
Aquinas *see* Thomas Aquinas
arbitration law 69–71, 78–79, 82; and contract law 79–80; trends in 86–87
Archdiocese of Los Angeles 136–37
Arendt, Hannah 183
Aristotle 165, 182
Aron, Ramon 120
ArtScroll 177
asset divestment *see* divestment

Association of Religion Data Archives (ARDA) 40, 42, 52
atheism 42, 49
Atteberry, Shawna 131
Augustine of Hippo (saint) 131
Austria 52
automobile market 172–73
autonomy: of churches 142, 146, 148, 149, 154, 157; personal 35, 112, 128, 188; political 139; religious 71, 80, 88
Azerbaijan 50

Bachya, Rabbenu 123
Baldwin Wallace University 19
Ball, John 111
bankruptcy law 178, 182, 189–92
Baptist churches/Baptists 14, 17, 145, 161
Beauvoir, Simone de 183
Belgium 49
Beneficial Financial Group 98
Berkovitz, Jay 77
Berman, Harold 148
Beth Din of America (BDA) 5–6, 64, 67–69, 71, 88; and American arbitration law 66–71; lack of criminal jurisdiction 82; lawyers at 72–76; on reasoned opinions 79; relationship with secular courts 84–85
beth dins 64–89, 186–87; advocates in 72–73; authority of 79–81; and bankruptcy arbitration 182; competition among 87–88; embrace of lawyers by 73–75; and the *kahal* 80–82, 85; and reasoned opinions 77; support for decisions by American courts 79–80; *see also* Jewish law
Bezos, Jeff 114

Biden administration 34
Bill and Melinda Gates Foundation 101
Blackhorse, Amanda 106
Board of Tax Appeals 94
*Bostock v. Clayton County* 188–89
Bourgeois Era 121, 122, 135
boycotts 1, 36
*Braunfeld v. Brown* 3
Brazil 127
Breyer, Stephen 34
Brooks, Wayne 128
Buber-Neumann, Margarete 116
Buechner, Frederick 130
Bureau of Internal Revenue 95; *see also* Internal Revenue Service (IRS)
*Burwell v. Hobby Lobby Stores, Inc.* 3, 31–32
Butler, Judith 183, 184–85

Calvin, John 131
Campbellites 134
capitalism 110, 115, 123, 125; American 109
Carlyle, Thomas 117–18
Carter, Stephen 186
Cathedral of Tomorrow 97
Catholic Church: Archbishop of Los Angeles 137; assault on 132; Code of Canon Law 137, 149, 152; and freedom 166–68; and habituation 163–67; hierarchy of 148–49, 154, 161; and the market 163, 168–75; in North America 140; political authority of 99–100, 145; property owned by, 99–100, 152; social teaching of, 124, 130; Supreme Tribunal of the Apostolic Signatura 137; theological anthropology of 6, 163–68, 175; trusteeism controversy 151–52; in the United States 140, 152; United States Catholic Bishops 33, 174; United States Catholic Conference 97; *see also* Little Sisters of the Poor
Catholic Worker movement 124
C.F. Mueller Company 95–96
charitable trusts 141, 149
charity 123, 132, 134–35
*Charter of Rights and Freedoms* (Canada) 157–58
Chaudhuri, Nirad C. 122
China 41–44, 49, 50, 60, 116, 127, 135
Chinese Communist Party (CCP) 42

choice architectures 172
Christianity: on accumulated wealth 122–23, 168; in China 44; and equality 114; and the equality of souls 119, 135; Evangelical 177; and free will 166; and liberalism 111–12, 116, 130; and the liberty of the will 110, 117, 128–29, 132; and love 132, 134; official discrimination against 44–45; on private property 132–33; on sin 126; on slavery 117–18; and socialism 123, 125; theology of 113, 118, 127, 135
*Christianity Today* (magazine) 98
Christ's Church of the Golden Rule 97
Church of Christ 134
Church of England 14; *see also* Anglicans
Church of Jesus Christ of Latter-day Saints *see* Mormon church
Church of Power 132
Church of Scientology 108
churches: Canadian 156–61; and civil law 148; internal rules of 147, 149; IRS determining status of 108; limits on ownership of real property 100; nonprofit status of 103; as private spheres 179; seizure of property by the state 99–100; tax-exempt status of 91–92, 94–98, 101–2, 107–9; *see also* ecclesiastical authority; ecclesiastical law; property disputes; *specific churches by name*
churching of America 39
civil courts *see* judiciary
civil liberties 58–59, 61, 63, 111
Civil Rights Act (1964) 189
Clark, John Bates 115–16
Clinton administration 27
colleges and universities: admissions bribery scandal 8–9; boards of trustees 18, 19–22; community colleges 8; divestment issue 9–10, 22, 23–24; endowment management 9–10, 12; enrollment statistics 16–17; German research universities 11, 15; governance structures of 18–23; nonprofit status of 9, 31; religion and 8–24; religiously founded 5; secularization of 11, 14, 24; state institutions 12
colonialism 12
commerce *see* economics; economy; markets

Commission on Higher Education 8
Committee on Preventive Services for Women 29
common good 169, 174
communism 111, 114, 124; Apostolic Christian 92
communitarianism 92–93, 121, 122
community colleges 8
Conestoga Wood Specialties 32
conflict minerals 36
Congregationalists 14, 17
Constant, Benjamin 112
consumerism 171, 173–74
contraceptive mandate 5, 25–26, 29–38; court cases 31–34
contraceptive methods 29–30, 36, 37
Coptic Christians 53
Coral Ridge Presbyterian Church 97
corporations: for-profit 1, 3, 30–33, 91, 92, 95–100, 121, 177, 178, 181; mission-driven 172, 173; not-for-profit 33, 37, 103, 149–50
Cover, Robert 149, 188
COVID-19 65–66, 130
cults 17, 44, 49
culture wars 5, 25, 30, 31, 34–38, 65, 177

Dane, Perry 150, 155
Dannelly, Clarence M. 11–12
data collection 40–41
Dawson, Lorne L. 17
Day, Dorothy 124
democracy: American 2, 4, 25, 38, 39; and elections 54–55, **56**, 62; and higher education 8–9, 10, 13; liberal 111, 137–38, 182, 187; and markets and the law 174–76; moral contexts of 6, 25; and performative litigation 105; and religion 1, 2, 4, 40, 146, 164, 174–76; and religious freedom 54–55; secular 137–38; social 112, 124–25; and value pluralism 174
Deneen, Patrick 121
denominationalism 14
denominations 14
Department of Health and Human Services (HHS) 29
Disciples of Christ 134
disestablishment 2, 100, 142
Dissenting Ministers 14
divestment 5, 22, 23–24; in higher education 9–10

Doe, Norman 149
*doux commerce* thesis 121, 170, 181, 182
Dulles, Avery Cardinal 148–49

ecclesiastical authority 6, 146, 152
ecclesiastical law 138, 139, 148; in a comparative context 155–60; and legal change 150–51
*Economic Justice for All* (US Catholic Bishops) 174
economics: Austrian 132; behavioral 171, 172, 175; and democracy 164; as "dismal science" 118; free market 1–2, 4, 6–7, 34–36; market 2, 88, 126, 138; and market efficiency 81, 114, 118, 126; and religion 164
economy: capitalistic 93; and justice 174; liberal 110, 111, 122; political 6, 24, 128, 130, 135; and politics 180; regulation of 25, 26, 35, 38; religious 39; of solidarity 111
education, ultra-Orthodox Jewish schools 66
egalitarianism 111, 118, 119
egoism 110, 120, 127
Egypt 52, 53
elections 54–55, **56**, 63
embryo research 35–36
Emerson, Ralph Waldo 187
Emory University (Emory College) 20, 21
Engels, Friedrich 123
England 135
Ensign Peak Advisors 90, 91, 98, 100, 105
entrepreneurs/entrepreneurship 1, 2, 115, 175
Episcopal Church (US) 139, 152–55, 156, 161
Episcopalians 17, 130
*Equal Employment Opportunity Commission v. Abercrombie & Fitch Stores* 189
equality: coerced 114, 115, 116; of comfort 116, 119; in goods and services 114–15; human 6; liberal plan of 120; of opportunity 114; of outcome 113, 114; of permissions 112, 113, 116; socialist 133; of souls 119, 135; of wages 115; of women 26; *see also* inequality
Erasmus 129

Esau, Alvin 158–59
Establishment Clause 104
ethics 121, 122, 125, 128, 129, 131; business 170; Christian 135, 168; virtue 165
ethnicity 57
*Evangelii Gaudium* (Pope Francis) 169–70

fair-trade items 36
Falun Gong 44
fascism 111
Federal Arbitration Act (FAA) 5, 69, 86
Federal Drug Administration (FDA) 29
feminist theory 178
Figgis, John Neville 141–42, 148, 150
Finke, Roger 17, 61
Finland 127
First Church of Cannabis 108
Fischel, Daniel 9
Fleischacker, Samuel 119
*folkhemmet* 124, 125, 127
Food and Drug Administration (FDA) 37
forced migration 62
for-profit corporations 1, 3, 30–33, 91, 92, 95–100, 121, 177, 178, 181
fortunetelling 107
fossil fuel divestment 9–10, 23–24
Foundation for Moral Law 33
Four Freedoms 117
Fox, Jonathan 44, 61
France 49, 135; ban on full-face coverings 44
Francis (pope) 129–30, 169–70
Frankfurt School 171
Free Church of Scotland 142
free market economics 1–2, 4, 6–7; and moral questions 34–36; *see also* economics
free trade 125, 164
free will 166
freedom: academic 11; of association 58; Catholic conception of 166–68, 176; of choice 173; of conscience 2, 25, 157; and constraint 170; of expression 46, 58; fundamental 29; internal 129; human 4, 6, 111, 164, 188; and identity 185–87; as liberal idea 113, 116–17, and the market 34–36, 162, 168, 176, 183; and obedience 130; of peaceful assembly 58; queer 19; and theology 163–64; virtue and 163–64;

*see also* liberty/liberties; religious freedom
fuel economy labeling 172–73

*Gelassenheit* 92
gender discrimination 184–85
gender stereotypes 184–85, 192
Germany 49, 135
Ginsburg, Ruth Bader 4, 178–79
Goodrich, Luke 146–47, 149, 151, 154, 155, 161
Gorsuch, Neil 188
grace 129, 131, 134, 163, 164, 166–69, 173, 175, 176
Grassley, Chuck 99
Great Conversion 127
Great Enrichment 125–26
Green, T.H. 113
Greenawalt, Kent 154
Gundersheim, Hayyim 77
Gunzburg, Aryeh Leib 77

habituation 163–67
halakhah (Jewish law) 5, 64, 66, 68, 73, 74, 76, 79, 82, 85, 88; *see also* Jewish law
Hart, David Bentley 122
Harvard University 15
hate crimes 53
headscarf ban 44, 189
health insurance 3–4, 25–38
Health Resources and Services Administration (HRSA) 29–30
Hegel, G. W. F. 183, 186–87
Henry VIII (king of England) 99
Hidary, Richard 72
Hill, Joe 120
HillaryCare 27
Hinduism 122–23
Hinn, Benny 99
Hobby Lobby Stores, Inc. 30–31, 32, 37
Holland 135
Hollister, Dana 137
Hong Kong 135
Hopkins, Ann 184–85
human rights 41, 43, 58–59, 63
Human Rights Council (Geneva) 46
humanism 129
Hume, David 111
Huntington, Samuel 56–57
Hutterische Bruder Gemeinde 93–94
Hutterische Gemeinde Elspring 94–95

Hutterite community 92–96
Hyer, Robert Stewart 21–22

identity: of citizens 187–88; gender 178, 185; LGBT 18; and the market 183; nature of 182–83, 185; performance of 184–87, 191, 192; personal 178; and religion 8; religious 7, 20, 178, 186, 187, 191, 192–93; sexual 188–89; of universities and colleges 9
illiberalism 116
*imago Dei* 123, 132
Independent Petroleum Association of America 9
India 53, 135
individualism 125, 139
inequality 113, 169; *see also* equality
innovism 115–16, 123, 125, 126
Institute of Medicine (IOM) 29–30
Institute of the Sisters of the Most Holy and Immaculate Heart of the Blessed Virgin Mary 136–37
intentionality 127, 130
Internal Revenue Service (IRS) 94, 99, 102–5
Ireland 135
Islam 123, 131; in China 44; discrimination against 49, 50; in Egypt 53; in India 53; *see also* Muslims
Islamic Republic of Afghanistan 41

Jahangir, Asma 43
James I (king of England) 131
Japan 127, 135
Jefferson, Thomas 2, 39
Jehovah's Witnesses 50
Jewish law 5, 64–65, 68, 71, 72, 74–75, 80–82, 88, 186; adherence to 88; on divorce (*get*) 81; enforcement of 83–86, 87; jurisdiction for arbitration 79–82, 86–87; and the market 88; and the production of reasoned opinions 76–79; *see also* halakhah (Jewish law)
John Paul II (pope) 132
John XXIII (pope) 132, 134
*Jones v. Wolf* 153, 156
Judaism 123, 131; and bankruptcy court 182; and kosher certification 85–86; market actors and 177; observant/enclavist 64–65; Orthodox 65–68, 87, 122; performance of 186–87; and the power of the *kahal* 80–82, 85; and secular litigation 66–68; use of communal sanctions in 83–86; violence against 53; *see also* beth dins; halakhah (Jewish law); Jewish law
judiciary: civil courts 64, 66, 69–71, 74, 79, 83–86, 139–40, 143–45, 147–49, 151–52, 156–57, 161; constitutive and declarative functions of civil law 148–50; and performative litigation 105–8; protection of religious freedom by 54–55, 63; and religious liberty law 65; restriction of religious freedom by **56**; secular law 64–65, 69, 74, 75, 79, 86, 87–88, 145, 160, 186; United States Court of Claims 94; *see also* arbitration law; performative litigation; rabbinical courts; Supreme Court
justice: economic 174; in the market 168; material 164

Kagan, Elena 34
*Kahan v. Rosner* 73–74
Kant, Immanuel 112
Kennedy, D. James 97
Klamer, Arjo 121
Knight, Frank 132, 133, 134, 135
Kocka, Jürgen 125
kosher certification 85–86, 177

Lahav, Alexandra D. 105
language 57
Lanham Act 106
Le Corbusier 16
Lenin, Vladimir 134
Leo XIII (pope) 132, 133, 134
Levelers 111
Levy, David 119
LGBTQ issues: employment discrimination 188–89; ordination 140, 156, 158; and property disputes 140; protection for LGBTQ people 178; same-sex marriage 10, 158, 177; transgender rights 1; and the United Methodist Church 10, 18–19, 23
liberalism 6, 110–35, 188; Christian 116, 130; critiques of 120; defined 111–13, 116–17; neo- 111, 130; "new" 112–13, 121; political 126
liberty/liberties: and Catholicism 164; civil 58–59, 61, 63, 111; defined

116–18; natural 119; of the will 110, 117, 128–29, 132; *see also* freedom
Lindsley, Philip 15
Little Sisters of the Poor 31, 32, 33–34, 37–38
*Little Sisters of the Poor v. Pennsylvania* 25–26, 31, 33–34
Lloyd George, David 113
Locke, John 2, 118, 120
Long, Russell 101
Louis XIV (king of France) 131
Luther, Martin 129
Lutherans 99

Madison, James 39
Magna Carta 113
Manifest Destiny 12
Mao Zedong 129
Maoism 124
market economy 88, 111, 126, 138
markets: and Catholic theology 168–74; civilizing effects of 170–71; corrupting influence of 171; as "free" spaces 162, 163; and law and democracy 174–76; as moral contexts 162–76; as public spaces 179–80; and religion in the commercial space 177–93; as social mechanisms 181
marriage, same-sex 10, 158, 177
Marsden, George 10–11
Marx, Karl 119, 123, 124
Marxism 171
Mason, Noah 96
Mataic, Dane 60, 61
Maurin, Peter 124
McConnell, Michael 4, 146–47, 149, 151, 154, 155, 161
McIntyre, James Francis 136, 137
McLean, Malcom 122
Mead, Sidney 39
Merriam, T.W. 132, 133, 134, 135
Methodist Episcopal Church, South 20, 21
Methodists 17; *see also* United Methodist Church
Middle Ages 126
Middle East 46, 62
Mill, John Stuart 112, 119, 120
Miscavige, David 108
modernity 88, 171
monopolies 116, 128
Montesquieu 170, 181

Mormon church 97, 98, 101, 102, 105–6, 109; profit-making by 90–92
Muslims 2, 44, 49, 53, 185, 189; Uighur 50; *see also* Islam

National Academies of Sciences, Engineering, and Medicine 29
National Academy of Medicine (NAM) 29
National Council of Churches of Christ 97
nationalism, religious 63
Nelson, Robert 126
neo-liberalism 111, 130; *see also* liberalism
neutral principles approach 139; in church property disputes 144–46; limitations of 150–51; pluralist understanding of 146–60
neutrality 138, 157–58, 161
New Deal 124
New Religious Institutionalism 150
New York University (NYU) 95–96
New Zealand 116
Niebuhr, H. Richard 14
Nielson, David 90–91
Nielson, Lars 90
nonprofit organizations 33, 37, 103, 149–50
Nordhaus, William 122
North Africa 46
Novak, Michael 133, 134

Obama, Barack 27
Obama administration 32, 172
Ogilvie, M.H. 158, 159
Oliver, John 99
Orthodox Union 68
Orwell, George 116
Oslington, Paul 119
Osteen, Joel 107

Paine, Thomas 112, 125, 181
*Pankerichan v. Djokic* 160
Paul the apostle (saint) 117, 131, 134
Paul VI (pope) 132
Peart, Sandra 119
performative litigation 105–8, 109; as democracy-forcing activity 105–6; non-SLAPP litigation 106–7; strategic lawsuits against public participation (SLAPP) 106
Perkins School of Theology 19

Perry, Katy 136, 137
Pew Research Center 40, 42
Pius XI (pope) 132
Planned Parenthood Federation of America 33
pluralism 6, 148, 175, 187–88; religious 179; value 174
politics: conservative 19; and the contraceptive mandate 29–31; cultural issues in 178; democratic 121; laissez-faire 125; moral context of 163, 176, 187; pluralism in 148; of recognition 183; role of religion in 42
Posner, Richard 4
Presbyterians/Presbyterian Church 14, 17, 97, 139, 140, 145; division over slavery 143
*Price Waterhouse v. Hopkins* 184–85, 192
product labeling 172, 173
Prohibition 122
property disputes 3, 136–61; in Canada 156–61; in the Catholic Church 136–37; common law standards 140–41, 145, 147, 152; and doctrinal fidelity 140–43; hybrid approach to 151, 155, 159, 161; implied trust approach 142–43, 157, 159; judicial adjudication of 139–46; and the neutral principles approach 139; neutral principles approach 144–46; neutrality in 138, 157–58, 161; over charitable trusts 141; pluralist approach 155–56, 160; polity approach to 143–44
property rights 146, 147, 148, 155, 156, 181
prosperity gospel 99
Protestant Episcopal Church *see* Episcopal Church (US)
Protestantism 100, 134; declining membership 17; in universities and colleges 10–11; *see also* Christianity; *specific Protestant denominations*
public policy 78, 81
Puritans 124
Putin, Vladimir 129

Quakers 121, 145
quietism 129

Rabbinical Council of America 67–68
rabbinical courts *see* beth dins

Rand, Ayn 120
Rarick, John 96–97, 98
Rauschenbusch, Walter 124
Rawls, John 114
Raz, Joseph 182
Reformed Churches 145
Regev, Eyal 16
religion: Chinese 50; and commerce 38; in the commercial space 177–93; as cultural component 56–57; decline in membership 16; and democracy 39–40; deregulation of 2; free exercise of 32, 39; and hate crimes 53; and identity 7, 8; new religions 17; non-registered 52; official 48–49; performativity of 185–86; prosperity gospel 99; relationship with the market 107–8, 182–83; and sociality 8; and tax law 91–92, 94; *see also* Christianity; Hinduism; Islam; Judaism; religious freedom
Religion and State Project (RAS) 40, 42, 52, 60
religious conflict 4, 56–58, **56**, 62
religious diversity 1–2, 57, 60, 65
religious freedom 1–2, 4–5, 32, 39–41, 81, 149, 157, 179, 182; consequences of denial of 55–63; constitutional guarantees of 41–42, *43*, 61; correlation with other freedoms and factors *59*; and democracy 54–55, 62; and economic development 59–62; and human rights 58–59; and Jewish law 82; for minority religions 44–46, *47*, 48–49; and political stability 59–62; promise and practice of 41–46; registration requirements 45, 50–52, 62–63; restriction of 5, 42–55; restrictions on proselytizing 45; and societal discrimination *54*; and transition of power *62*
Religious Freedom Restoration Act (RFRA) 31–32
Richman, Barak 4
Rienzi, Mark 30
rights: human 41, *43*, 58–59, 63; negative 175; property 146, 147, 148, 155, 156, 181; transgender 1; of women 32
Roman Catholic Church *see* Catholic Church
Romanticism 171

Roosevelt, Franklin 117
Roosevelt, Theodore 113
Rorty, Richard 124
Rousseau, Jean-Jacques 113, 114, 127–28
Rumbold, Richard 111
Russia 50, 51–52, 116, 129; *see also* USSR
Russian Orthodox Church 49, 140

Sandel, Michael 121
Saudi Arabia 49
Scotland 135
Second Vatican Council 136
sectarianism 10, 13–14
sects 13–15, 16, 17, 49
secular law *see* judiciary
secularism 59, 138
secularization: market-driven 5; narratives of 2; of universities and colleges 11, 14, 24
self-governance 82, 171
Self-Realization Fellowship 97
self-sufficiency 130
Sellers, Charles C. 121
Sen, Amartya 117
separationism 179
sermons, monitoring of 42, 63
Settlement and Removal Acts 119
Shaheed, Ahmed 43
Shakespeare, William 115
Shaw, George Bernard 126
slavery 3, 117–18, 129, 131, 186–87
slotting fees 172
Smith, Adam 111, 118–20, 125, 130, 181
social contract 128
social Darwinism 120, 128
social democracy 112, 124–25
socialism 113–14, 121, 124, 125, 126, 127, 133; Christian 123–24, 125; democratic 111, 113
sociology of religion 14
South Africa 22–23
South Central Jurisdictional Conference (SCJC) 10, 18–20, 23
Southern Methodist University (SMU) 10–11, 18–23
Soviet nations (former) 46, 62
Soviet Union 128; *see also* Russia
Spartacus 111
Stalin, Joseph 129
Stanford University 21–22

Stark, Rodney 17
sterilization procedures 29
stoicism 129
strategic lawsuits against public participation (SLAPP) 106
Sunstein, Cass 172–73
Supreme Court: on arbitration 78; and the contraceptive mandate 25–26, 31–34; on employment discrimination 184, 188–89; and the Establishment Clause 104; on higher education endowments 12; on the Lanham Act 106; religion and state cases 2–4; on religious property disputes 151, 153
Sweden 116, 124, 135
synagogues 53, 68, 81, 83, 84, 179

Talmud 72, 76–77, 79, 88
Tamari, Meir 123
Tax Anti-Injunction Act 104
tax law 6, 91–92, 94; concerning church property 100; Italian 96–97; and nonprofit organizations 103–4; and religious wealth 102; tax exemptions for churches 94–98, 101–2, 107–9; Tax Reform Act (1969) 98
Tax Reform Act (1969) 98
#TaxTheChurches 107
Taylor, Charles 183
televangelists 99
Thatcher, Margaret 111
theology: Abrahamic 110; Christian 113, 118, 127, 135; on liberty of the will 129; moral 165; of the people 129
Third Plenary Council of Baltimore 152
Thomas, Clarence 33–34
Thomas, Mary Martha 21
Thomas Aquinas 123, 133, 134, 165, 174
Thoreau, Henry David 125
Tichnor, George 15
Tillich, Paul 110, 126, 132
Tinder, Glenn 118
tithing 7, 182, 190–92
Tocqueville, Alexis de 39, 55
Todorov, Tzvetan 116
Tolstoy, Leo 112
Truman, Harry 8
Trump administration 33
trusteeism controversy 151–52
Turner, Paul Venable 16
Turner, R. Gerald 18

Uighur Muslims 50
United Arab Emirates 60
United Church of Canada 158
*United Church of Canada v. Anderson* 158
United Methodist Church 10, 18–20, 23, 139; theology schools associated with 18–19; Traditional Plan 10, 18; *see also* Methodists
United Nations 41, 43, 58; Framework Convention on Climate Change (UNFCC) 9; Special Rapporteur on freedom of religion 43, 46, 55–56; Universal Declaration of Human Rights 41, 43, 58
United States: Bourgeois Revaluation in 135; Catholic Church in 33, 97, 140, 152, 174; and the churching of America 39; colonial 12, 60, 152; *see also* US Constitution
United States Catholic Conference 97
United States Conference of Catholic Bishops 33, 174
Universal Declaration of Human Rights 41, 43, 58
universities *see* colleges and universities
University of Chicago 21–22, 128, 132
University of Kansas 13
University of Nashville 15
US Constitution: Establishment Clause 104, 146; First Amendment 1, 3, 4, 71, 103, 106, 159; Fourteenth Amendment 71; Free Exercise Clause 146
USSR 128; *see also* Russia

value pluralism 174
Vanderbilt University 20, 22
Vatican 96, 97, 152
Verennes, Fernand de 55–56
Villa San Giuseppe 136–37
virtue ethics 165
virtue(s): encouragement of 163, 174; growing in 167; and law 169; and markets 170; as operative habits 165
Voltaire 120, 125, 181

Walzer, Michael 121, 122
War on Drugs 122
Warren, Earl 3
Washington Redskins 106
*Watson v. Jones* 3, 143–46, 147, 151, 153
Waverly property 136–37
wealth: Christian view of 122–23, 168; extraction of 2; of Hutterites 93; of the Mormon church 90–91, 98, 100–102, 105; of the Orthodox Jewish population 67, 87; and the Prosperity Gospel 131; religious 92, 96–97, 98–102, 103, 109
Weber, Max 13, 110, 128
Wee Frees 142
Wegener, Carl Richard 110, 126, 132
whistleblower complaints 90–92, 98, 100, 105–6, 109
Williams, H.H. 125, 126
Wilson, Brian 14
Wollstonecraft, Mary 112, 125
women: equality for 26; rights of 32; and gender stereotypes 183–85, 192; Roman Catholic 31–34, 37–38, 136–37

Xi Jinping 124, 129

Yale Report 15–16
Yale University (Yale College) 12, 15, 101
Yeltsin, Boris 49
Yeshiva University 67–68

Zamagni, Stefano 129–30
Zondervan 177
Zoroastrianism 123
*Zubik v. Burwell* 31, 32–33